Advanced NXT

The Da Vinci Inventions Book

Matthias Paul Scholz

Apress®

Advanced NXT: The Da Vinci Inventions Book

Copyright © 2007 by Matthias Paul Scholz

ISBN-13 (pbk): 978-1-59059-843-6

ISBN-10 (pbk): 1-59059-843-1

Printed and bound in the United States of America 9 8 7 6 5 4 3 2 1

Lead Editors: Matthew Moodie, Jim Sumser
Technical Reviewer: Jim Kelly
Editorial Board: Steve Anglin, Ewan Buckingham, Gary Cornell, Jonathan Gennick, Jason Gilmore,
    Jonathan Hassell, Chris Mills, Matthew Moodie, Jeffrey Pepper, Ben Renow-Clarke,
    Dominic Shakeshaft, Jim Sumser, Matt Wade, Tom Welsh
Project Manager: Kylie Johnston
Copy Edit Manager: Nicole Flores
Copy Editor: Jennifer Whipple
Assistant Production Director: Kari Brooks-Copony
Production Editor: Laura Cheu
Compositor: Susan Glinert Stevens
Proofreader: Lori Bring
Indexer: Carol Burbo
Artist: April Milne
Cover Designer: Kurt Krames
Manufacturing Director: Tom Debolski

Distributed to the book trade worldwide by Springer-Verlag New York, Inc., 233 Spring Street, 6th Floor, New York, NY 10013. Phone 1-800-SPRINGER, fax 201-348-4505, e-mail orders-ny@springer-sbm.com, or visit http://www.springeronline.com.

For information on translations, please contact Apress directly at 2855 Telegraph Avenue, Suite 600, Berkeley, CA 94705. Phone 510-549-5930, fax 510-549-5939, e-mail info@apress.com, or visit http://www.apress.com.

The source code for this book is available to readers at http://www.apress.com in the Source Code/Download section.

To the memory of Stanislaw Lem (1921–2006)

Contents at a Glance

Contents

About the Author

MATTHIAS PAUL SCHOLZ has a degree in mathematics obtained at the University of Bayreuth, Germany, and works presently as a system engineer. He has held IT-related positions in various companies in Germany over the past 12 years, specializing in model-driven development and distributed environments. He has been an active member of the LEGO MINDSTORMS community since 2000. Scholz was one of the developers of the open source leJOS platform for the RCX, took part in the LEGO MINDSTORMS Developer Program, and is presently one of the 20 members of the LEGO MIND-STORMS Community Partners Program. Furthermore, he is one of the contributors to the popular The NXT STEP blog and maintains the German-language sister blog, Die NXTe Ebene. His own MINDSTORMS NXT-related web site is at `http://mynxt.matthiaspaulscholz.eu`.

About the Technical Reviewer

JIM KELLY is a freelance technical writer in Atlanta, Georgia. He obtained a bachelor's degree in English from the University of West Florida and a bachelor's degree in industrial engineering from Florida State University. He has been writing and editing for more than nine years. He is currently a member of the LEGO MINDSTORMS Community Partners Program and works with other members to improve and test the MINDSTORMS NXT and other products. Jim is the author of the Apress books *LEGO Mindstorms NXT: The Mayan Adventure* and *LEGO Mindstorms NXT-G Programming Guide*.

Acknowledgments

First of all, I would like to thank my most amiable wife for her support and patience with all the evening, late-night, and weekend hours I spent on the book in the past months.

Special and very cordial thanks go to Jim Kelly who encouraged me to write this book, opened doors for me, and not only provided warmhearted guidance and indispensable advice but also acted as a tech editor for the book.

Also, I'd like to thank all the other aficionados out there whose commitment and mad rapture for LEGO MINDSTORMS NXT filled me with the energy to complete all the work for the book. In particular, I'd like to mention Steven Canvin from LEGO, Maureen Reilly from NXTLOG, Brian Davis, Steve Hassenplug, Philo, and The NXT STEP gang. Thanks also to the guys from the leJOS NXJ project, John Hansen for NXC, Ralph Hempel for pbLua, and Daniele Benedettelli and Lukas Probst for their tutorials. These people are only a small section of all the enthusiastic LEGO weirdos that form a bustling community I'm proud to be a part of. Please bear with me if I forgot to name someone who particularly deserves it.

I am amazed and grateful for the work done by the production team for this book, in particular Kylie, Jennifer, and Laura from Apress, who did a prodigious job, and I'd like to voice my particular gratitude for being that dedicated and so very patient with me.

Preface

Robots have been a source of fascination to me since my childhood. That was during the time of the first *Star Wars* trilogy, with very humanlike robots appearing on the screen, such as C-3PO, who still reminds me of some friends of mine, and not so humanlike others, such as R2-D2 (who nevertheless also reminds me of some people I know). There were the books of Stanislaw Lem and Douglas Adams that discuss the philosophical questions related to the creation of artificial beings. Do androids dream of electric sheep? I still wonder.

Yet all my attempts to build something similar on my own failed. The gizmos I'd assembled from wood and plastic not only looked strangely different from the ones I had in mind, but also didn't do anything (besides fall apart frequently). The time was not ripe for building robots of your own, unless you had a degree in electronic engineering, high soldering capabilities, and a well-endowed bank account to acquire all the special electromechanical parts required.

This all changed dramatically when in 1998 the LEGO Group released the LEGO MINDSTORMS system. At once it was possible to build robots with a technology that I and almost everyone else I knew was used to since childhood: LEGO bricks. In fact, I considered LEGO to be only a toy then and my trunk full of bricks had long ago changed possession to my little brother. But it didn't take long to realize the potential of the new product line. I was even more surprised to find out that there was a MINDSTORMS community out there that to a large part was composed of people of my age, my professional IT background, and my interest in technics, in particular in robotics. Consequently, I bought some of the kits and expansions and indulged in the open source movement that was rapidly growing and bustling with energy. That is, I became one of the developers of the leJOS project, dedicated to providing a Java implementation for the MINDSTORMS RCX Brick.

So the millennium went by with creating robots and trying to overcome the limitations of the RCX, whose technical parameters were already outdated in 1998. An update was overdue, but instead, the kits were beginning to disappear from the shops and it seemed that LEGO was resting on the laurels of MINDSTORMS, which had developed into the best-selling product in the company's history.

Fortunately that wasn't the case at all.

In 2005, rumors began to spread that a successor to the RCX was to be expected. Indeed, LEGO announced the MINDSTORMS Developer Program (MDP) and asked for applications. I instantly jumped in—without much hope—as virtually everyone I knew in the community did the same. How great, though, was my joy when I received a confirmation that I was to be one of the blessed 100? As a matter of fact, I didn't believe it in the beginning, suspecting that it was just a cruel joke by my friends.

It wasn't, and what was to follow were months of fun, devotion, and creative energy. The days had not enough hours and the kits not enough parts to implement all the ideas that were appearing in my head and in those of the most interesting and different people I've met in the program. Well, one needs to bring home the bacon, but I realized then how tedious your (otherwise satisfying) everyday job is able to appear when you long to race home and complete the time machine you are tinkering with.

One of the ideas that arose rather early was to combine my NXT-related activities with another topic of interest to me—medieval history. It was only a small step to notice that the mechanical works of one of the greatest engineers ever, Leonardo da Vinci, would suit the subject tremendously well. However, I never dreamt of really writing a book on it, and most likely it wouldn't have come into being if Jim Kelly—whom I'm proud to be connected to by the MDP, the blog we both write for, and last but not least, the books in this MINDSTORMS series—hadn't encouraged me to do so.

Hence, here it is. I hope you enjoy it.

Who This Book Is For

This book is about building quite complex LEGO NXT robots with a lot of different parts. You will learn techniques to master certain challenges in building real-world gadgets with LEGO and how to make best or at least good use of special parts that are contained in the NXT kit or in other ones. You also should get a feeling for how to transform contraptions from the "real" world into LEGO devices and how to use the motors and various sensors the NXT kit provides.

That said, some of the robots are rather sophisticated and comprise a lot of different parts that are arranged in a sometimes complicated manner. Therefore, absolute beginners who do not feel at least basically at ease with LEGO TECHNIC and studless building might prefer to make themselves familiar with these topics before trying to tackle the robots introduced in this book.

As for the software, a fundamental understanding of the basic principles of programming is recommended. I introduce five different environments for creating and running programs in the NXT, where almost each one is based in a particular development paradigm. It goes without saying that there's always the option of concentrating on one single environment and leaving the others out; but even so, some experience with the programming paradigm in question—for instance, with object-oriented programming in the case of leJOS—might prove useful. Also, when it comes to the software, programming newbies might wish to address some tutorials before implementing the programs in the book.

For the NXT environments used in the book, though, no previous knowledge is required. I explain in detail not only their installation and configuration, but also the language constructs, which are displayed by example in a step-by-step manner.

In the end, you should be familiar with the strategies to implement standard challenges for NXT robots in the different languages and have an overview of the options available for programming the NXT and know which one best fits your background and taste.

How This Book Is Structured

This book is organized around chapters that recreate five inventions of Leonardo da Vinci using LEGO. Each of these chapters consists of the following:

- A lecture on the historical background

- A discussion of the hardware challenges the invention imposes on a LEGO model and the solution

- Complete step-by-step building instructions

- Programming instructions for each of the five programming environments the book uses

Chapter 1: Introduction

This chapter consists of a tour through Leonardo's life and five of his most famous inventions to be built with LEGO. It also introduces the NXT and its components and provides a glimpse of the NXT community and some of its most prominent sites.

Chapter 2: A 3,000-Foot Look at NXT Programming Environments

This chapter discusses the five different programming environments used in this book: the official LEGO MINDSTORMS NXT Software, RobotC, NXC, pbLua, and leJOS NXJ. It focuses on those that allow running programs directly on the Brick—autonomous robots rather than those confined to remote control from an external device such as a computer or a cell phone.

Chapter 3: The Armored Car

This chapter is the first robot chapter. It deals with Leonardo's design of an armored car, a machine like today's military tank. Like the following four chapters, it provides a historical background, a discussion of the LEGO hardware challenges and their solutions, the building instructions, and the programming of the robot with five different programming environments.

Chapter 4: The Catapult

This chapter introduces one of the catapults Leonardo designed and shows how to build it with LEGO. You will encounter the device he invented to set up kinetic energy and the touch sensor.

Chapter 5: The Revolving Bridge

This chapter shows how to build Leonardo's revolving bridge with LEGO. You will gain insight into motor synchronization and learn how to make use of the ultrasonic sensor.

Chapter 6: The Aerial Screw

This chapter presents a LEGO implementation of Leonardo's aerial screw, also—but misleadingly—known as the "helicopter." It's an introduction to mimicking curved structures and to the usage of the light sensor.

Chapter 7: The Flying Machine

This chapter showcases another machine invented by Leonardo for the purpose of flying and how to build it with LEGO. Its "flapping wings" make it different from the aerial screw. You will learn how to use wires to run mechanical parts and to remotely control a NXT robot.

Chapter 8: Outlook: What NXT?

This is a discussion of the conceivable steps the reader may take from here. It discusses possible refinements of the preceding five robots and the possibility of remotely controlling them. It sheds some light on other inventions of Leonardo's that might be created with LEGO, and finally introduces some web sites and books recommended for further reading.

Appendixes

This book contains four appendixes. The first provides step-by-step guides to the installation and configuration of the five different programming environments in this book. The second contains a copy of Leonardo's letter of application to the duke of Milan that is mentioned frequently in the book. The final two appendixes are a glossary and a bibliography.

Prerequisites

To complete the programming examples in the book, you will need five different programming environments for the NXT. The first one is contained in the retail version of the NXT kit, while the others are available on the Internet, either for free or as trial versions. Appendix A provides all the information you need to download, install, and configure them for this book.

Downloading the Code

The source code for this book is available to readers at the Apress web site at `http://www.apress.com` in the Source Code/Download section. You can also check for errata and find related titles from Apress.

Additional material related to the book such as updates, videos and more can be downloaded from my web site at `http://mynxt.matthiaspaulscholz.eu`.

Contacting the Author

If you are eager to contact me for feedback, questions, or suggestions, feel free to use the contact page on my web site at `http://mynxt.matthiaspaulscholz.eu/contact`. I always try to respond to any approach by a reader as soon as possible.

CHAPTER 1

■ ■ ■

Introduction

*I have been impressed with the urgency of doing. Knowing is not enough; we must apply.
Being willing is not enough; we must do.*

—Leonardo da Vinci

This book is on two topics that at first glance may appear rather disconnected: Leonardo da Vinci and LEGO MINDSTORMS NXT. Yet, on reconsideration you might notice that not only do the stupendous mechanical designs of Leonardo have much in common with NXT robots, but so do Leonardo—the inventor and engineer—and modern NXT robot builders.

Leonardo's machines were based on established designs and existing mechanical parts but went beyond the tradition by combining high-technology components of his time with conceptual audacity and brilliant ingenuity, thus creating devices that aroused the admiration of his contemporaries as well as people today. Same goes for NXT robots and their creators—though certainly to a more minor extent. LEGO TECHNIC is a well-known and established way of building LEGO machines, while NXT may be justifiably considered as some kind of high-technology gadget. And already creations of stunning imaginativeness are appearing on the scene, pushing the possibilities of NXT robotics farther and farther beyond the limits.

So what stands more to reason than combining these two topics, thus bridging the centuries and reviving the thoughts of one of the most brilliant minds in mankind's history?

Most likely the majority of people know Leonardo as an artist, as the creator of such renowned works as the *Mona Lisa* or *The Last Supper*. But as you will see in the course of this chapter, his faculties, interests, and achievements were much more widespread.

You will take a look into Leonardo's life, examining five of his most prominent inventions. After that you will endeavor your first tour through the LEGO MINDSTORMS NXT universe.

Always keep in mind, though, that the following ramble can only provide a selection of the capabilities and achievements of this stupendous universal genius.

An Invention-Driven Tour Through the Life of Leonardo da Vinci

No doubt Leonardo di ser Piero da Vinci is one of the most ingenious men of modern history. Justifiably, he's also one of the most well-known: almost 500 years after his death, he hasn't ceased to arouse the imagination and admiration of contemporary people.

Media on Leonardo da Vinci is legion today (for a short selection, refer to the bibliography in Appendix D). To provide even an abstract of the many different aspects of his life, appreciating his capabilities on the areas of anatomy, art, and science, would decidedly be beyond the scope of this book. Instead, I will try to unveil his scientific career by throwing some highlights on a selection of his mechanical designs that may both serve as an illustration of the different fields of technological research he excelled in as well as help you approach his life and his way of thinking.

Renaissance Man

Like no other man, Leonardo personifies the *Renaissance*, a term meaning *rebirth* and denoting a time half a millennium ago when the focus of the Occident's highbrows shifted from metaphysical considerations to matters that from today's view may be considered "physical": interest in the human being itself; the scientific (rather than the philosophical) heritage of the antique; the different phenomena mankind encounters in nature; and the use of mechanical inventions for everyday life challenges. It's not without reason that the artwork that has become *the* symbol for the Renaissance is one of Leonardo's creations: *The Vitruvian Man* (Figure 1-1).

■**Note** Giorgio Vasari, who wrote the first biography of Leonardo in his "Vite de' più eccelenti architettori, pittori e scultori italiani" ("The lives of the most excellent Italian architects, painters, and sculptors") in the 1550s, said that when famous Florentine artist Andrea del Verrochio saw Leonardo's work on the angel in *The Baptism of Christ*, he was so amazed that he resolved never to touch a brush again.

Even though there are other famous men such as Michelangelo, Albrecht Dürer, or Galilei Galileo who are connected to the Renaissance in the public mind, Leonardo da Vinci most likely represents more than anybody else the synthesis of all-embracing curiosity, open-mindedness, and ingenuity that characterized the Renaissance polymaths—qualities that seem to have become regrettably rare in today's fragmented scientific landscape.

■**Note** Some other famous Renaissance artists such as Rafael and Michelangelo lived and worked in Rome when Leonardo moved there from Milan in 1513, but it seems Leonardo did not come into contact with them. Maybe he was too consumed with his own works then, as he had resumed his theoretical researches on the laws of optical reflection, in particular in connection with parabolic and concave mirrors. It is a topic he had come in contact with previously during his early apprentice years in Verrochio's workshop, where *concave mirrors*—collecting and amplifying the sun's light—were used for metallurgic purposes. It is said that it is here that Leonardo witnessed the welding of the two hemispheres to the golden ball that is located on top of the Florentine dome today.

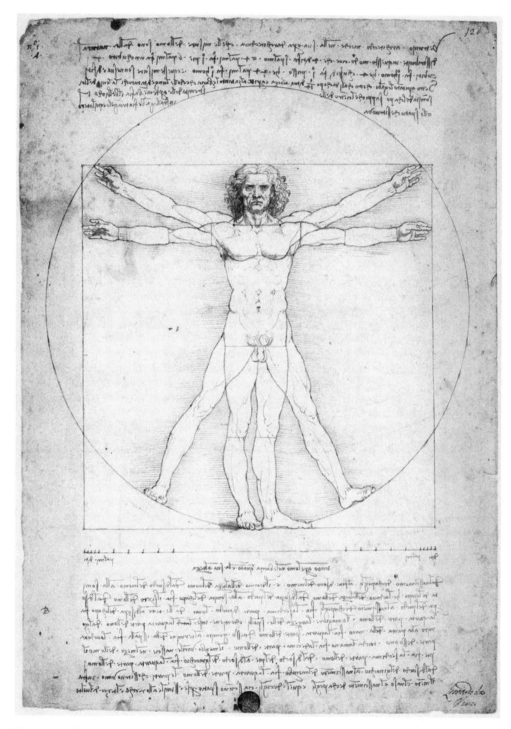

Figure 1-1. *The proportions of the human body in the manner of Vitruvius*

HISTORY OF LEONARDO

Leonardo spent much of his lifetime living in Milan. But he was no born Milanian; his place of birth on April 15, 1452, was Anciano, a small Tuscany village near Vinci, located in the vicinity of Florence.

It is popularly believed that his mother was a peasant woman to whom his father, the wealthy Florentine notary Piero, was not married. Though not uncommon these days, illegitimate children in most cases did not have it easy back then. However, Leonardo was lucky. His father brought him to live with him and his wife at Vinci when he was five years old. In 1460, the family moved to Florence. Here Leonardo most likely received an excellent education. His later claims of being "almost illiterate" may be considered as intentional understatements.

At age 14, he became a *garzone* (studio boy) in the workshop of the famous Florentine sculptor Andrea del Verrochio, a possible indication of the parental diligence toward him. Verrocchio today is most well-known for his impressive equestrian statue of Bartolomeo Colleoni in Venice, but his workshop in Florence processed orders in many different areas: painting, bronze statues, bells, construction machines for the building of the Florentine dome, mechanical theater gadgets, metallurgic works, and armory. It was here where Leonardo started to develop his interest in military devices, though he was nominally employed as a painting apprentice, where he obviously excelled as well.

By 1482 when he left Florence for Milan, Leonardo was an independent master. In 1498, the French conquered the Duchy of Milan, driving the Sforzas out of power. Leonardo stayed there for one more year and left in 1499. It has been said that the reason for this decision was because the French archers used his life-size clay model of his planned *Gran Cavallo* horse statue for target practice. As a matter of fact, it was not the first time his artistic plans had been impacted by the war; in 1495, 70 tons of bronze that had been set aside for the *Gran Cavallo* was instead cast into weapons for the duke during a previous French assault.

After Leonardo returned to Milan in 1508, he was again driven away when in 1513 Swiss mercenaries hired by the city's patricians drove out the French. Leonardo moved to Rome where Giovanni di Medici, the son of the former Florentine sovereign Lorenzo (Lorenzo eventually became the infamous Pope Leo X), instructed his brother Guiliano to gain valuable acreage by draining the Paludi Pontine (Pontinian swamps) south of the Eternal City. Guiliano was happy to engage Leonardo for this sophisticated project.

Leonardo obviously had deeply impressed his French employers during his second stay in Milan. In 1517, the French King Francois I (nicknamed "le Roi-Chevalier," the Knight King) invited him to France to work as his first royal engineer. Leonardo moved into the manor house Clos Lucé, also called "Cloux," which was located next to the king's residence at the royal Chateau Amboise and which is a museum today open to the public. The king was a genuine admirer of his new first engineer ("No man had ever lived who had learned as much about sculpture, painting, and architecture, but still more that he was a very great philosopher," as he said), and eventually the two men became friends, though very unequal in age (Francois was 42 years younger).

Francois granted Leonardo and his assistants generous pensions that enabled Leonardo to concentrate on his theoretical studies about flying in his last two years of life. Now and then he performed some jobs also for the court that aroused stunned admiration—hydraulic systems for fountains, for instance, or, on the occasion of a visit of Florentine merchantmen, a mechanical lion (the symbol of Florence) that automatically opened its breast to spread lilies (the symbol of the French crown) on the delighted audience.

Leonardo died May 2, 1519, in the arms of King Francois. His remains were later moved to the chapel of Saint Hubert inside the castle; however, there is no longer any trace of them today, as many tombs were destroyed during the 16th century Wars of Religion.

Five Designs

This section explains the five designs you will build in this book:

- The armored car
- The catapult

- The revolving bridge
- The aerial screw
- The flying machine

The Armored Car

The armored car is one of Leonardo's most well-known designs. As with all of his inventions, it came to us by drawings produced by Leonardo himself, an exceptionally gifted draftsman. The armored car resembles the concept of the military tank invented at the beginning of the 20th century (Figure 1-2).

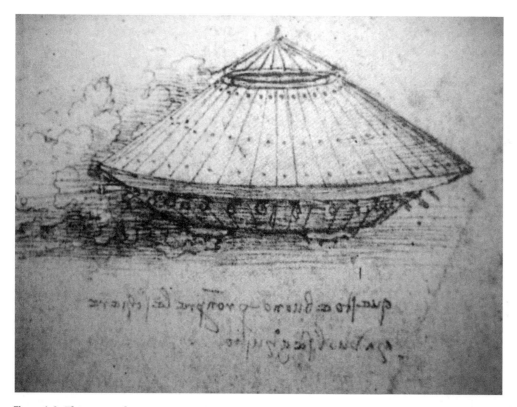

Figure 1-2. *The armored car*

Leonardo apparently drew this sketch between 1482 and 1485 when he was living in Milan for the first time. The drawing of the armored car may have been attached to a letter that Leonardo wrote or had had written (in the times of no word-processing software it was common to have important documents written by a paid expert) to the Duke of Milan, Ludovico Sforza, nicknamed "Il Moro," as an application of employment. Appendix B contains a translation of the complete text of this letter of application. Though we do not know the reception it got, machines of war were undoubtedly of major interest to a North-Italian sovereign in the politically unstable last decades of the 15th century. In the case of Ludovico that interest decidedly was a valid one, as the French drove the Sforzas out of Milan only some years later.

We may wonder about Leonardo's dealings in military aspects and may even find it reprehensible, but we must not forget that at this time, war was not considered unethical but rather was looked at as some kind of art—at least by those who did not directly suffer from it. Furthermore, it squared with the interest of the Renaissance engineers in technical methods, as machines of war were among the most complex classical devices. And last but not least, the rulers were willing to spend incredible sums for military technique—not unlike today—but even more interesting to engineers, potentates were the most important employers of their profession in times when unemployment insurance did not exist.

The Catapult

Leonardo's work on the catapult is another example of his interest in military devices. In contrast to the scientists in the medieval times, he did not confine himself to just copying the classical knowledge but used it as a base for enhancements and amendments, true to Newton's famous citation "If I have seen further it is by standing on ye shoulders of Giants" 200 hundred years later. Such is the case with the catapult; Leonardo invented a new spring mechanism that could generate higher energy for throwing projectiles farther (Figure 1-3).

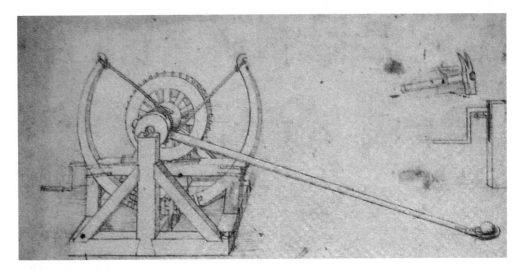

Figure 1-3. *The catapult*

Though fire weapons had already been established by the end of the 15th century and had found their way onto the European battlefields, they still suffered from a lot of "teething troubles." Hence, the well-proven concept of catapults was widely used, particularly at sieges where their multiple advantages—ease of use, high firing rate, high range, and the ability to launch a wide variety of different projectiles—provided a gain against cannons when using artillery against fortresses.

Leonardo made many designs for different types of catapults during his life, many of them during his early Florentine years. The one in question appears to have been produced during the first years of his work for Ludovico Sforza in Milan. It may have also been attached to the letter of application with the armored car.

We do not know how many of his military designs during his time in Milan made it into real deployment. Technical difficulties, impracticalities, and the fact that Leonardo was not employed by the duke as a military engineer but as the director of parades and festivities, might imply that many of his plans never left the theoretical stage. It's also possible the duke was not able to recognize the significance of Leonardo's designs and may have preferred other more practical and traditional competitors for the job. After all, Leonardo's position enabled him to run his own workshop alongside some apprentices. This gave him the opportunity to continue his studies without too many financial worries. During this time period, six major paintings, including *The Last Supper*, and a flood of technical drawings were created.

The manuscript for the catapult is part of Leonardo's Codex Atlanticus, which is preserved in the Biblioteca Ambrosiana in Milan. Many of Leonardo's drawings are collected in *codices*, collections of loose papers compiled by different collectors over the centuries. In most cases they are arranged not according to their original chronological order but, as was the custom in earlier periods, by a topical or even aesthetical scheme.

■**Note** These codices are today distributed over the museums of the world. For example, the Codex Leicester, a folio of scientific observations and illustrations on natural phenomena such as water, light, and gravity, was acquired by Microsoft's founder Bill Gates in 1994 and is put on public display once a year in a different city around the world. In 2007, it will be exhibited from June to August in the Chester Beatty Library in Dublin, Ireland.

The Revolving Bridge

The revolving bridge is contained in another manuscript that came to us with the Codex Atlanticus. It's an example of another area of Leonardo's interest: *hydrodynamics*, the science of the flow of water (Figure 1-4).

Leonardo dealt with studies on this topic during almost all of his scientific life. He believed water and air are similar substances and thus follow similar laws of flow. This was a surprisingly modern approach and was of particular interest to him in regard to his research on human flying, which you will read about in a later section.

Fortunately for him (and for the world), this interest squared perfectly with a practical need of his time: water was one of the major sources of energy then. The north Italian plain was plastered with water mills in these times. Furthermore, the rare roads were in bad shape and were more like paths than anything else. Hence, rivers and the sea were of utmost importance for transportation of goods and people.

As a consequence, cities such as Florence and Milan, with no direct access to the sea, were keen to spend a great deal of financial and material resources on making use of the rivers and any evolving engineering disciplines.

In Florence, young Leonardo was engaged in a canal project to make the Arno river navigable from Florence to the Mediterranean Sea. He was the first to propose this enhancement, according to Giorgio Vasari, the writer of Leonardo's first biography. In Milan, Leonardo made further contact with hydraulic engineering, learning a lot about it from Milan's impressive set of the so-called *navagli*, a network of inner-city canals. These experiences proved helpful when Leonardo turned his attention toward another water-related topic of even more military importance than today: bridges.

Figure 1-4. *Hydrodynamic study*

As cross points between streets and rivers, the two thoroughfares of transportation, bridges were of paramount relevance in military strategies. Bridges formed bottlenecks that could detain enemy troops. But this advantage could also be turned into a disadvantage if the enemy got a hold of the structure. Toward the end of his first decade in Milan, Leonardo developed a simple but effective concept to cope with this hazard: the revolving bridge. In his design, the bridge can be rotated around one of its end pylons (Figure 1-5). This way it could be moved away from the bank the enemy troops were approaching from, depriving them of the possibility to cross the river.

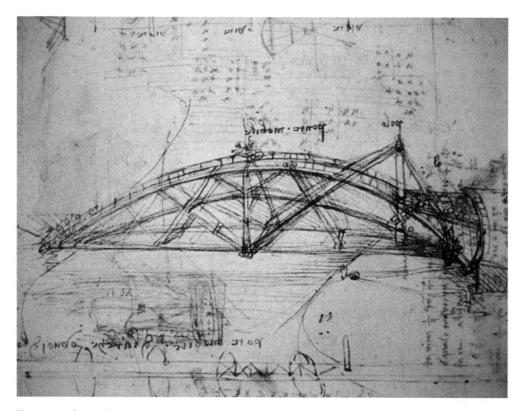

Figure 1-5. *The revolving bridge*

It is not known, though, if this bridge was ever been built somewhere around Milan.

When Leonardo left the city in 1499, he took his hydraulic knowledge with him and after three years of travel where he worked in different northern Italian cities, he found a cordial reception by the rulers of a city that was (and is) connected to water like none other: Venice.

As the Ottoman Empire had conquered Constantinople only five years before and was aggressively breaking into Venice's eastern borders, the Serenissima was in desperate need for skilled military engineers who had hydraulic knowledge also. As a result, in 1502, Leonardo joined the service of Cesare Borgio, who ruled the city as the doge. For the next two years, Leonardo planned and monitored the building of a defensive system on rivers, and even escorted the doge to a campaign in the Romagna. As an interesting side note, Leonardo did not appear to have many moral qualms about also working for the "other side"—an attitude he seemed to share with military suppliers of today.

■Note Also in 1502, Leonardo planned a 720-foot bridge as part of an engineering project for Sultan Bajazet II. This bridge would be made completely from wood and was to span the Golden Horn, an inlet at the mouth of the Bosporus. Though it was never built in his time, in 2001 a Norwegian group reproduced it near the capital of Oslo, almost precisely 500 years after his first drawing (Figure 1-6).

Figure 1-6. *The Norwegian version of Leonardo's bridge project on the Golden Horn*

Leonardo decided to leave the Venetian service after two years and return to Florence. He changed his employer but not his profession. The Florentine Republic engaged him both as a military advisor as well as a hydraulic engineer. Again, both occupations were not completely separate, as one of his first projects was the intended diversion of the Arno River near Florence's old enemy, the city of Pisa, in order to disconnect it from its water supply. Other projects also dealt with the Arno, but were of a more civil nature, such as the plan to extend the navigability of the river and reinforce the embankment near Florence to prevent floods. For that, Leonardo developed some of his largest machines, huge structures intended for use in canal building. It was also in these Florentine years between 1504 and 1508 when Leonardo painted the *Mona Lisa*.

The Aerial Screw and the Flying Machine

The beginning of the 16th century saw the maturing of Leonardo in an area in which he never presented any of his designs to a paying customer. No doubt this was due to their highly advanced and principally theoretical nature, for the matter in question was no less than the ability of human beings to fly.

OBSCURE MANUSCRIPTS

In spite of their advanced nature (or due to it), Leonardo's mechanical achievements did not contribute to the development of science and technology and did not influence technological progress in the early phase of modern history. His drawings were either obscure to his contemporaries and their offspring or totally unknown and remained so for 300 years. But in the 19th century, engineers were able to appreciate Leonardo's grasp of the mechanical.

More than 5,000 pages of his manuscripts are still available today. Apart from some superficial mentions of Leonardo and his works in some almanacs in the 16th century, these drawings are the only sources of his scientific research that have survived as far as we know.

Leonardo did not publish or otherwise distribute the contents of his notebooks. He did not wish for anybody to see or use his manuscripts. Apart from some drawings he produced for presentation to potential clients, his notes were intended for internal use, as some sort of mind maps. He even took up the habit of laying down the (often just fragmentary) textual explanations next to the actual drawings in mirror writing. In other words, he wrote from right to left so the finished text was the mirror image of normal writing, as shown in the illustration; he did so presumably in order to prevent possible business rivals from stealing his ideas.

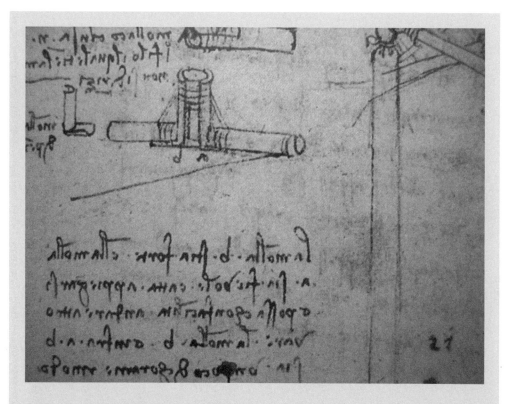

Furthermore, Leonardo was left-handed, which would have made writing from left to right pretty cumbersome for him. Writing feathers were shaped to be used by "ordinary" right-handed people then. This left-handedness, though, has helped to distinguish manuscripts written by him from similar ones from this period of time.

Due to the worksheet nature of his manuscripts, many of them were reengineered and extended in the course of Leonardo's life, sometimes even with nontechnical content. This is what made his manuscripts obscure and ambiguous to external readers. In modern times, people are apt to attach concepts of today's world to them. For example, some people inaccurately think he invented the helicopter when he drew the aerial screw. We have to be very careful with such misinterpretations, though there are instances where Leonardo's ideas appear to anticipate modern inventions indeed.

Leonardo was fascinated by flight all of his life and had become convinced that a human being could fly by his own muscle power, an idea he was deeply committed to and didn't give up until his death: ".... you will see the human being with big wings created by him, who will lean against the resistance of air, vanquishing it, being able to outplay and to rise above it," he wrote in 1486. In his opinion, the principal issue was to develop enough energy for the lifting mechanism. That belonged to a class of problems that could be solved by engineering: amplifying the power generated by a human's body by mechanical means. Navigability once the person was in the air was apparently not in the focus of his efforts, as there are not any noteworthy steering contraptions found in any of his according designs.

As previously mentioned, Leonardo considered air a substance that is a lightweight relative of water and thus would follow similar mechanical laws. This general idea led him in 1485 to the design of an *aerial screw*, a device that should "screw" itself into the air like a screw into water (Figure 1-7).

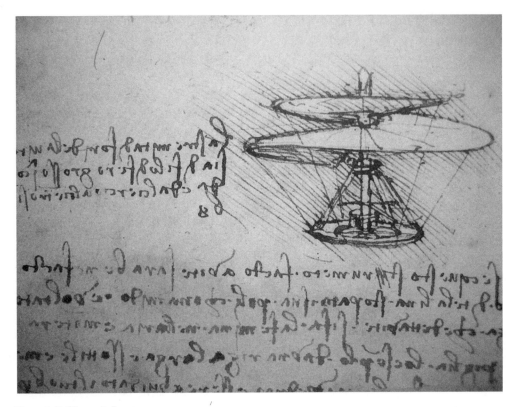

Figure 1-7. *The aerial screw*

In his opinion, the only major problem to solve was the generation of a revolution speed fast enough to make the whole device leave the ground. Obviously, the concept of lift and different levels of pressure on parts moving through the air was unknown to Leonardo, disqualifying the aerial screw as a helicopter; the aerial screw follows a completely different approach.

Leonardo developed many of his ideas for flying contraptions from his anatomical studies. In his opinion, the basic mechanical setup of all living creatures was similar. Hence, these capabilities were not out of the question (e.g., he intensely studied flying fish), in particular when appropriately supported by mechanical means.

Hence his approach toward flying was two-fold. On one hand, he followed the path of creating machines that should amplify man's power as far as possible. One or more pilots were meant to stand upright, sometimes even being required to move their heads and legs in addition to their arms to achieve maximum exploit of the body's muscles. On the other hand, he tried to mimic the mode of operation of birds, insects, and other flying animals, as in the case of his famous design of the flying machine (Figure 1-8).

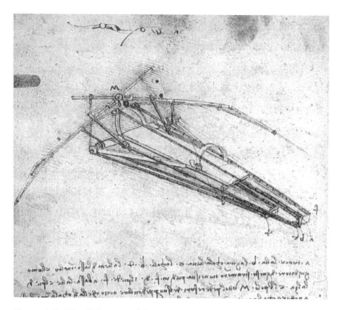

Figure 1-8. *The flying machine*

It was in the first decade of the 16th century that Leonardo wrote a treatise on the flight of birds. Though he tinkered with small models of many of his designs for empirical studies, there is no evidence that any of his flying machines—including the aerial screw and the flying machine—had ever been actually built during his lifetime. However, in our time some of them have been built and tested. His plan for a parachute has been certified to work by a skydiver who used it to jump out of a balloon 9,000 feet above the ground.

LEONARDO'S THEATER STAGE SET FOR ORPHEUS

Leonardo designed an ingenious theater stage set for the popular myth of Orpheus, shown in the following figure. It comprised two hemispheres that could be modeled and painted according to artistic need. They could be opened, closed, and rotated. Hence, with a dramatic theatrical effect, the underworld scene could be brought to the spectators' view by a circular and opening movement, with Pluto emerging on a platform from below accompanied by devils and furies.

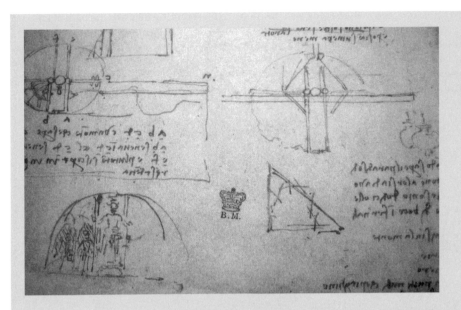

It might seem surprising for an engineer to be involved in the theater. However, when considering that Leonardo held the position of director of parades and festivities during his first years in Milan, and that the fine arts and mechanical gadgets played an important part in the Renaissance, Leonardo's activities in that area do not appear that far-fetched. As a matter of fact, it was his capability as a musician that gave the impact for his initial visit to Milan in 1481. Having built a silver lyre in the shape of a horse's head, he presented it to Duke Lorenzo di Medici (nicknamed "Il Magnifico"), the ruler of Florence. The duke, who was given more to diplomacy and good relations with his neighbor cities than to war, considered the beautiful lyre an ideal gift of peace for the authorities of Milan. The duke felt that young Leonardo, who could not only play the lyre very well, but was considered by his contemporaries to be exceptionally talented, handsome, and charming, was ideally suited for the diplomatic mission of delivering the lyre to Ludovico Sforza. Leonardo not only delivered the splendid lyre to Ludovico but also played it in a musician's competition and, according to his biographer Vasari, "played the (horse-shaped) lyre better than any other musicians at Ludovico's court."

Leonardo designed a lot of machines intended for use in performances and already had acquired some reputation as a stage engineer during his first sojourn in Milan. For the Milanese paradise feast he created a set of revolving hemispheres populated with actors impersonating the planets.

Yet, it likely was primarily not that part of his curriculum that induced the new rulers of Milan, the French, to offer him a position as *peintre et ingenieur ordinaire*. As a means of strengthening their position, the French were in need of skilled military engineers, and Leonardo still had an according reputation in the city. Eventually, in 1508, he accepted the offer and moved to Milan again. Here he not only turned to designing and building fortresses but again became concerned with hydraulic projects, this time with sluices, for a possible connection between Milan and Lake Como in the Alps. It was also during these years that he created the theater stage set for Orpheus.

Note In Vasari's biography of Leonardo, he said "[T]he greatest of all Andrea's pupils was Leonardo da Vinci, in whom, besides a beauty of person never sufficiently admired and a wonderful grace in all his actions, there was such a power of intellect that whatever he turned his mind to he made himself master of with ease." Because there is no known portrait of Leonardo in his youth, the only hint of how the great man may have looked is in two supposed self-portraits in his later years. One of these is shown in Figure 1-9.

Figure 1-9. *Supposed self-portrait of Leonardo*

The LEGO MINDSTORMS NXT

Now that you are acquainted with Leonardo and his life, let's take a look at the other topic this book deals with: LEGO MINDSTORMS NXT. In this section you will become familiar with the components that make up the new NXT, bridging Leonardo's world and applying this knowledge to his mechanical designs and reviving them with modern means.

In 1998, LEGO released the first generation of its MINDSTORMS line, the RCX: kits consisting of electric motors, sensors, LEGO bricks, and LEGO TECHNIC pieces grouped around a central controlling unit. Along with a bunch of extension kits, it developed into the most successful product in the company's history. Eight years later its successor, the LEGO MINDSTORMS NXT, finally saw the light of day, first in the United States in August 2006, and two months later in Europe.

The NXT ships in two versions:

- The retail version with 577 parts.

- The education base set with only 431 parts, but with a rechargeable battery and charger. It lacks the retail version's programming software, which is sold separately under different licenses for schools.

Hardware

Let's take a look at the hardware components of the NXT. There are four main categories:

- The central controlling unit: the NXT Brick
- Output devices: motors
- Input devices: sensors
- Means of communication: Bluetooth

The NXT Brick

The central component of the NXT is the programmable controller, also known as The Intelligent Brick (Figure 1-10). It's the NXT's brain, featuring a 32-bit ARM7 microcontroller with 256K flash and 64K RAM memory—running at 48MHz—and a second 8-bit AVR microcontroller with 4K flash and 512B RAM memory, running at 4MHz.

The four input ports are used for connecting the sensors, while the three output ports are for attaching the motors (Figure 1-11). The connections are digital, hence it is possible to extend the amount of available sensor and motor ports by adapters.

Figure 1-10. *The NXT Brick*

As shown in Figure 1-11, the connections are made using cables that resemble telephone cables, though the end connectors are mirrored, allegedly to prevent children from connecting their NXT to the telephone box. One of the input ports is IEC 61158 Type 4/EN 50 170–compliant, meant to be used for future high-speed expansions.

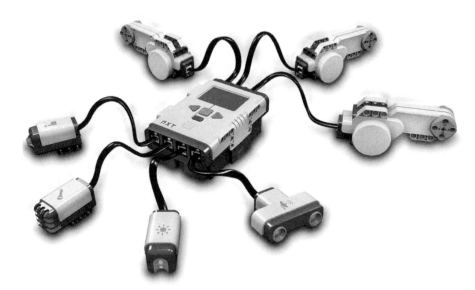

Figure 1-11. *The NXT Brick with motors and sensors attached*

The connection to the PC can be established over a USB cable attached to a USB 2.0 port next to the output ports or over the Brick's Bluetooth connectivity, which is also a means for communication with other Bluetooth-enabled devices such as PDAs or mobile phones.

On top of the Brick, there is a 100 × 64 pixel LCD display and four buttons that control the Brick's operating system: orange for on/off; dark gray for clear/back; and two light-gray buttons for navigating the menus displayed on the LCD.

A built-in speaker provides 8kHz sound quality over a sound channel with 8-bit resolution and a 2kHz–16kHz sample rate.

The Brick is powered by six AA batteries that do not come with the retail kit, or a rechargeable battery pack that comes with the education base set.

Oh, and if you always wanted to know how the Brick looks inside, see Figure 1-12.

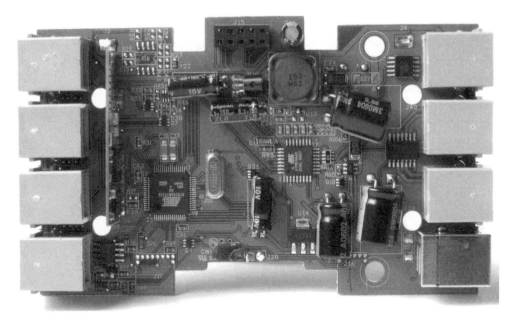

Figure 1-12. *The Brick's inner life (Image courtesy of Jürgen Stuber)*

■**Caution** Don't try opening the Brick at home!

Motors

The NXT kit comes with three motors (Figure 1-13).

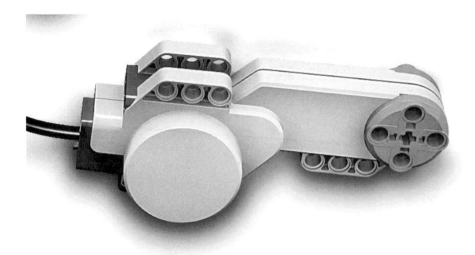

Figure 1-13. *A NXT motor*

You will notice that they appear rather large and bulky compared to the RCX motors. This is due to the high inner gearing that makes the motors much more powerful and reliable than the RCX's motors (Figure 1-14). But as a result, NXT robots are much larger than RCX ones.

Figure 1-14. *Inner gearing of the NXT motor (Image courtesy of LEGO Education)*

NXT motors are *servos*. That means that their internal position and state can be controlled from an external unit—in this case the NXT Brick. This is done using the in-built rotation sensor, enabling the Brick to control the motor very accurately. It can be rotated precisely up to 1 degree or run at a particular speed. Furthermore, two motors can be easily synchronized, which allows for precise straight driving. Anyone who has built a mobile RCX robot will quickly remember the problems these robots have staying on a straight course.

Since the controlling Brick can track changes of a motor's state, a motor can also be used as a "wired remote control."

Sensors

Sensors allow the NXT robot to get insight about and respond to the outer world. To this end, the NXT kit comes with four types of sensors; the kit contains one of each. There are additional sensors available, created and sold by third-party vendors.

Touch Sensors

The touch sensor is like a bumper; it enables the robot to detect press-and-release events. This kind of sensor can be used to detect very near obstacles. Figure 1-15 shows a touch sensor.

Figure 1-15. *The touch sensor*

Light Sensors

The light sensor is a rudimentary device that lets the robot "see" in a very limited sense. Measuring the amount of light that reaches the sensor's inlet, it allows for distinction between bright and dark, similar to an amoeba. Figure 1-16 shows a light sensor.

Figure 1-16. *The light sensor*

Though there's no built-in color detection, areas of different colors will give rise to different numerical values of reflected light. After all, these are not absolute but relative values, depending for instance on ambient light. This makes color detection with the light sensor pretty unreliable and context-dependent. The light sensor also has a small lamp to emit a red light, which is useful for illumination of dark environments and for amplification of reflected light.

Sound Sensors

The sound sensor is the robot's "ear." It can detect sounds in two different modes. First, it uses a mode called *adjusted decibels (dbA)* that mimics the way the human ear actually measures ambient sound. This means that the sensitivity of the sensor is adapted to the sensitivity of the human ear, ignoring very low or very high frequencies. The other mode, called *standard decibel (db)*, is simpler and plainly registers the whole frequency bandwidth equally.

Figure 1-17 shows a sound sensor.

Figure 1-17. *The sound sensor*

The sound sensor will deliver its results as percentages of its maximum volume of 90 decibels (which is equal to the noise of a lawn mower). For instance, values up to 5% reflect silence, 5–10% reflects distant talking, and 10–30% reflects nearby talking or low music.

It stands to reason that this kind of measurement does not allow for very precise control of the robot by sound. In particular, it's not meant to be used for voice recognition or the like.

Ultrasonic Sensors

The ultrasonic sensor is a type of sensor that is new to the MINDSTORMS world and has not been available with the RCX. Its eyelike shape might be considered to be like the robot's eyes, indeed enabling it to have a look at what's around it. Figure 1-18 shows an ultrasonic sensor.

Figure 1-18. *The ultrasonic sensor*

The sensor works in the way bats or submarines detect objects, with sonic signals of high frequency that are reflected by an object and received by the sensor again. The sensor is able to compute the distance to the object by measuring the running time of a single signal. Hence, the sensor can be used to attain two kinds of information—whether an object reflects signals at all, and if so, how far away it is. Depending on its mounting on the robot and the kind of object it detects, the LEGO ultrasonic sensor's detection range is up to 100 inches.

The ultrasonic sensor mainly serves as a means for touch-free object detection. Its great advantage to the touch sensor is that no physical contact with the object is required. This makes it possible to avoid objects much earlier. Yet, there's a drawback to this also. The sensor can't be used in an area where another ultrasonic sensor is actually at work. The sensor's signals will be interlaced with the signals of the other. Furthermore, since the signals are not labeled as its own, it will not be able to distinguish the reflection of its signals from the emission of the other sensor. Moreover, surfaces that swallow up or disperse signals, such as soft, round, or very jagged ones, are hard to detect and apt to be missed.

Bluetooth

Bluetooth is an industrial specification for wireless personal area networks and provides a way to connect and exchange information between different kinds of devices, such as PDAs, mobile phones, computers, cameras, and so on, via a globally unlicensed short-range radio frequency. Figure 1-19 shows a Bluetooth adapter.

Figure 1-19. *A Bluetooth adapter*

In addition to the USB cable discussed in the earlier section on the NXT Brick, the NXT allows for wireless communication also by providing Bluetooth Class 2 connectivity. Thus, an NXT Brick can talk to and receive messages from other Bluetooth-enabled devices such as a computer, a mobile phone, or other NXT Bricks up to the distance of approximately 10 meters.

The Bluetooth connectivity is established using the LEGO MINDSTORMS NXT Software (Figure 1-20).

Figure 1-20. *LEGO MINDSTORMS NXT Software utility for the NXT Bluetooth connectivity*

In particular, this connectivity can be used to upload or download programs or other software artifacts from or to the Brick or to remotely control the robot.

The Brick can be connected to up to three other devices at a time. However, it can only communicate with one at a time.

The NXT device can be made invisible to other devices. The Bluetooth connectivity can even be switched off completely, mainly to save battery power.

It should be noted that NXT supports only particular Bluetooth stacks, for instance the Bluetooth software included in Microsoft Windows XP Service Pack 2 and WIDCOMM Bluetooth Software for Windows version 1.4.2.10 SPS or newer. A complete list can be found on the official LEGO MINDSTORMS NXT web site at http://mindstorms.lego.com/.

Software

Like any programmable device, the NXT requires a good deal of software. Without it the Brick and its attached hardware components would simply be a collection of plastic and metal lying motionless on your table.

To bring a NXT robot to life, you need some things that pretty much all computerized gadgets depend on:

- Operating system: the firmware
- Data store: the NXT file system
- Administrative tools: the Try Me feature and the programming software

Firmware

The NXT Brick brings along its own *firmware* (a piece of software that is embedded into hardware), which can be thought of as the operating system of the NXT. Since it is stored in the flash memory, it will not be erased if you switch off the NXT or remove the batteries.

The firmware comes with the kit and has to be downloaded from the PC to the NXT at least once. However, you may erase it or reload it as often as you wish (well, almost—there's a limit of around 70,000 times after which the involved hardware components won't work reliably any more), for instance, when there are updated versions of the firmware available. New versions of the firmware are released frequently; the official version at the time of the writing of this book was 1.05.

You can even replace it with other kinds of appropriate firmware that may offer better performance, particular features, or support for a special programming language. An example of the latter is RobotC, a language for the NXT that runs on its own separate firmware. This firmware has to be downloaded to the NXT before you can use the language.

You will have a look at RobotC in the following chapter.

In summer 2006, LEGO released a software developer's kit (SDK) that included documentation for interfacing with the MINDSTORMS NXT driver on the PC or Mac as well as documentation for the executable file format on the NXT and how the firmware's Virtual Machine (VM) executes these files. Moreover, the company published the firmware itself as open source in December 2006.

NXT File System

The NXT's flash memory also contains a file system named Table of Contents (TOC). It is used to store persistent artifacts such as programs and data files and allows for a maximum number of 63 items. You can inspect the file system by using a utility of the LEGO MINDSTORMS NXT Software (see Figure 1-21). Note the different types of files on the Brick, as displayed on the left panel.

Figure 1-21. *LEGO MINDSTORMS NXT Software utility for inspecting the NXT file system*

Try Me

The NXT comes with a built-in program that provides a graphical menu on its display. Here you can do several administration tasks such as switching the Bluetooth connectivity on or off, connecting to other devices, starting or stopping programs, or getting information on the state of your Brick.

One of the most helpful features is the Try Me function. Using it, you can test all the sensors and motors attached without having to write a program for it. For instance, you can attach one or two motors to the output ports and run them in a given sequence, or test the reaction of an ultrasonic sensor.

Programming Software

The NXT kit also provides its official programming environment, the LEGO MINDSTORMS NXT Software. We already have encountered it in the hardware section and will have a look at in Chapter 2.

The NXT Community

When LEGO at the end of 2005 announced the NXT, a community for it was instantly created on the World Wide Web. The Internet appears to be the perfect platform for NXT aficionados. This community is still growing, with new blogs, private NXT-related sites, and new videos every week.

This section takes a short look at some of the most prominent and popular parts of the community.

The MINDSTORMS Developer's Program

At the end of 2005, the LEGO Group's robotics team announced a program called MINDSTORMS Developer Program (MDP). An exclusive group of 100 people was provided with beta versions of LEGO MINDSTORMS NXT kits to test them and help guide the product development process for NXT. Another more limited handful of LEGO aficionados (called "MUPpets" based on the name of the project: MINDSTORMS USERS Program) were included in the actual product development. There was no application process, and the existence of this group was not made public.

During the winter of 2005/2006, more than 96,000 robotics enthusiasts from 79 countries between the ages of 18 and 75 applied online for the MDP. In February 2006, the 100 lucky ones (including this book's author) were chosen and given access to an online forum that was set up to provide feedback. The members of the program were and still are under a nondisclosure agreement, whereas some parts of the MDP were allowed to be made public after May 1, 2006.

Until the official end of the program in August 2006, most of the members were extremely busy with exchanging ideas on the NXT with LEGO and influencing the product to be released. All parties participating in the MDP consider it a tremendous success today. It's not surprising, therefore, that LEGO set up a successor, called the MINDSTORMS Community Partners (MCP) program where approximately 20 people, partly chosen from the MCPs, are meant to help establish and deepen the connection between the NXT community and the LEGO Group.

LEGO.com MINDSTORMS Community NXT

Some of the major results of the MCP, information on some of its most committed members, and a lot of interesting robots can be found on LEGO's official community page at http://mindstorms. lego.com. This site is also the place for announcements, press releases, and company news regarding the NXT product. It also features downloadable media such as wallpapers, desktop icons, and a web site toolkit for building your own NXT web site. It is the exclusive source for new releases of the LEGO MINDSTORMS NXT Software. Moreover, LEGO has started to provide building instructions for advanced robots designed by the LEGO robotics team, including the recent sound-playing robot and a truly prodigious classic cuckoo clock.

However, the most interesting feature on the web site arguably is NXTLOG, most likely the largest repository for NXT robots on the Web. It's a fully moderated community where members may upload their NXT projects with photos, descriptions, and building instructions, thus sharing their designs with the community. Each week projects are chosen as "Projects of the Week." By April 2007, there were more than 1,800 projects published. Everyone, including those who do not have a project of their own to contribute, is welcome to get inspired by the contents of NXTLOG. Hence, whenever you are out of ideas for your next NXT, feel free to have a look there.

MINDSTORMS Education NXT

When LEGO launched LEGO MINDSTORMS in 1998, it also developed LEGO MINDSTORMS for Schools, the educational version of the MINDSTORMS concept. It was meant to help students become familiar with science, technology, engineering, and math. To this end, LEGO MINDSTORMS for Schools combines the LEGO MINDSTORMS system with the very popular programming software ROBOLAB.

Today, LEGO MINDSTORMS for Schools is used in more than 25,000 educational institutions world-wide, from elementary schools to universities.

The educational branch of LEGO, called LEGO Education, has been very active in supporting teachers in providing new ways of teaching traditional curriculum areas. The basic idea is making the teaching and learning of science and technology an adventure by focusing on firsthand experience with construction, mechanisms, energy, and programming techniques. The traditional way of memorizing external knowledge is discouraged here; instead, students are asked to use their individual problem-solving skills and imagination in challenges while cooperating with their fellow students.

LEGO has created a separate version of the NXT kit for the educational branch. With the arrival of this kit, the MINDSTORMS Education NXT site (http://www.legoeducation.info/nxt) was created. It is targeted particularly at teachers and other educators, but other people can also find a lot of interesting material there, including a NXT blog, building instructions for a lot of unique robots, and a store where you can buy a lot of NXT-related items; some of them available exclusively.

The NXT STEP

With *blogs* (web sites where entries are made in journal style and displayed in a reverse chronological order) becoming enormously popular in the past few years, those related to the NXT have also sprung up like mushrooms. One of the earliest and still most popular blogs is The NXT STEP (http://thenxtstep.blogspot.com), founded by MDP James Kelly in March 2006 and coauthored by a lot of other members of the MDP (including, once again, this book's author).

The NXT STEP has gained a reputation for not only being very active and often the first blog to spread news on the NXT but also for setting a high standard for qualified content. The blog has become pretty popular since its creation; it's listed on the official LEGO NXT community page and reached its 900th post as of April 2007, with more than 30,000 unique visitors in that month.

nxtasy.org

Another increasingly successful means of communication in communities are *forums*, essentially web sites composed of a number of member-written threads, where each thread entails a discussion or conversation in the form of a series of posts. It stands to reason that this kind of exchanging of information is perfect for a NXT robot community, and it's no surprise that today there are a lot of NXT-related forums to be found on the Web. One of the first was nxtasy.org (http://nxtasy.org), founded by Eric Salinas in June 2006. It quickly became the largest online forum for the NXT, having gained almost 750 members by March 2007.

Besides the forum and several subforums that deal with NXT software, hardware, projects, and other general topics, there are frequent challenges to the members. In addition, there's an active blog with prominent contributors and a repository with a lot of interesting NXT robot projects.

mynxt.matthiaspaulscholz.eu

I'll take the opportunity here to draw your attention to my own NXT-related web site at http://mynxt.matthiaspaulscholz.eu. It's linked to many of the previously mentioned sites and has found and is still finding the interest of a lot of people. For instance, around 3,000 unique visitors went to the site as of March 2007.

The site features a bunch of robots created by me along with their building instructions, links to NXT-related tools, programming languages, and other NXT-related information on the Web as well as a Middle-European-focused events page and a contact page where you can send messages to me; I always try to respond.

It goes without saying that the NXT universe is growing still, and there's an abundance of other interesting web content out there related to the NXT.

For a list of some other sites that I consider worthwhile, refer to Appendix D of this book.

Summary

In this introductory chapter, you made a tour through Leonardo's life, built around some of his most prominent inventions. You should now be familiar with him and his major works and be able to put them into perspective with the historical context of the Renaissance era as well as appreciate their uniqueness. You also met the latest member of the LEGO MINDSTORMS family, the NXT, and learned about its components and capabilities. I hope that you are looking forward to implementing Leonardo's inventions with LEGO, as you will do in the following chapters.

Last but not least, I introduced some of the main protagonists of today's NXT online community. You should know by now where to start when making your first steps with the NXT. In the following chapter, I will acquaint you with some of the most interesting programming environments.

CHAPTER 2

■■■

A 3,000-Foot Look at NXT Programming Environments

He who loves practice without theory is like the sailor who boards ship without a rudder and compass and never knows where he may cast.

—Leonardo da Vinci

Building a NXT robot is fun and the result is commonly pleasant to behold. Yet, a robot that does not actually do anything is not a real robot; a *robot* is defined as "an electromechanical device that can perform autonomous or preprogrammed tasks." The fun of looking at a newly built robot is nothing next to the pleasure of watching your own creation walking, driving, grabbing, avoiding, recognizing—in a nutshell, behaving—even if its behavior is sometimes (some might say *most of the time*) different from the one you originally intended.

To that end, a robot needs to be programmed. Programming a robot can be as much fun as building it. On the other hand, it can turn into drudgery if you use the wrong tool, the wrong language, or the wrong program design. Mind that *wrong* in this sense means "not suited for the context." There is not *one* tool or *one* language for the domain of NXT robot programming. A tool or language that fits a particular task or given skill better than another might not be suitable in a different programming challenge. The trick is to choose the right tool for the right context.

On the following pages you will take a tour through some existing programming environments for the NXT that will provide you with a toolbox to choose from and the knowledge of what to choose when. There are a lot of programming environments available—some commercial, some provided by the community—but I will concentrate on the ones that are executable directly on the Brick, in contrast to those that run on the computer and control the Brick remotely, which in my view does not comply completely with the concept of autonomous robots.[1]

Of course, this is just a 3,000-foot view. Discussion of the details of the programming environments or their advantages and drawbacks is out of the scope of this book. However, you can find some reading recommendations in Appendix D on this topic. For each of the environments discussed in this chapter, there's an associated paragraph in Appendix A that will help you install and configure it on your machine as well as download the programs and run them on your Brick.

---

1. For a pretty complete overview on presently available programming environments for the NXT, see Steve Hassenplug's site at http://www.teamhassenplug.org/NXT/NXTSoftware.html.

LEGO MINDSTORMS NXT Software

The LEGO MINDSTORMS NXT Software is the software that comes with the NXT retail kit. It is the software developed and distributed by the LEGO Group itself and is endorsed by the company for programming NXT robots. The following image shows the LEGO MINDSTORMS NXT Software loading.

The LEGO MINDSTORMS NXT Software is available for Windows XP and the Mac and was developed for LEGO by National Instruments, an Austin, Texas–based company specializing in automated test environments and virtual instrumentation software. National Instruments produces the proprietary LABVIEW programming platform that uses a dataflow language, called G, with a graphical syntax. ROBOLAB software, the programming software created for the original LEGO MINDSTORMS for Schools product by National Instruments in 1998, is based on LABVIEW. LEGO MINDSTORMS NXT Software was built on top of LABVIEW. Consequently, the programming language used in the LEGO MINDSTORMS NXT Software was named NXT-G.

In the next section I illustrate the basic concepts of that programming language so you will understand the different areas of the IDE later on.

NXT-G

NXT-G is a *dataflow language*—NXT-G programs are modeled as directed graphs of the data flowing between operations. This modeling is done using a graphical notation, comprising *blocks*, which visualize operations, and *sequence beams*, which control the flow of your program. The beams indicate the sequence in which the blocks connected by them will be executed when the program actually runs on the Brick (Figure 2-1).

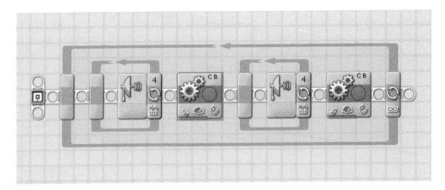

Figure 2-1. *Dataflow in a simple NXT-G program*

In contrast to popular imperative languages such as BASIC, C, and Java, there is no sequence of commands that the programmer is laying down in a textual way. Instead, NXT-G programs are created by using drag-and-drop to place different types of blocks on the work area and connect them with beams and data wires. Before downloading such a program to the Brick, the program automatically gets compiled into assembler code that can be executed by the firmware. The LEGO MINDSTORMS NXT Software allows for creating your own blocks in addition to those that initially come with the software. You can also import blocks created and published by other NXT-G programmers.

Blocks

By default, the software offers a wide variety of NXT-related blocks.[2] In addition to the blocks in the following sections, there are a number of other utility blocks, for instance for data type conversion, mathematical operations, generation of random numbers, access to the Brick's file system, and more.

Output Control

Control for output devices such as motors, sound, and LCD is provided by the following blocks:

- *Motor block*: Controls the movement of one single motor.
- *Move block*: Controls and synchronizes the movement of two or more motors.
- *Rotation sensor block*: Counts the degrees or full rotations of a motor.
- *Sound block*: Plays a tone or a sound file.
- *Display block*: Displays text, an image, or a custom shape on the NXT's LCD screen.

Input Control

Control for input devices such as sensors is provided by the following blocks:

- *Touch sensor block*: Provides access to the present state of a touch sensor.
- *Sound sensor block*: Serves as a sound detector that provides the current sound value and sends true or false when the sound value is above or below a given level.
- *Light sensor block*: Measures ambient light on a light sensor or turns on or off the light sensor's lamp.
- *Ultrasonic sensor*: Checks for reflections of signals detected by an ultrasonic sensor.

Communication

Communication is handled by the following blocks:

- *Send message block*: Sends Bluetooth messages.
- *Receive message block*: Receives Bluetooth messages.

Program Flow

Control on the program's general flow is achieved by using the following blocks:

- *Wait block*: Lets the program pause until a certain sensor value is reached or a certain amount of time has passed by.
- *Loop block*: Repeats a portion of the program until a condition is complied with, such as elapsed time, the number of repetitions, a logic signal, or a sensor state.

---

2. It has been announced that future versions of the LEGO MINDSTORMS NXT Software will have additional blocks.

- *Switch block*: Chooses between two or more sequences of code according to a particular condition.
- *Stop block*: Stops a running program, running motors, lamps, and sounds.

Other Blocks

There are some blocks that do not fit the previous categories:

- *Timer block*: Reads or resets the value of three built-in timers that start counting when a NXT-G program starts.
- *Record/play block*: Allows for the recording of movements of the robot. Once you've recorded a sequence of movements, you can switch the block to "play" mode; the robot will repeat the recorded movements.

Custom Blocks

One of the most useful features of the LEGO MINDSTORMS NXT Software is the ability to create and use custom blocks. *Custom blocks* may be seen as user-defined subprograms consisting of sequences of blocks connected by beams and data wires.

Creating a custom block, a so-called *My Block*, is easy; just use the My Block Builder on the Custom Blocks palette by selecting a number of blocks in the work area and grouping them together into your own block with a customized icon (Figure 2-2).

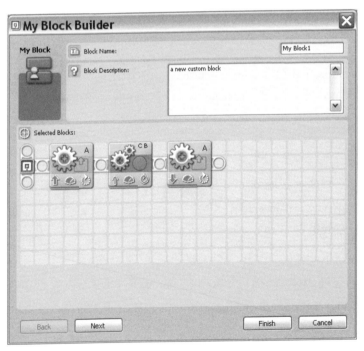

Figure 2-2. *Defining your own custom block*

The newly created My Block will appear on the Custom palette and can be used in further programs like any other block and shared with others (Figure 2-3).

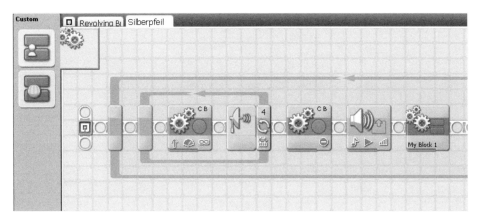

Figure 2-3. *Using a custom block*

Variables

NXT-G also supports the concept of *global variables*. Whenever you need to set a value that should be globally accessible by other blocks, you might consider defining such a variable.

Variables are defined using the Define Variable command in the Edit menu of the IDE. Your new variable has to be named and its type of data has to be specified; however, only Text, Number, or Logic variable types are possible here (Figure 2-4).

Figure 2-4. *Defining a variable in NXT-G*

Variables can then be used in a program by simply dragging and connecting a variable block to the program graph (Figure 2-5).

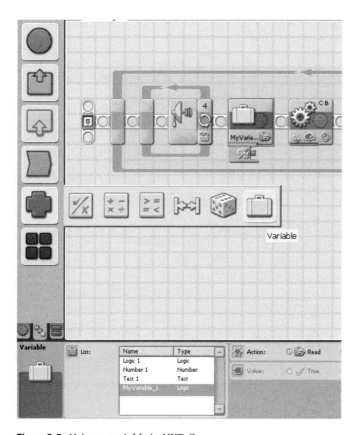

Figure 2-5. *Using a variable in NXT-G*

Note that variables are of particular importance when using custom blocks; they are a means to mimicking the passing of parameters to the block.

Data Wires

You might have already asked yourself how actual data values are passed between blocks. To this end, NXT-G offers the concept of *data wires*, model elements visualized as lines (Figure 2-6).

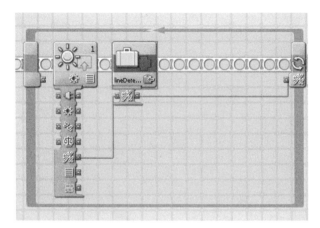

Figure 2-6. *A data wire passing a data value between two blocks*

Each block possesses a *data hub*, where the types of values it can provide are accessible. By connecting the ports on the data hubs of two blocks, the target block at the end of the wire can access the value stored in the source block at the wire's beginning.

IDE

Once you install and start the LEGO MINDSTORMS NXT Software, you can see the integrated development environment (IDE), as shown in Figure 2-7.

The IDE consists of six different areas that enable you to perform all the tasks that are required to write programs for the NXT, to download them to the Brick, and to run them there:

- *Toolbar*: The area that allows you to trigger most frequently used commands
- *Programming palette*: The store for the different types of blocks
- *Work area*: The canvas to compose your programs on
- *Configuration panel*: The area to configure the separate blocks on the work area in detail
- *Controller*: The tool to compile, download, and run programs
- *Robo Center*: The bridge to the NXT community

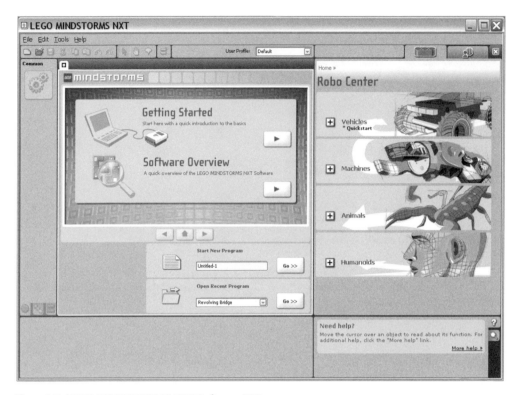

Figure 2-7. *LEGO MINDSTORMS NXT Software IDE*

Toolbar

On the toolbar, you can start the most frequently used commands, such as loading or saving programs, administrating your custom blocks, updating the firmware, and calling help. Figure 2-8 shows the toolbar.

Figure 2-8. *LEGO MINDSTORMS NXT Software IDE toolbar*

Programming Palette

The programming palette is the container for the model elements that you can use in your program. For more productive work, it's separated into three tabs:

- *Common palette*: Contains the most frequently used blocks
- *Complete palette*: Contains all available blocks
- *Custom palette*: Contains the blocks you've created yourself or imported

Figure 2-9 shows the programming palette.

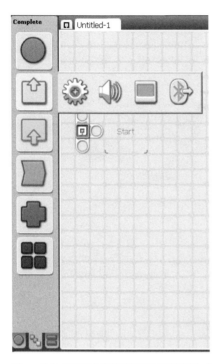

Figure 2-9. *LEGO MINDSTORMS NXT Software IDE programming palette*

Work Area

The work area is where the actual programming takes place. Blocks are dragged from the palette and connected to beams here (Figure 2-10).

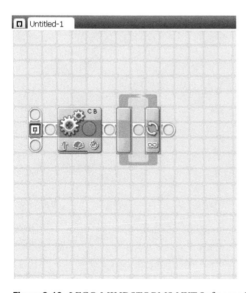

Figure 2-10. *LEGO MINDSTORMS NXT Software IDE work area*

Configuration Panel

You will use the configuration panel to configure the blocks that are part of your program. Each block has a set of configuration settings that will be displayed and may be filled with values when the block is selected in the work area. Figure 2-11 shows the configuration panel.

Figure 2-11. *LEGO MINDSTORMS NXT Software IDE configuration panel*

Controller

The controller is the administration tool that lets you view the present state of your NXT Brick or Bricks in terms of availability, memory, and power. Moreover, it's the trigger for downloading to and running programs or pieces of programs on the Brick (Figure 2-12).

Figure 2-12. *LEGO MINDSTORMS NXT Software IDE controller*

After the program has been compiled, you will download it to the Brick, as shown in Figure 2-13. The compiled assembler code is transferred to the Brick's memory.

Figure 2-13. *LEGO MINDSTORMS NXT Software IDE downloading programs*

Robo Center

The Robo Center is not directly connected to programming but serves as a bridge to the NXT community. Here you find not only onscreen building instructions for four advanced robots but also a portal to the LEGO.com MINDSTORMS community NXT web site where you can get challenges and download NXT-G–related material such as sample programs, sound files, and additional building instructions. Figure 2-14 shows the Robo Center.

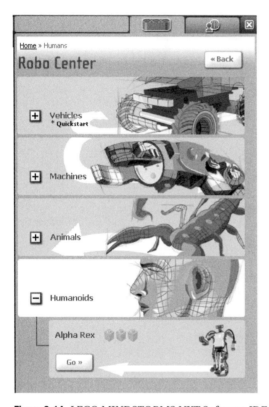

Figure 2-14. *LEGO MINDSTORMS NXT Software IDE Robo Center*

Example Program Snippets

To illustrate all these concepts, let's have a look at some typical robot programming tasks and how they are implemented in a NXT-G program. I keep them very simple to prevent implementation details hiding the big picture. Note that you will see complete programs in the following chapters.

Driving

Assume that you have a four-wheeled robot where the two rear wheels are each driven by a motor (Figure 2-15).

Figure 2-15. *The four-wheeled robot[3]*

You want the robot to drive straight. Since the robot will drive until you manually switch it off, you will begin with attaching a loop block to the starting point of each NXT program, configuring it to run forever. Inside this loop you place the move block for driving straight (Figure 2-16).

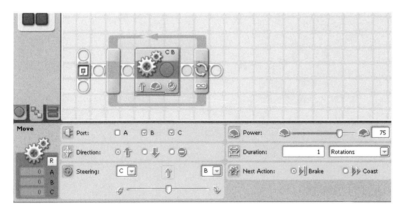

Figure 2-16. *NXT-G driving straight*

Stopping

How do you stop the robot using NXT-G programming? Simply enough: you use a move block configured to stop the two rear motors (Figure 2-17).

---

3. Building instructions for this robot, called Silberpfeil, can be found on my web site at http://mynxt.matthiaspaulscholz.eu.

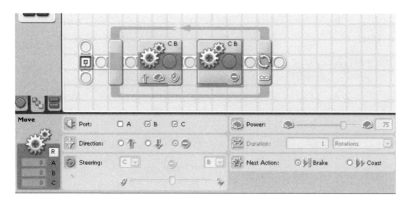

Figure 2-17. *NXT-G stopping motors*

Rotating

To rotate, you drag a move block onto the beam that drives the motors 45 degrees (Figure 2-18).

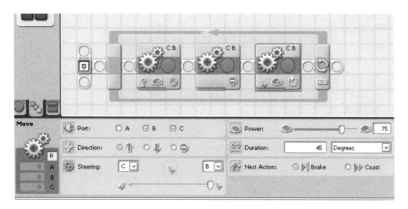

Figure 2-18. *NXT-G rotating*

Accessing and Handling Sensor Values

Assume that you have an ultrasonic sensor attached to the Brick and you want to detect objects with it that are closer than 50 inches. For this, you use a loop block, configuring it to run a move block until the ultrasonic sensor triggers an according detection event (Figure 2-19).

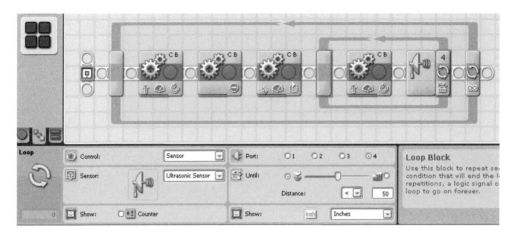

Figure 2-19. *NXT-G ultrasonic detection*

Playing Sounds

Playing a sound with NXT-G is easy. A particular type of block, the sound block, allows not only for playing tones but also for playing complete sound files saved in the NXT-proprietary .rso file format (Figure 2-20).

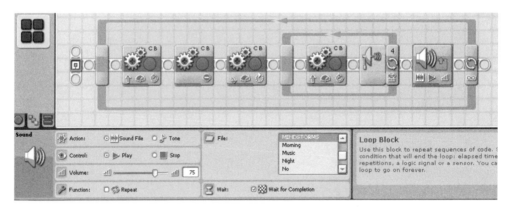

Figure 2-20. *NXT-G playing sounds*

RobotC

RobotC is a programming environment based on the popular functional programming language C. It was developed by the CMU Robotics Academy, an institute of the Carnegie Mellon University in Pittsburgh, Pennsylvania, that is "committed to using robotics to excite children about science and technology and to help create a more technologically literate society," as its web site states. Figure 2-21 shows RobotC.

Figure 2-21. *RobotC*

While a 30-day evaluation version can be downloaded for free, RobotC is a commercially available product, with a price of around $50. Presently, RobotC is available for Windows XP only but plans for Mac support have been announced already by the Robotics Academy.

An interesting point with RobotC is that it is cross-platform, supporting not only the NXT but also its MINDSTORMS predecessor, the RCX, and the popular VEX, a robotics kit produced by Innovation First, Inc. It is claimed that programs written for one of these platforms are portable to others with only little change. This is made possible by a *Virtual Machine* (VM), a layer that provides the glue between the code laid down in the RobotC language and the hardware it runs on, and that glue is necessarily different on each target platform. Hence, RobotC programs are run by an interpreter that does not operate on the native instruction set of the robotics controller but on the instructions of the VM (these VM instructions are called *bytecode*). Other high-level programming languages such as Java and C# are based upon this very concept. Yet, it is different from the one the original C language and NXT-G are following.

While performance often is a crucial point for interpreted languages, RobotC prides itself on providing better performance than NXT-G on the Brick. This is due to the use of a particular RobotC-specific firmware that differs from the official NXT one. Hence, before RobotC programs can be run, the official firmware has to be replaced by RobotC's on the Brick.

There are other features that make RobotC attractive to programmers such as real-time debugging (which is pretty difficult with NXT-G), an optimizing bytecode compiler, and support for almost all concepts of the powerful C language.

IDE

The IDE of RobotC is rather clear, consisting of a menu bar and an editor (Figure 2-22).

Figure 2-22. *RobotC's IDE*

Menu Bar

The menu bar is the place where you can start commands such as opening or saving programs, selecting the target platform, connecting to the NXT Brick, downloading RobotC's firmware, and compiling and downloading programs (Figure 2-23).

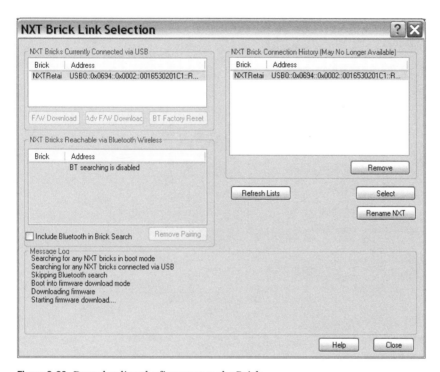

Figure 2-23. *Downloading the firmware to the Brick*

It's also from here where you start the debugger (Figure 2-24).

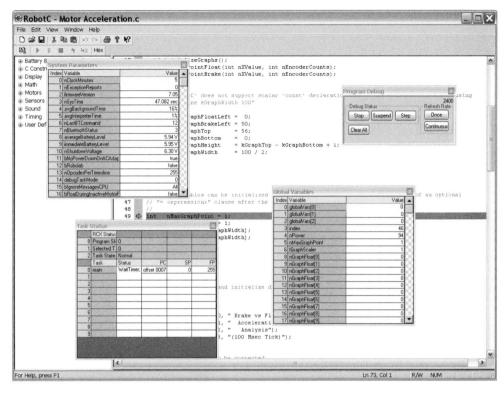

Figure 2-24. *RobotC's real-time debugger*

Editor

The editor is separated into two parts: a tree that lists language elements, and the actual editing section. The elements in the tree can be dragged into the editing section, thus helping the programmer easily gain an overview of the language elements and save on typing. The editing section is the place where you actually write your program code. It features syntax highlighting, code completion, and intelligent indenting.

Example Program Snippets

You will now implement the simple sample program snippets with RobotC that you developed with NXT-G in the previous section.

Driving

Again, you need an infinite loop for the endless execution of the program. The two motors are run by two separate commands:

```
// endless loop
while(true)   {
        // run motors B and C at a power level of 75%
        motor[motorB] = 75;
        motor[motorC] = 75;
}
```

Stopping

You stop the motors in a similar way to running them—just set the power to 0:

```
// stop motors B and C
motor[motorB] = 0;
motor[motorC] = 0;
```

Rotating

Run motor A by reading the variable nMotorEncoder that is the degrees counter:

```
// rotate motor by 45 degrees
nMotorEncoder[motorA] = 0;
while(nMotorEncoder[motorA] < 45 ) {
    motor[motorA] = 75;
}
motor[motorA] = 0;
```

Accessing and Handling Sensor Values

You need a loop for executing some statements until the ultrasonic sensor detects an object nearer than 50 inches:

```
const tSensors ultrasonicSensor = (tSensors) S1;
do {
    // perform some statements
    ...
    // do so while ultrasonic sensor does not detect
    // an object nearer than 50 inches
} while(SensorValue(ultrasonicSensor) > 50);
```

Playing Sounds

Play a tone by using the PlayTone convenience method predefined by RobotC:

```
// play a tone (frequency 500, duration 50 * 10 ms)
PlayTone(500, 50);
```

NXC

Not eXactly C (NXC) is a C-style language that can be used to program the NXT Brick. Programs written in NXC are compiled to run on the original LEGO NXT firmware.

NXC is built on top of the assembler language NBC that was the first language to appear on the scene next to the LEGO MINDSTORMS NXT Software. Its first beta release was published by MCP member John Hansen just one day after the first stage of the nondisclosure agreement expired for the beta-test team on May 1, 2006. Hansen was already rather well-known as a coauthor with David Baum of the popular Not Quite C (NQC), a C-style language that was widely used for programming the NXT's predecessor, the RCX.

NXC is published under the Mozilla Public License (MPL), which means among other things that you can download and use it for free (http://bricxcc.sourceforge.net/nxc). Hansen has also upgraded the IDE, called Bricx Command Center (BricxCC), for NQC and other programming languages for development with NBC. It's available at http://sourceforge.net/projects/bricxcc. Let's have a look at it now.

IDE

The Bricx Command Center runs on Microsoft Windows only and is presently available in version 3.3 (Figure 2-25).

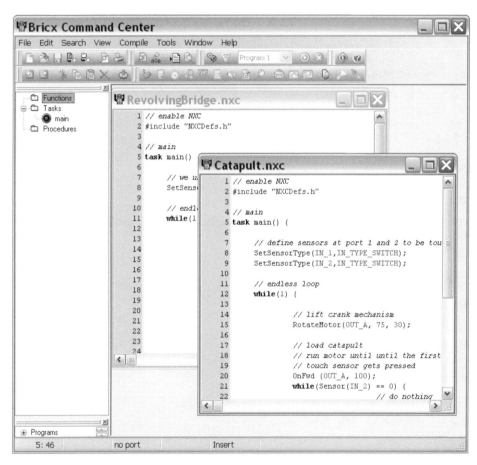

Figure 2-25. *The Bricx Command Center*

The IDE comprises the three classical components:

- A menu bar
- A toolbar providing buttons for the most frequently used features of the menu bar
- An editor

Menu Bar

BrickCC's menu bar provides support for features such as the usual file operations, enhanced editing commands, and compiling and downloading programs to the Brick. The Tools menu that lists a lot of useful tools for the Brick is shown in Figure 2-26.

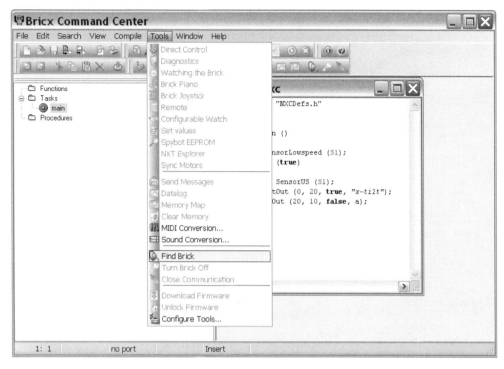

Figure 2-26. *BricxCC's Tools menu*

Another menu item worth having a look at is Preferences, where you can play around with a multitude of different configuration settings (Figure 2-27).

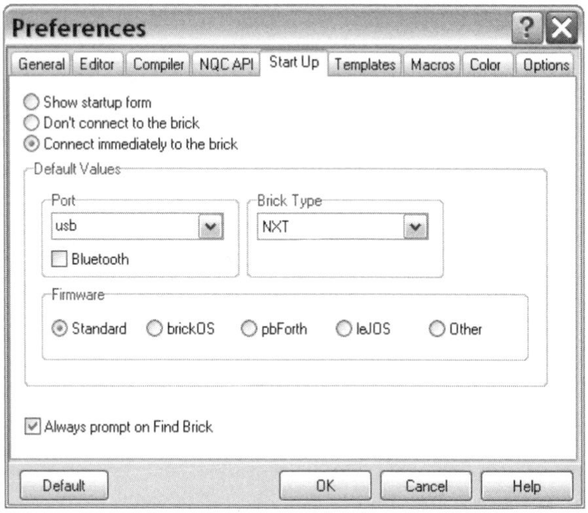

Figure 2-27. *BricxCC's Preferences menu*

Editor

The editor is separated into two parts: a tree that lists language elements, and the actual editing section (Figure 2-28).

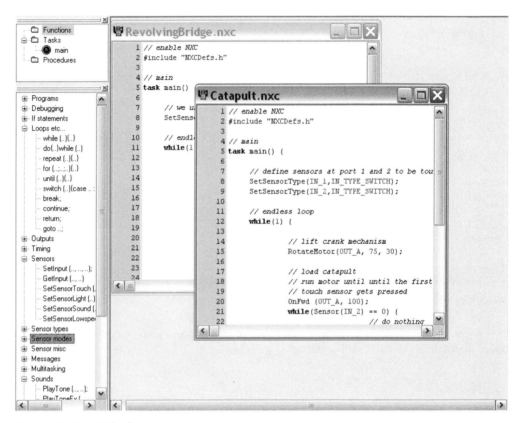

Figure 2-28. *BricxCC's editor*

The editor provides high-level support for creating NXC programs with most of the features you would expect in a modern IDE.

Example Program Snippets

To get a feeling of how an NXC program looks, let's implement the sample program snippets you developed with NXT-G and RobotC in the previous sections.

Driving

To drive forward, you run the two motors B and C synchronized. The synchronization is simply done by using the OnFwdSync function with OUT_BC as the first argument:

```
// run motors B and C synchronized on a power level of 75%
// the third argument 100 means that both motors run in the same direction
OnFwdSync (OUT_BC, 75, 100);
```

Stopping

To stop, use the Off function:

```
// stop motors B and C
Off(Out_BC);
```

Rotating

To rotate motor A, you use the RotateMotor function:

```
// rotate motor by 90 degrees
RotateMotor (Out_A,75,90);
```

Playing Sounds

To play sounds, use the following command:

```
// play a tone of frequency 500 and duration 5000 ms
PlayTone (500, 5000);
```

pbLua

pbLua is a new text-based programming language for the NXT developed in 2006 by Ralph Hempel, one of the renowned pioneers of the LEGO MINDSTORMS community. Hempel is a firmware expert, one of the four MUPpets, and the author of a number of books on the NXT's predecessors (Figure 2-29).

Figure 2-29. *pbLua*

pbLua is based on Lua, a lightweight programming language that was developed by a team at the Pontifical Catholic University in Rio de Janeiro. It was originally designed for extending applications but today also serves as a general-purpose, stand-alone language. Like RobotC, Lua (and thus pbLua) is not compiled into native code that can be directly executed by the operating system. Instead, it is translated into bytecode that is interpreted by an OS-specific VM.

Since Lua relies more on providing metamechanisms for extending the language semantics than on bringing along a broad set of language features, its core is kept rather small and lightweight and has a reputation for being very fast. Along with its automatic garbage collection and dynamic typing, it's not only ideal for scripting and rapid prototyping but very well-suited for being ported to embedded systems.

At the time of this writing, pbLua was available for free as a beta 3 version from Hempel's site, http://www.hempeldesigngroup.com/lego/pbLua.

pbLua does not come with its own programming environment, although there is a Lua plug-in for Eclipse. Appendix A deals with how to use pbLua and the plug-in.

Example Program Snippets

Lua is based on the concept of *associative arrays*, also known as *lookup tables*. Functions and data are kept in maps and may be accessed using a key of any type. These maps can be dynamically created, changed, and iterated.[4] For instance, a typical call to a function would look like this:

```
nxt.OutputSetSpeed(3,0,0,0)
```

where nxt is a lookup table and OutputSetSpeed the key of a function. In this case the nxt table and its functions come with pbLua already, but you are free to extend it, of course.

Driving

To run the motors you access the according function keys in the (predefined) nxt table:

```
-- configure motor B and C to run in "brake" mode
nxt.OutputSetMode(2,2)
nxt.OutputSetMode(3,2)
-- set the power of the motors to 75 %
-- 32 means "run mode"
nxt.outputSetSpeed(2, 32, 75, 0)
nxt.outputSetSpeed(3, 32, 75, 0)
```

Stopping

To stop the motors you set the power to 0%:

```
-- set the power of the motors to 0 %
nxt.outputSetSpeed(2, 0, 0)
nxt.outputSetSpeed(3, 0, 0)
```

Rotating

You need to enable regulation to make use of the tachometer feedback built into the NXT motor and set the tachometer to the desired value of degrees:

```
-- enable regulation for motor A
nxt.OutputEnableRegulation(1,1)
-- rotate 90 degrees
nxt.OutputSetSpeed(1,32,75,0)
nxt.OutputSetTachoLimit(1,90)
```

leJOS NXJ

leJOS, currently in version 3.0, is a tiny open source Java-based operating system that was originally designed for the NXT's predecessor, the RCX, and was and still is very popular for programming with Java. With the appearance of the NXT, the leJOS community made efforts to port leJOS to run on the NXT. An alpha release of leJOS for the NXT, called leJOS NXJ, can be downloaded at http://www.lejos.org. There is a strong presumption that LeJOS NXJ will soon develop into a mature and productive platform for the NXT (Figure 2-30).

---

4. You can even use maps as values in other maps, thus creating a hierarchy of lookup tables.

Figure 2-30. *leJOS NXJ*

leJOS NXJ consists mainly of three parts:

- A VM for the execution of Java bytecode
- An API for NXT programming on top of this VM
- Additional software tools

It does not provide its own IDE but endorses the usage of one of the Java IDEs already established in the market. For use of leJOS NXJ with Eclipse, see Appendix A.

Example Program Snippets

Let's take a look now at the programming tasks you have encountered already and how they are solved with leJOS NXT.

Driving

To drive, you simply set the speed and call the forward method on the motors in question. Note that with leJOS NXJ, *speed* denotes degrees per second; the maximum value is 900:

```
// switch on speed regulation
Motor.B.regulateSpeed(true);
Motor.C.regulateSpeed(true);
// set speed
Motor.B.setSpeed(600);
Motor.C.setSpeed(600);
// run motors
Motor.B.forward();
Motor.C.forward();
```

Stopping

Stopping is very simple; just call the stop method on the motors in question:

```
// stop motors
Motor.B.stop();
Motor.C.stop();
```

Rotating

To rotate motor A by 90 degrees, use the following command:

```
// rotate
Motor.A.rotateTo(90);
```

Accessing and Handling Sensor Values

To access and handle sensor values, first configure the sensor in question and then run a loop that checks the sensor in each cycle:

```
// configure the touch sensor on input port 1
TouchSensor touchSensor = new TouchSensor(Port.S1);
// do something until touch sensor gets pressed
while(!touchSensor.isPressed()) {
        // do something here
}
```

Playing Sounds

Playing a sound with leJOS NXJ is very easy:

```
// play a sound of frequency 500 that takes half a second
Sound.playTone(500, 500);
```

Summary

In this chapter, I introduced some programming environments that enable you to develop and run programs directly on the NXT robot. You should now have some insight on the basic concepts and features of the LEGO MINDSTORMS NXT Software, RobotC, NXC, pbLua, and leJOS NXJ and rate their potential use for you.

In the next chapter, you will use the programming environments introduced in this chapter to implement NXT programs for Leonardo da Vinci's invention of the armored car.

CHAPTER 3

■ ■ ■

The Armored Car

I will make covered vehicles, safe and unassailable, which will penetrate the enemy and their artillery, and there is no host of armed men so great that they would not break through it. And behind these the infantry will be able to follow, quite uninjured and unimpeded.

—Leonardo da Vinci

In this chapter, you will have a closer look at the first of Leonardo's prominent inventions covered in this book. You will create an NXT-driven LEGO robot and program it with the environments introduced in Chapter 2.

In the end, you will not only have gained insight into one of Leonardo's most thrilling designs and the hazards of engineering in the Renaissance, but also an understanding of different aspects of building around the NXT and the challenges and possible solutions of robot programming.

Historical Background

Leonardo da Vinci drew his sketch of the armored car—part of the Manuscript Popham, located today in the Biblioteca Reale in Torino, Italy—sometime around 1485 in Milan. It's likely that it was presented to the Duke of Milan, and thus appears neat and well laid out (Figure 3-1).

Its carriage was designed to support many light cannons, set up in a 360-degree firing range. For propulsion of the considerable weight, he designed a fancy, geared mechanism with cranks that could be pulled by men or draught animals located inside the carriage. A conical cover made of wood was meant to protect the crew. On top of the whole structure, a sighting turret granted the advantage of having a harbored outlook to the battlefield on a mobile platform.

Like the other engineers and artists during the Renaissance, Leonardo was eager to adopt antiquated ideas, using his inspiration for inventions and enhancements of classical concepts. For example, the armored car adopts the concept of the chariot and the "war tortoise," a rectangular formation of soldiers on the battlefield holding their shields on the side open to attack. When the men in the middle held up their shields above them, the resulting structure was almost impenetrable to the enemy. The small gaps between the shields allowed room for lances or spears.

The tremendous military technology improvements of the 15th century spawned new challenges to contemporary war strategy. With the appearance of fire weapons on the battle fields, usefulness of traditional tactics, weaponry, and fortress architecture rapidly decreased. Strategies became mandatory to integrate the firearms' ever-growing and already immense potential into battle operations and to cope with the threat they imposed both on troops and fortresses.

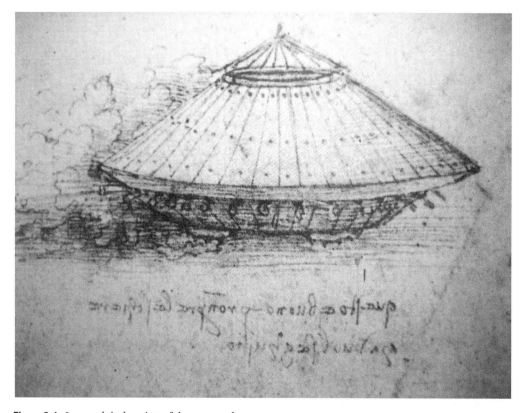

Figure 3-1. *Leonardo's drawing of the armored car*

This need became even more urgent as Italy had become Europe's battleground by the end of the 15th century. The factors that had made possible the cultural explosion of the Renaissance in Northern Italy—wealth, peace, being in the heart of European trade, natural resources—also made it a target in the European turf war that shredded the Italian political landscape until the 19th century.

Since 1490, two generations of Italians were faced with continuous war, as the kings of France, England, and Spain, the Pope, and the emperor of the Holy Roman Empire tried to establish control on the "fulcrum of Europe" with legions of mercenaries highly trained for killing.

In this atmosphere of imminent war, engineers and artists like Leonardo spent a lot of their imaginative power for military devices, and their employers were willing to spend enormous sums of money for their real or imaginary military needs.

Though an entrancing vision, Leonardo's armored car was technically unrealizable, according to all authorities, and certainly has never been built. The whole device would have been much too heavy to be moved over an uneven battleground. Any draught animal would have been uncontrollable in the narrow and dark interior once the cannons started firing, and there's even a design flaw in the drawing: the arrangement of the gears would have turned the front and rear wheels in different directions (Figure 3-2).

■**Note** There is some presumption that the "design flaw" in Leonardo's armored car may have been intentional. It's likely that Leonardo took that measure in order to keep his designs from being stolen.

Figure 3-2. *Detail of the armored car's gearing mechanism*

Special Challenges

When building the armored car, there are a couple challenges to overcome: how to interpret Leonardo's sketches, and how to build the gearing mechanism with LEGO.

Interpreting the Design

When venturing the task of building any of Leonardo's inventions with LEGO, there's always the particular problem of interpreting the drawings appropriately. Leonardo's figures were mainly meant as mere sketches for internal work, far from being well-formed blueprints or building instructions comprehensible for other people.

This is the case with the sketch of the armored car; many of the details are left to the speculation of the beholder. Yet, we are lucky because modern computer-aided design (CAD) tools have been able to create 3D computer models of many of Leonardo's inventions, although the results still require a good deal of interpretation. But they are still much better than trying to refer to the often obscure and fragmentary originals.

The comprehensive Leonardo3 web site (http://www.leonardo3.net) with a wealth of information on Leonardo and his inventions includes many computer-generated images. Also, particularly helpful to me is the book *Leonardo's Machines: Da Vinci's Inventions Revealed* by Domenico Laurenza, Mario Tadei, and Edoardo Zanon (David & Charles Publishers, 2006), a magnificent folio with an abundance of 3D CAD images, exploded views, and background information.

Building the Gearing Mechanism

How will you mimic the gearing mechanism with LEGO? How will you integrate the NXT motors in the propulsion chain? Figures 3-3 and 3-4 show a possible solution.

Figure 3-3. *The armored car's gearing mechanism rebuilt with LEGO*

Figure 3-4. *Attachment of a motor to the axis that drives the gearing*

Building the Armored Car

Figure 3-5 shows the final built armored car. Note that the upper ends of the beams that form the cover are attached with strings to the main axis of the car to enhance the stability.

Figure 3-5. *The armored car*

The following images (Figures 3-6 through 3-41) provide step-by-step instructions on how to build the armored car.

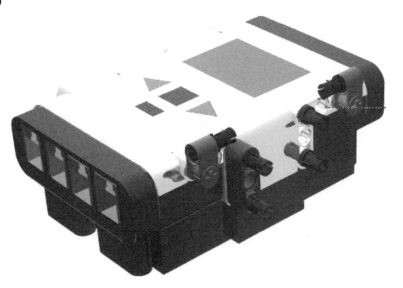

Figure 3-6. *Building the armored car: step 1*

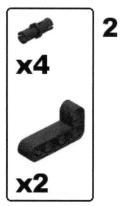

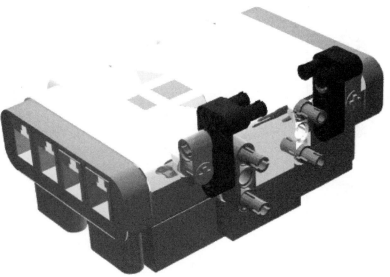

Figure 3-7. *Building the armored car: step 2*

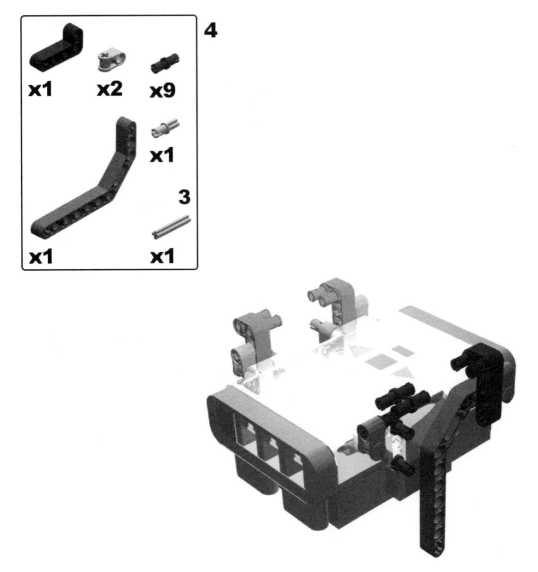

Figure 3-8. *Building the armored car: steps 3 (rotate model) and 4*

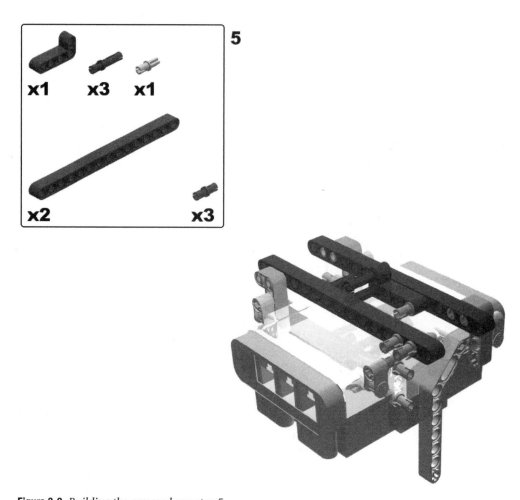

Figure 3-9. *Building the armored car: step 5*

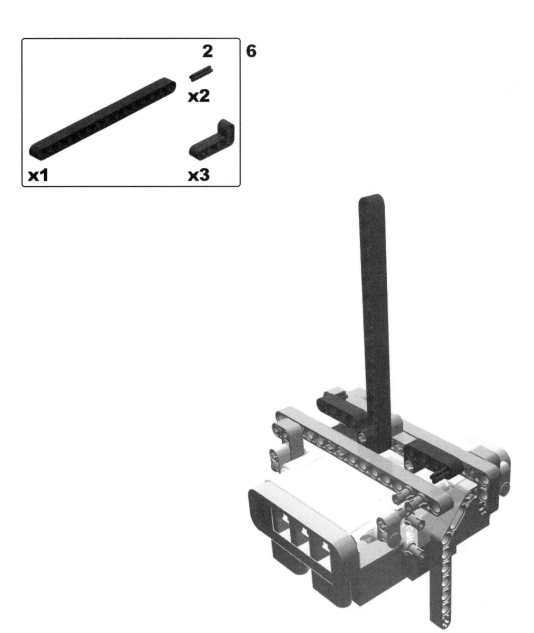

Figure 3-10. *Building the armored car: step 6*

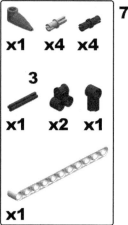

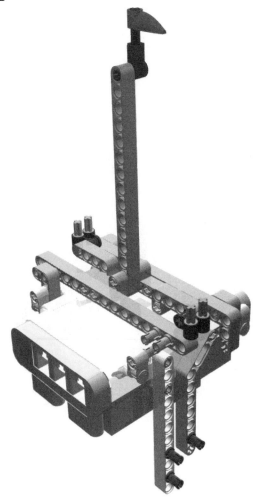

Figure 3-11. *Building the armored car: step 7*

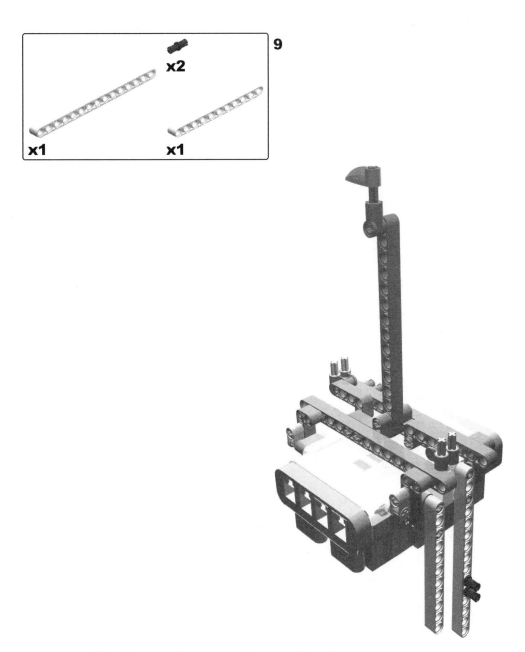

Figure 3-12. *Building the armored car: steps 8 (rotate model) and 9*

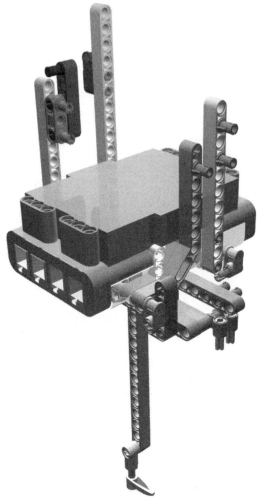

Figure 3-13. *Building the armored car: steps 10 (rotate model) and 11*

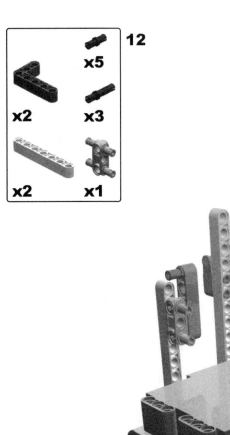

Figure 3-14. *Building the armored car: step 12*

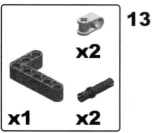

Figure 3-15. *Building the armored car: step 13*

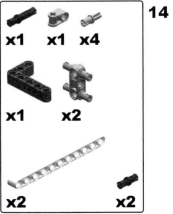

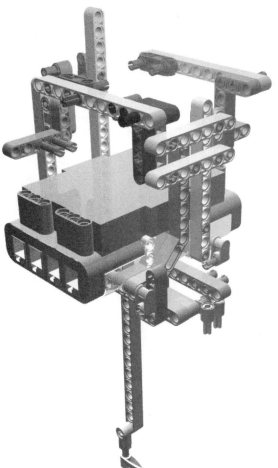

Figure 3-16. *Building the armored car: step 14*

Figure 3-17. *Building the armored car: step 15*

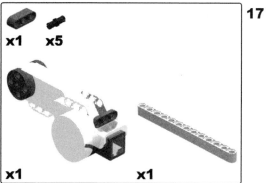

Figure 3-18. *Building the armored car: steps 16 (rotate model) and 17*

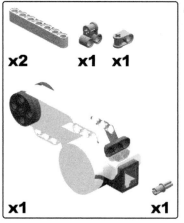

Figure 3-19. *Building the armored car: step 18*

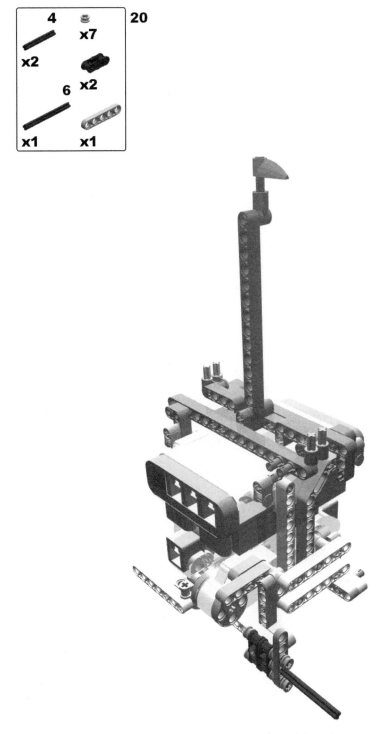

Figure 3-20. *Building the armored car: steps 19 (rotate model) and 20*

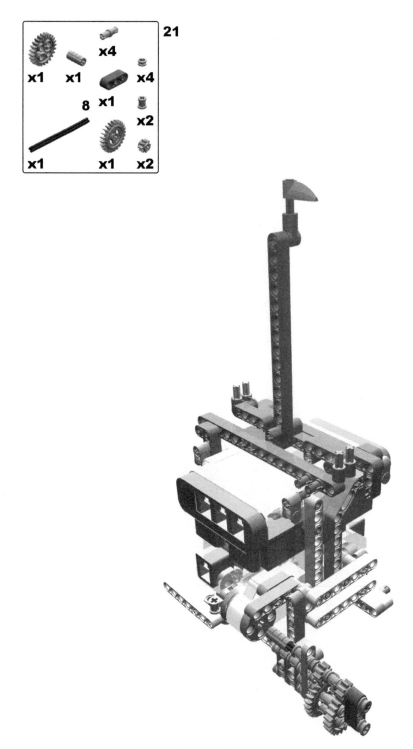

Figure 3-21. *Building the armored car: step 21*

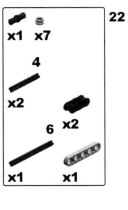

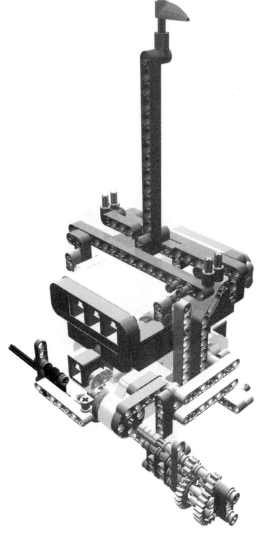

Figure 3-22. *Building the armored car: step 22*

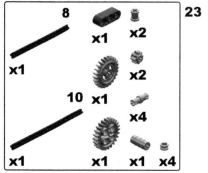

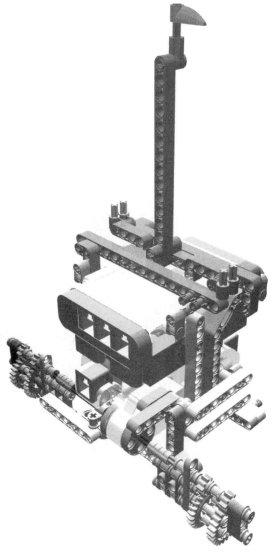

Figure 3-23. *Building the armored car: step 23*

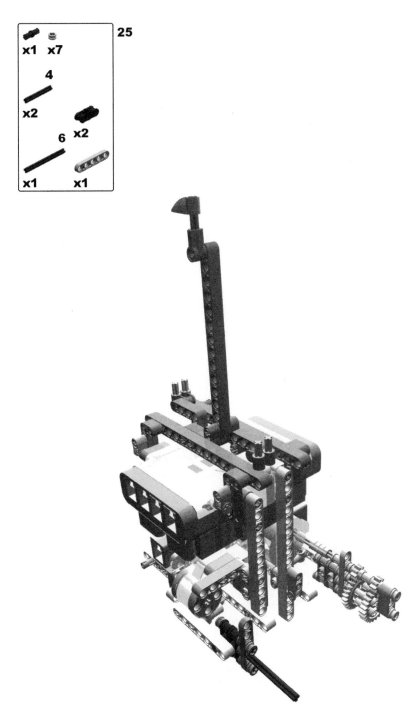

Figure 3-24. *Building the armored car: steps 24 (rotate model) and 25*

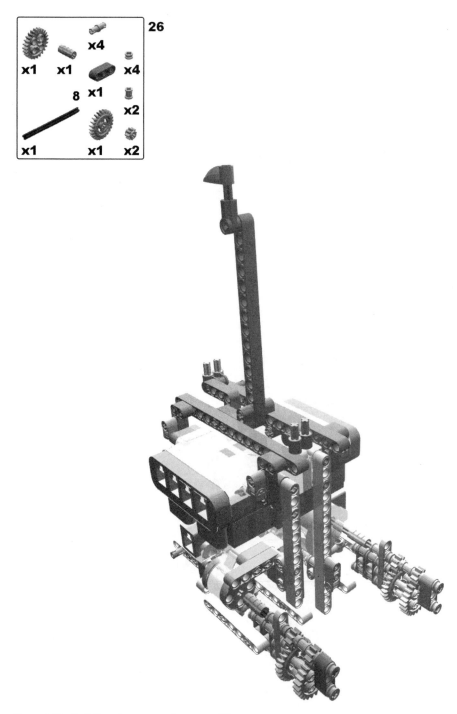

Figure 3-25. *Building the armored car: step 26*

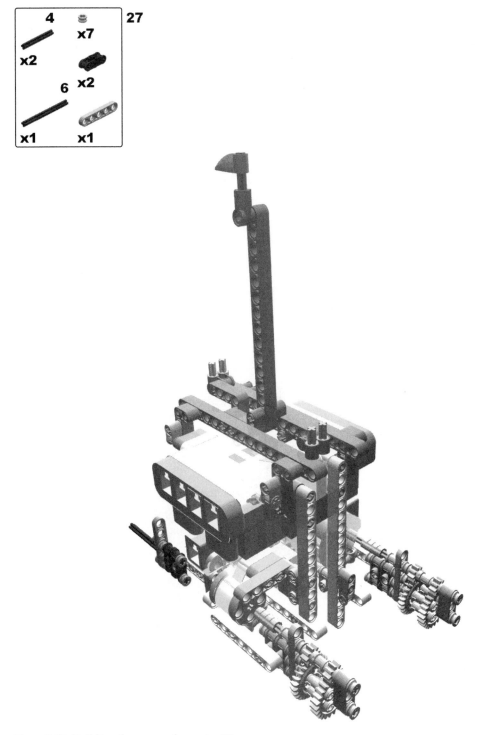

Figure 3-26. *Building the armored car: step 27*

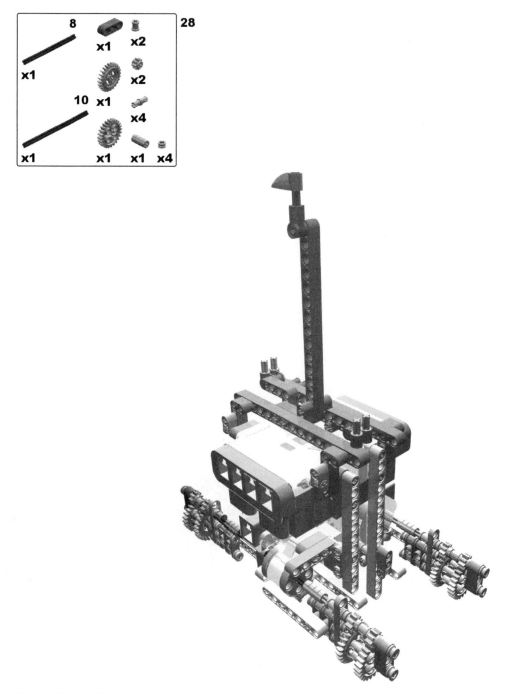

Figure 3-27. *Building the armored car: step 28*

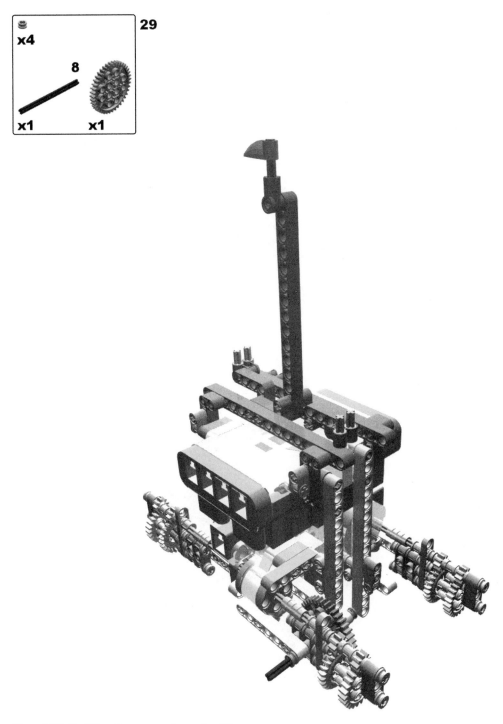

Figure 3-28. *Building the armored car: step 29*

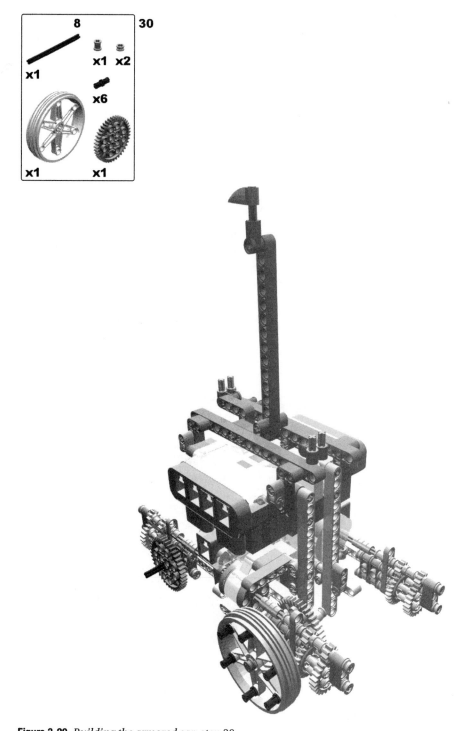

Figure 3-29. *Building the armored car: step 30*

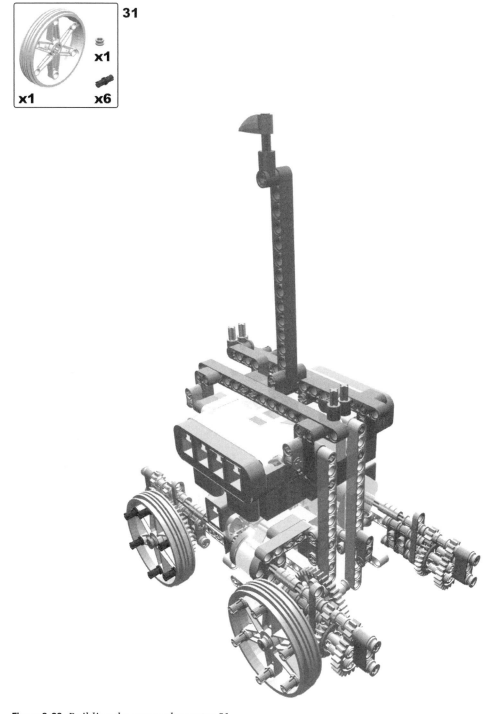

Figure 3-30. *Building the armored car: step 31*

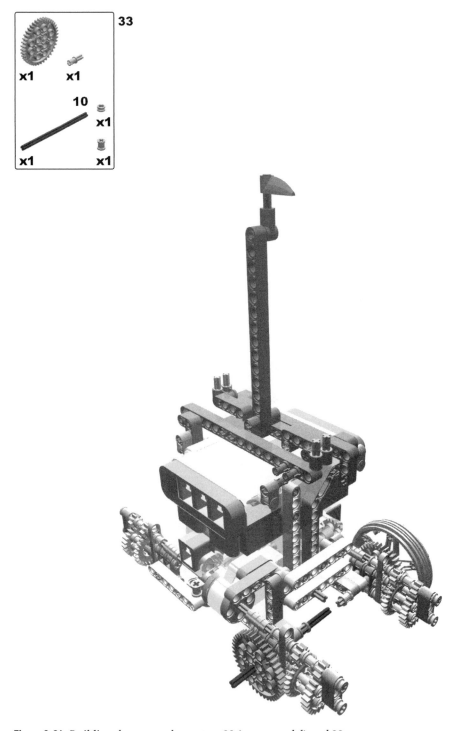

Figure 3-31. *Building the armored car: steps 32 (rotate model) and 33*

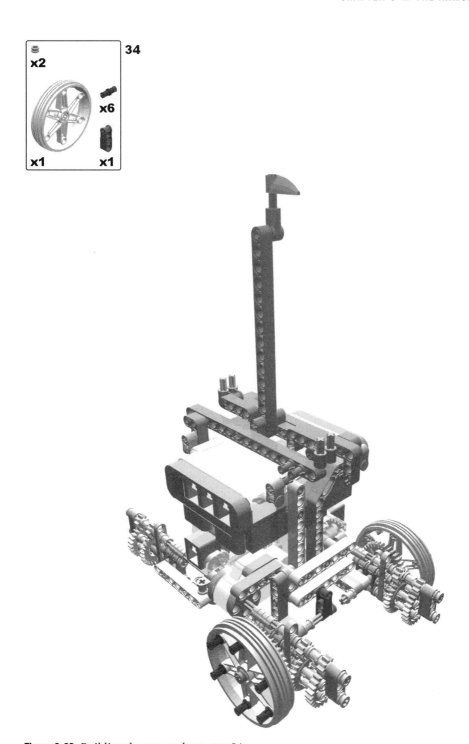

Figure 3-32. *Building the armored car: step 34*

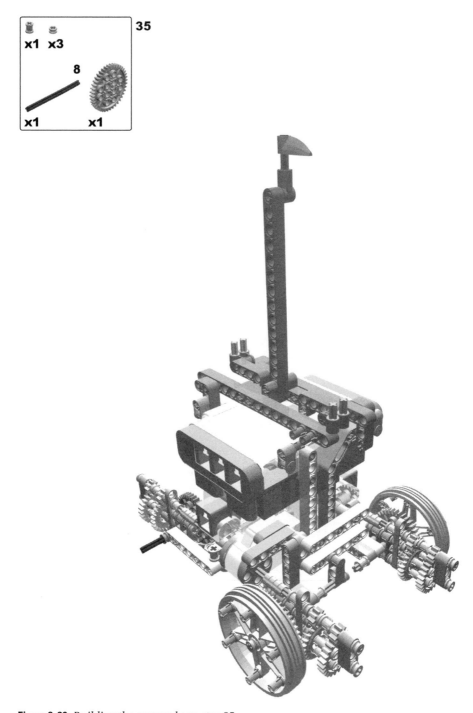

Figure 3-33. *Building the armored car: step 35*

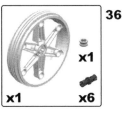

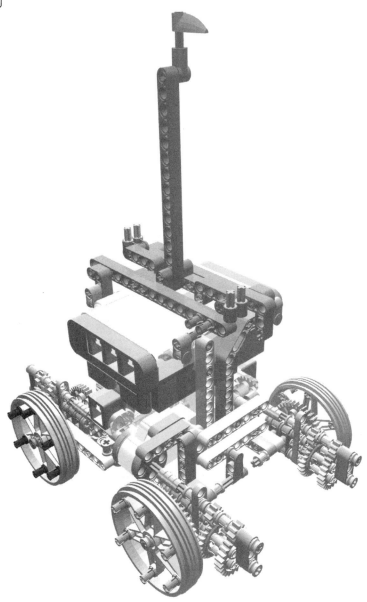

Figure 3-34. *Building the armored car: step 36*

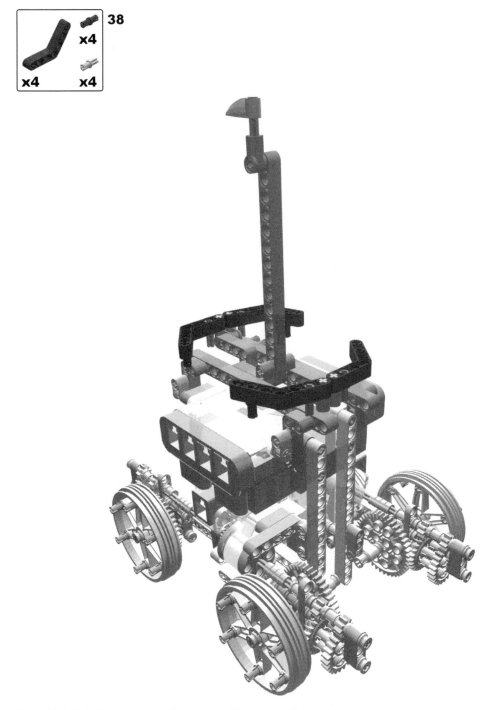

Figure 3-35. *Building the armored car: steps 37 (rotate model) and 38*

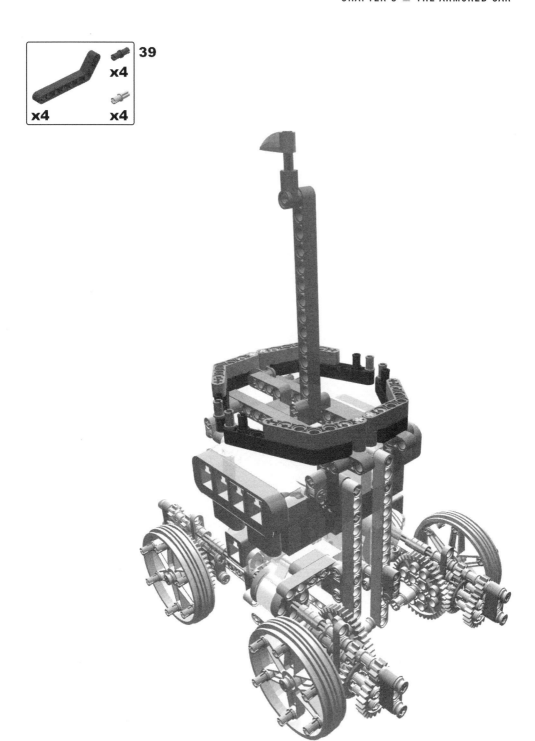

Figure 3-36. *Building the armored car: step 39*

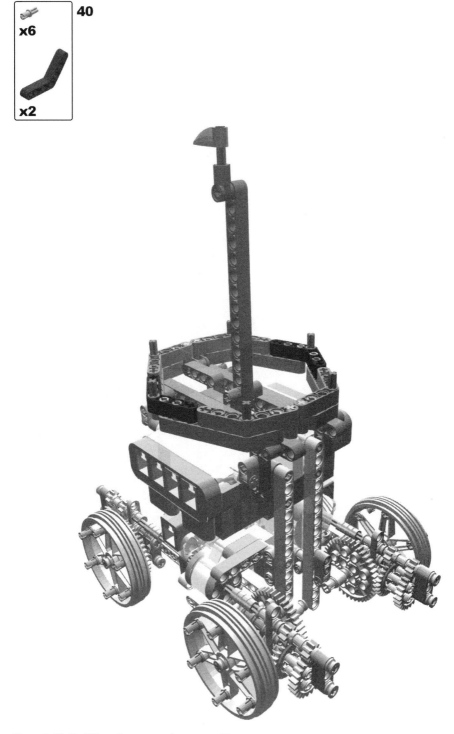

Figure 3-37. *Building the armored car: step 40*

Figure 3-38. *Building the armored car: step 41*

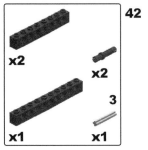

Figure 3-39. *Building the armored car: step 42*

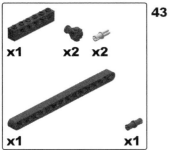

Figure 3-40. *Building the armored car: step 43*

Figure 3-41. *Building the armored car: step 44*

To complete the model with cannons and the cover, just add the remaining five cover substructures and attach the cannons appropriately (Figure 3-5). Figure 3-42 shows the bills of material.

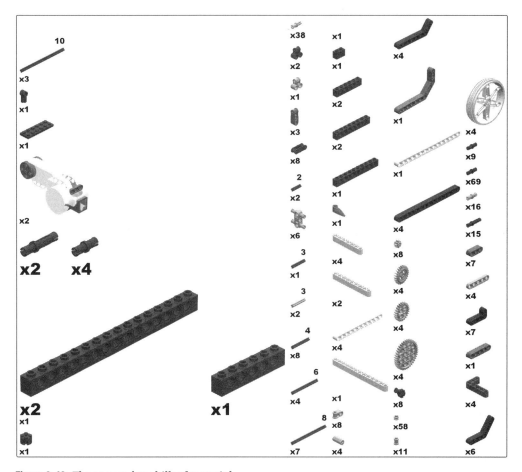

Figure 3-42. *The armored car bills of material*

Programming the Armored Car

Since by design the armored car has rather limited capabilities for movement, you will create a rather simple program for it. This program will give you a good initial grip on the different programming environments.

This section shows you how to program the armored car to simply drive forward, using each of the different programming tools discussed in Chapter 2. Figure 3-43 illustrates the general flow of the program.

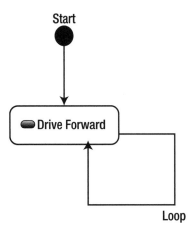

Figure 3-43. *The armored car program*

LEGO MINDSTORMS NXT Software

Let's start with programming the robot with NXT-G. Since the armored car drives around until you manually switch it off, start with attaching a loop block to the starting point of each NXT program, configuring it to run forever (Figure 3-44).

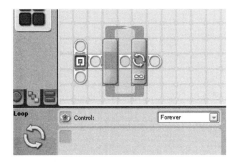

Figure 3-44. *The global forever loop block*

Inside of this loop, place a move block for driving straight. Note that due to the particular technical setup, the two motors have to spin in opposite directions. As the complete logic is contained in a forever loop, the robot will drive straight until you switch it off. Figure 3-45 displays the complete program.

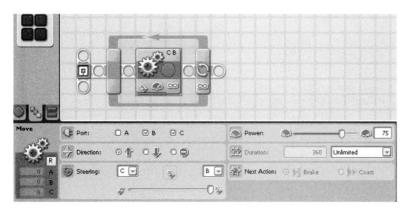

Figure 3-45. *Driving straight with a move block*

RobotC

RobotC programs are organized in units called *tasks* that represent executable pieces of code. Tasks may call other tasks that can be thought of as *subprograms*.

Yet, for simplicity again, we will not call subtasks, but define the simple top-level task main:

```
task main() {

}
```

You want the motors B and C to run synchronized:

```
task main() {

    // motor B and C should run synchronized
    nSyncedMotors = synchBC;
    // motor C has to rotate in the opposite direction
    nSyncedTurnRatio = -100;

}
```

Again, you need an infinite loop for the endless execution of the program:

```
task main() {

    . . .
nSyncedTurnRatio = -100;

    // endless loop
    while(true) {

    };
}
```

When you run a motor, the other motor will run in the opposite direction because they are synchronized accordingly:

```
task main() {

    . . .
    while(true) {

        // run motors B at a power level of 75%
        // motor C spins synchronized in the opposite direction
        motor[motorB] = 75;
    };
}
```

That's it! Here's the complete RobotC program for the armored car:

```
task main() {
    // motor B and C should run synchronized
    nSyncedMotors = synchBC;
    // motor C has to rotate in the opposite direction
    nSyncedTurnRatio = -100;

    // endless loop
    while(true) {

        // run motors B and C at a power level of 75%
        // motor C spins in the opposite direction
        motor[motorB] = 75;

    }

}
```

NXC

Let's turn to programming the armored car with NXC now.

Tasks are the top-level elements of NXC programs also:

```
// main
task main() {

}
```

You have to include the NXC header to use the particular NXC functions:

```
// enable NXC
#include "NXCDefs.h"

// main
task main() {

}
```

Again, you need an infinite loop for the endless execution of the program:

```
. . .
task main() {
```

```
    // endless loop
    while(true) {

    }

}
```

Finally, use the OnFwdSyn function to run the two motors B and C synchronized:

```
. . .
task main() {

    // endless loop
    while(true) {

            // run motors B and C synchronized on a power level of 75%
            // the third argument 100 means that both motors
            // run in the opposite direction
            OnFwdSync (OUT_BC, 75, 100);

    }

}
```

The following is the complete NXC program for the armored car:

```
// enable NXC
#include "NXCDefs.h"

// main
task main() {

    // endless loop
    while (true) {

            // run motors B and C synchronized on a power level of 75%
            // the third argument 100 means that both motors
            // run in the opposite direction
            OnFwdSync (OUT_BC, 75, 100);

    }
}
```

pbLua

Using pbLua, you will define the ArmoredCar function and configure the motors B and C:

```
-- function ArmoredCar
function ArmoredCar()

    -- configure motors B and C to run in "brake" mode
    nxt.OutputSetMode(2,2)
    nxt.OutputSetMode(3,2)

end
```

Next, run the infinite loop for the endless execution of the program:

```
. . .
function ArmoredCar()

    -- configure motors B and C to run in "brake" mode
    nxt.OutputSetMode(2,2)
    nxt.OutputSetMode(3,2)

    -- loop forever
    while 1 do

    end

end
```

Run the two motors on a power level of 75%:

```
. . .
function ArmoredCar()

    . . .
    while 1 do

      -- set the power of the motors to 75%
      -- 32 means "run mode"
      nxt.outputSetSpeed(2, 32, 75, 0)
      nxt.outputSetSpeed(3, 32, -75, 0)

    end

end
```

Finally, run the ArmoredCar function:

```
. . .
function ArmoredCar()

    . . .

end

-- run the ArmoredCar function
ArmoredCar()
```

Done! The complete pbLua program for the armored car is as follows:

```
-- function ArmoredCar
function ArmoredCar()
    -- configure motors B and C to run in "brake" mode
    nxt.OutputSetMode(2,2)
    nxt.OutputSetMode(3,2)

    -- loop forever
    while(1) do
```

```
        -- set the power of the motors to 75%
        -- 32 means "run mode"
        nxt.outputSetSpeed(2, 32, 75, 0)
        nxt.outputSetSpeed(3, 32, -75, 0)

    end
end

-- run the ArmoredCar function
ArmoredCar()
```

leJOS NXJ

Java programs are organized in components called *classes*. The entry point for execution of a stand-alone executable class is a main method:

```
package org.nxtdavinci.armoredcar;

public class ArmoredCar  {

    public static void main(String [] args) throws Exception {
    }
}
```

To use parts of the leJOS NXJ API, you need to import the according packages:

```
package org.nxtdavinci.armoredcar;

import lejos.nxt.*;

public class ArmoredCar  {

    public static void main(String [] args) throws Exception {
    }
}
```

Set up speed regulation for the motors B and C and set the speed to 600 rpm, which is two-thirds of the maximum value:

```
. . .
public class ArmoredCar  {

    public static void main(String [] args) throws Exception {

        // switch on speed regulation
        Motor.B.regulateSpeed(true);
        Motor.C.regulateSpeed(true);

        // set the speed of the motors to 600 rpm
        Motor.B.setSpeed(600);
        Motor.C.setSpeed(600);

    }

}
```

The infinite loop for forever running the two drive motors looks like this:

```
. . .
public class ArmoredCar {

    public static void main(String [] args) throws Exception {

        . . .
        Motor.C.setSpeed(600);

        // loop forever
        while(true) {

        }

    }

}
```

Finally, run the two motors in opposite directions:

```
. . .
public class ArmoredCar {

    public static void main(String [] args) throws Exception {

        . . .
        // loop forever
        while(true) {

            // run the motors in opposite directions
            Motor.B.forward();
            Motor.C.backward();

        }

    }

}
```

Here's the complete leJOS NXJ program for the armored car:

```
package org.nxtdavinci.armoredcar;

import lejos.nxt.*;

public class ArmoredCar {

    public static void main(String[] args) {

        // switch on speed regulation
        Motor.B.regulateSpeed(true);
        Motor.C.regulateSpeed(true);
```

```
    // set the speed of the motors to 600 rpm
    Motor.B.setSpeed(600);
    Motor.C.setSpeed(600);

    // loop forever
    while(true) {

        // run the motors in opposite directions

        Motor.B.forward();
        Motor.C.backward();


    }
  }

}
```

Summary

In this chapter, you built your first LEGO NXT implementation of an invention of Leonardo da Vinci, his famous armored car, and programmed it with five different contemporary environments. Building this model should have given you a good idea of what it's like to build a mechanism with LEGO, in particular, facing the challenges, knowing how to solve them, and integrating a controlling unit like the NXT into an original design. Furthermore, you learned basic yet real approaches using the different NXT programming environments. You are able now to write simple programs of your own with these environments.

In the next chapter, you will deepen your knowledge with another invention of Leonardo's that is also related to military aspects: the catapult. You will also use the first type of input device, the touch sensor.

CHAPTER 4

The Catapult

Simplicity is the ultimate sophistication.

—Leonardo da Vinci

In this chapter, you will build Leonardo's catapult. Although it may seem to be a rather traditional military weapon, you will see that Leonardo didn't deal in vain with it and added some ingenious and unique details. You will learn how to use the motors, the touch sensor, and the different programming environments.

Historical Background

Leonardo made more than one draft for different kinds of catapults. The one in question hails from the time when he moved to Milan at the beginning of the 1580s (Figure 4-1). It's not unlikely that like the armored car, the sketch of the catapult was attached to his letter of application to Duke Ludovico.

Figure 4-1. *Leonardo's drawing of the catapult*

Today, the sketch is part of the Codex Atlanticus preserved in the Biblioteca Ambrosiana in Milan. It reveals to us a fancy design of the core component of a catapult: the device that generates, stores and sets free the mechanical energy that propels the hurling part. Principally, there are two concepts for doing so: creating the power by torsion of ropes or wooden arms (an *onager*), or doing so using the gravity of a falling weight (a design known as a *trebuchet*).

Leonardo's catapult is of the onager type. Nevertheless it's of singular brilliance because it uses a double leaf spring instead of the classical straight arm. With this, the catapult was not only much more compact but also able to convey a much higher level of mechanical energy to the hurling arm, resulting in a greater range and enhanced penetrating power. The released power must have been so huge that the catapult had to be fixed to the ground with ropes and blocks. In fact, Leonardo was not so much interested in the catapult itself but in the spring mechanism and the basic aspects of generating power with these kinds of mechanical devices.

■ **Note**   Most likely, some spring configurations were contained in Leonardo's "Treatise on Machine Elements," apparently a milestone in the theoretical research on mechanical elements such as wheels, gears, screws, and springs. Unfortunately, this treatise has been lost, so we know of it by reports only.

When we think of military capabilities, we tend to associate fire weapons with more modern times and classical artillery with earlier eras. But we must not forget that the adoption of and transition to new technologies is always a gradual process, in particular in epochs that have not seen such a high frequency of change as the days we live in now. Hence, classical, or we might even say *antique*, weapons used in medieval warfare for a long time did not vanish altogether from Renaissance military strategies. Instead, they were still in use after combustion-powered arms were invented.

The catapult was a distance weapon already used by Alexander's troops during the conquest of the Persian realm. It was deployed extensively in medieval warfare, which consisted to a large degree of sieges and engagement of fortified military installations. Here, the catapult was at its best, using its particular strengths to stand up against the firearms of the Renaissance age. First, its firing mechanism was rather simple; so, in contrast to a cannon, it did not require highly trained (and thus expensive) specialists. Next, catapults had a high firing rate as well as a high firing range, in particular compared to the very slow field guns at the end of the 16th century.

■ **Note**   The catapults used at the siege of Lisbon in 1147 are reported to have been capable of throwing a 60 kilogram stone every 15 seconds over a distance of up to 300 feet.

Catapults didn't require transportation over large distances into enemy space but could be constructed on site since they were mainly built of material—wood and ropes—that could be acquired locally, a considerable advantage against the clumsy fire weaponry in times of almost nonexistent or at least very bad streets.[1]

In addition to this, catapults were very versatile weapons that could hurl a variety of projectiles against the enemy, including stones, arrows, stink pots, or incendiary composites—even beehives. Indeed, catapults were the first weapons to be used for biological warfare since it was not uncommon to fire carcasses of diseased animals or human beings that had perished in epidemics into the besieged fortress. We know that on some occasions, even living captives were hurled as a means to demoralize the defenders.

---

1. Consequently, Leonardo invented a cannon that could be disassembled for easier transportation and then reassembled on the battlefield.

Apparently, with the evolution of modern artillery, catapults lost their importance in warfare and eventually vanished from the battlefields in the 16th century. Yet for Leonardo and his fellow engineers, improving these sorts of weapons was still a worthwhile occupation and of interest to their potential employers.

Hardware Challenges

It's easy to see that there are two major components of the catapult that impose particular difficulties when building them with LEGO: the double leaf spring and the crank mechanism for loading and firing.

The Double Leaf Spring

Building elastic parts with LEGO is not trivial, especially when they need to have a curved shape. I solve this by using a combination of short straight and bent beams, thus creating a sufficiently round structure that is stable and elastic on one hand and nevertheless capable of storing enough kinetic energy to provide a sufficient amount of thrust to the catapult's arm (Figure 4-2).

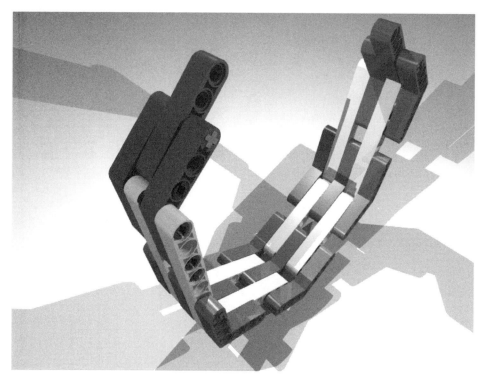

Figure 4-2. *The double leaf spring*

The Crank Mechanism

The mechanism that drives the spring has to serve two purposes: first, it is required to drive the spring's gear wheel to bring the catapult's arm into loading position and close each leaf at the same time, thus building up kinetic energy for firing. Second, it needs to allow for release of the wheel in a flash so that the power stored in the leaves is set free in an instant.

I provide a solution that meets these two requirements by setting up a *worm gear* on the bottom of the great gear wheel. A worm gear is able to sustain the large force that acts upon the gear wheel's teeth and to prevent the wheel from slipping or turning back. On the other hand, it does not allow for a quick release of the wheel, so you have to add an additional degree of freedom to the whole worm gear assembly. The complete axle can be lowered to let the gear wheel, the leaf spring, and the attached arm spin freely (Figure 4-3).

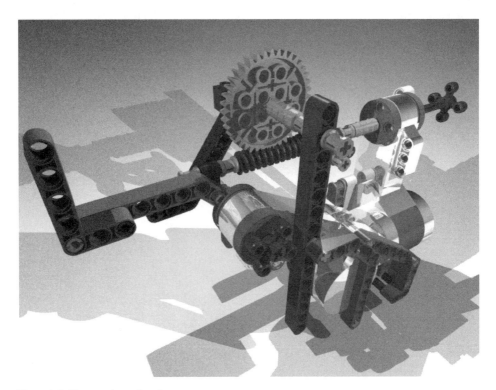

Figure 4-3. *The crank mechanism*

Building the Catapult

Figure 4-4 shows the completed catapult robot. Now you will build the catapult and integrate the NXT Brick as a controlling unit.

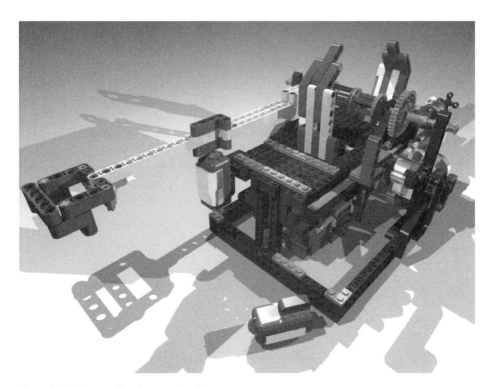

Figure 4-4. *The completed catapult robot*

The following images (Figures 4-5 through 4-40) show step-by-step instructions on how to build the catapult.

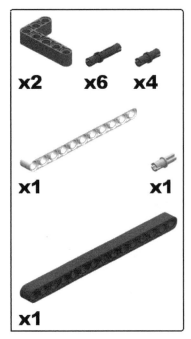

Figure 4-5. *Building the catapult: step 1*

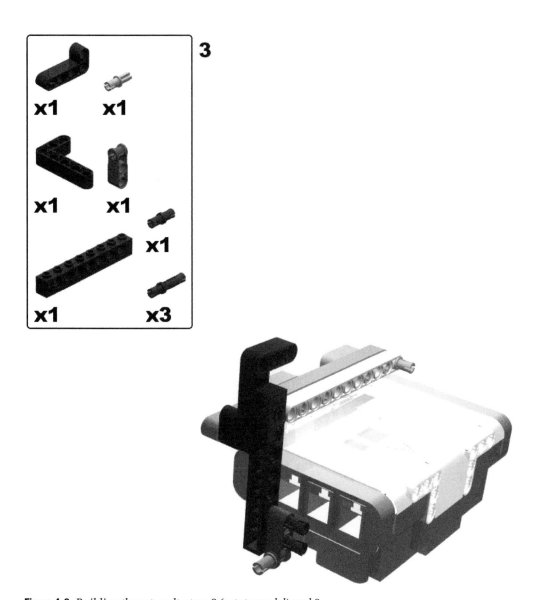

Figure 4-6. *Building the catapult: steps 2 (rotate model) and 3*

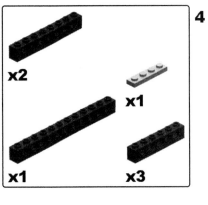

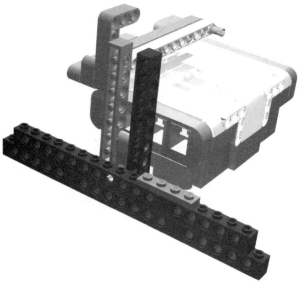

Figure 4-7. *Building the catapult: step 4*

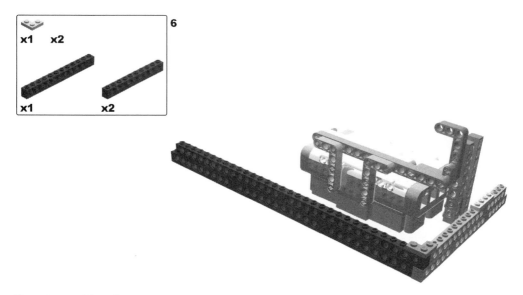

Figure 4-8. *Building the catapult: steps 5 (rotate model) and 6*

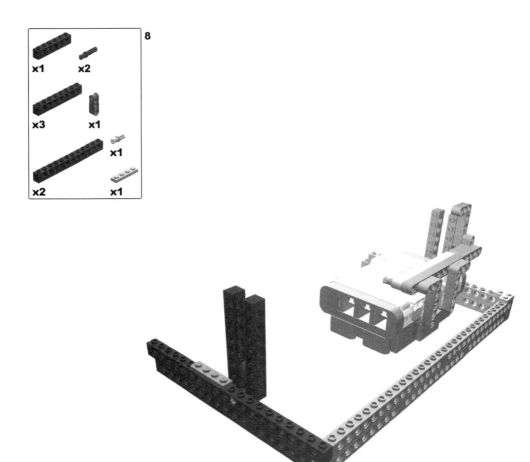

Figure 4-9. *Building the catapult: steps 7 (rotate model) and 8*

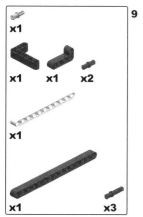

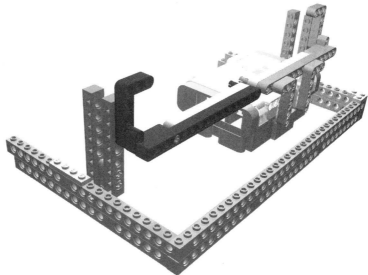

Figure 4-10. *Building the catapult: steps 9*

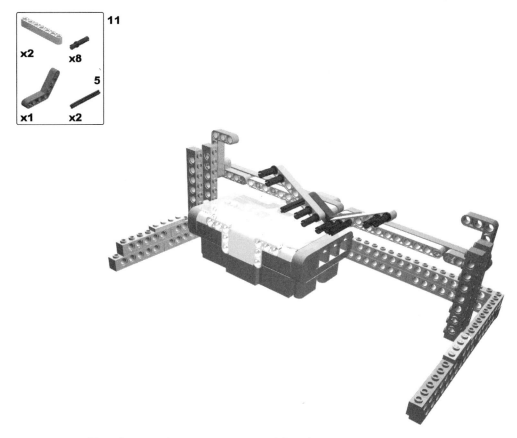

Figure 4-11. *Building the catapult: steps 10 (rotate model) and 11*

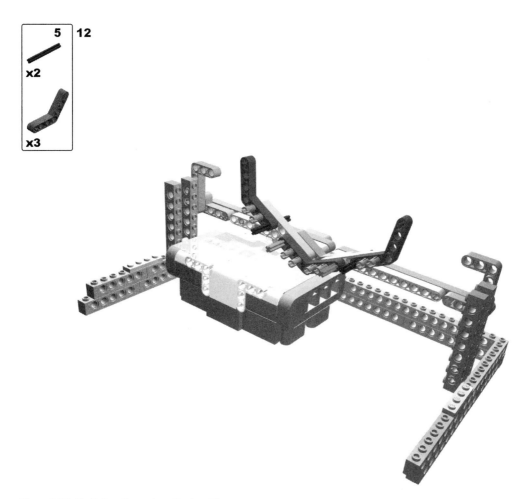

Figure 4-12. *Building the catapult: step 12*

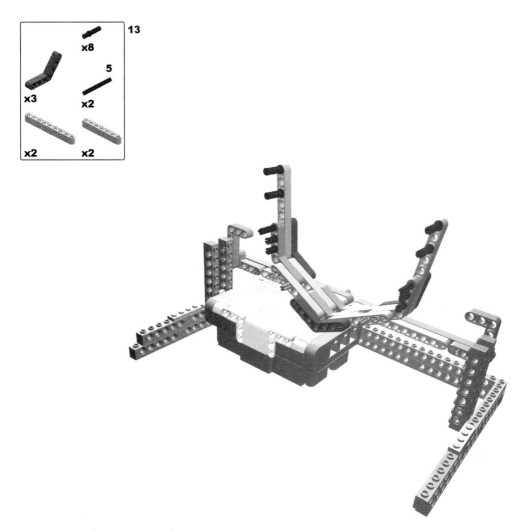

Figure 4-13. *Building the catapult: step 13*

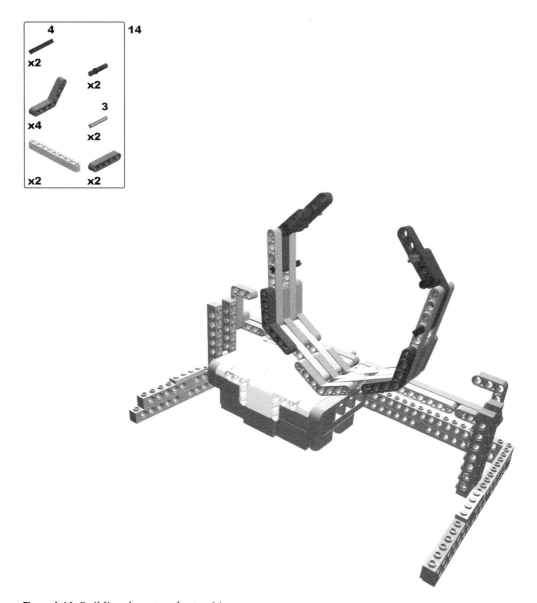

Figure 4-14. *Building the catapult: step 14*

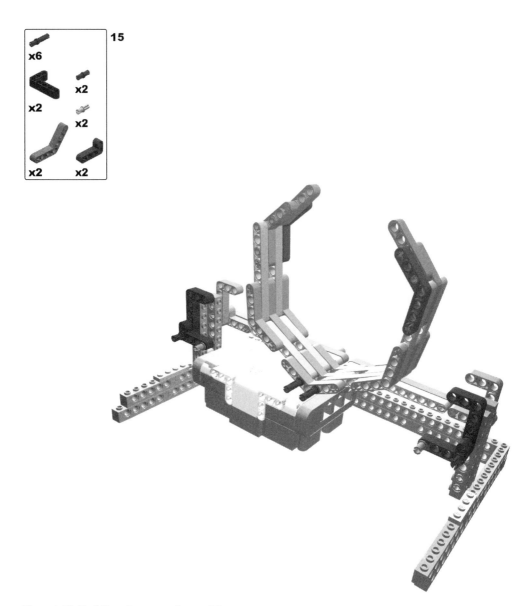

Figure 4-15. *Building the catapult: step 15*

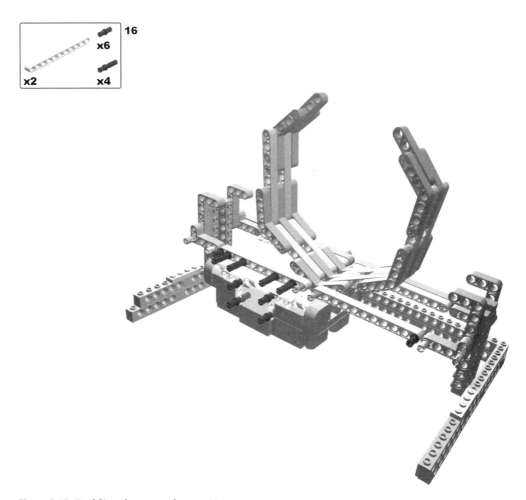

Figure 4-16. *Building the catapult: step 16*

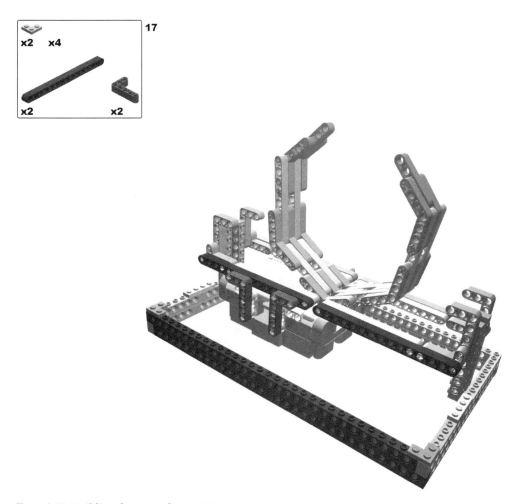

Figure 4-17. *Building the catapult: step 17*

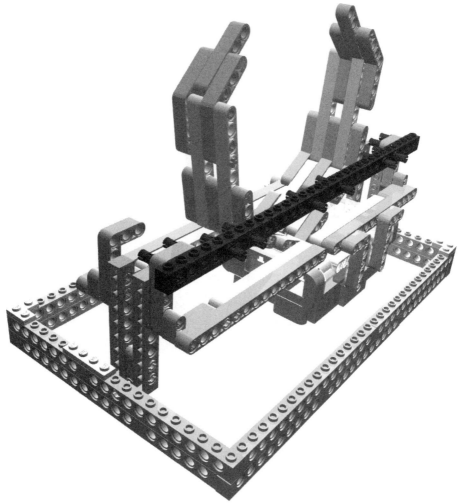

Figure 4-18. *Building the catapult: steps 18 (rotate model) and 19*

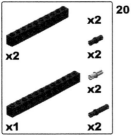

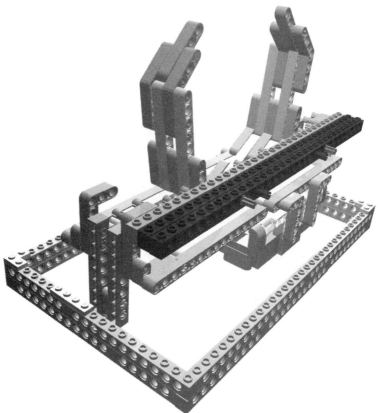

Figure 4-19. *Building the catapult: step 20*

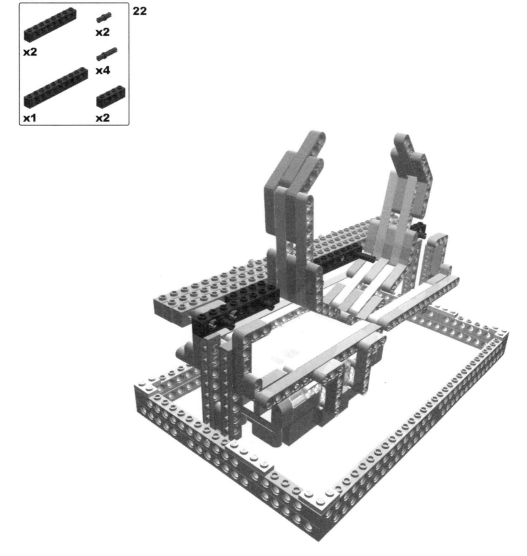

Figure 4-20. *Building the catapult: steps 21 (rotate model) and 22*

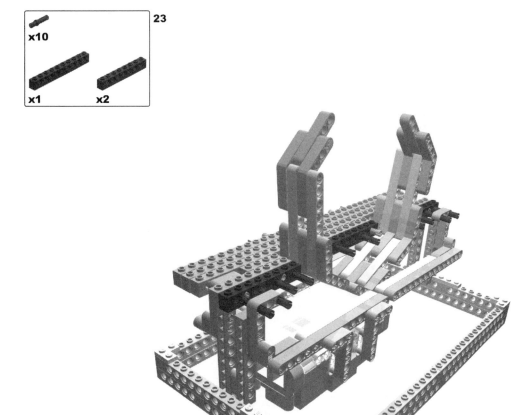

Figure 4-21. *Building the catapult: step 23*

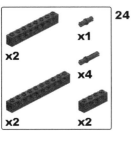

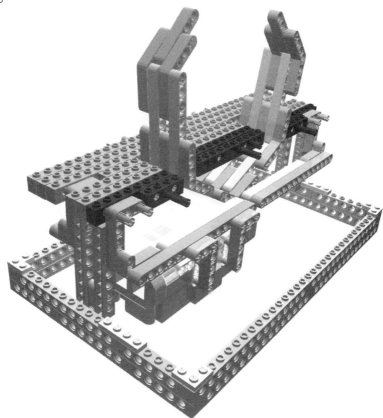

Figure 4-22. *Building the catapult: step 24*

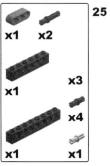

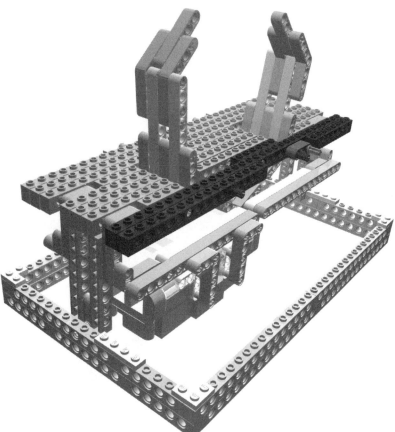

Figure 4-23. *Building the catapult: step 25*

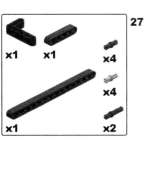

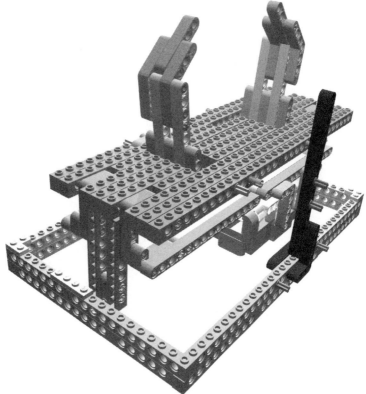

Figure 4-24. *Building the catapult: steps 26 (rotate model) and 27*

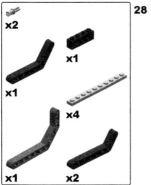

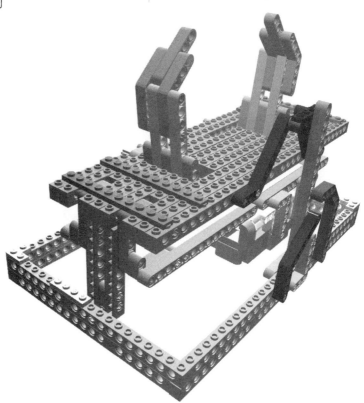

Figure 4-25. *Building the catapult: step 28*

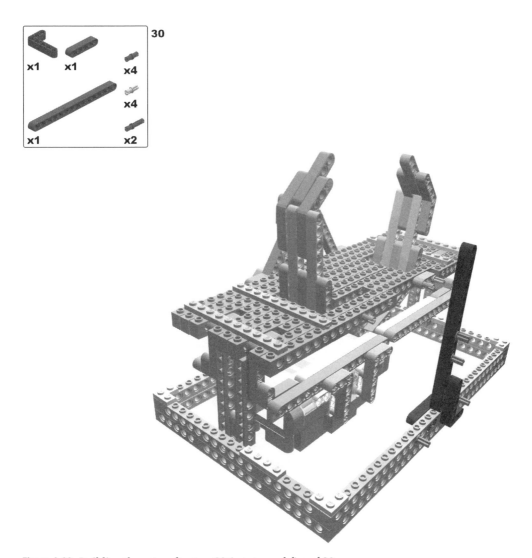

Figure 4-26. *Building the catapult: steps 29 (rotate model) and 30*

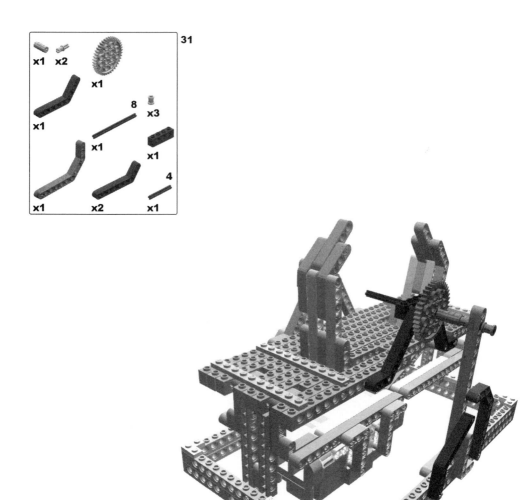

Figure 4-27. *Building the catapult: step 31*

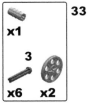

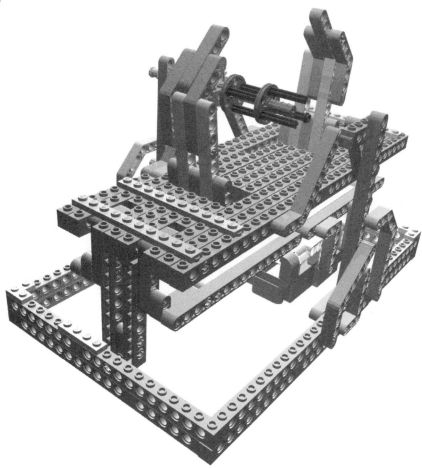

Figure 4-28. *Building the catapult: steps 32 (rotate model) and 33*

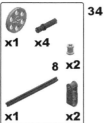

Figure 4-29. *Building the catapult: step 34*

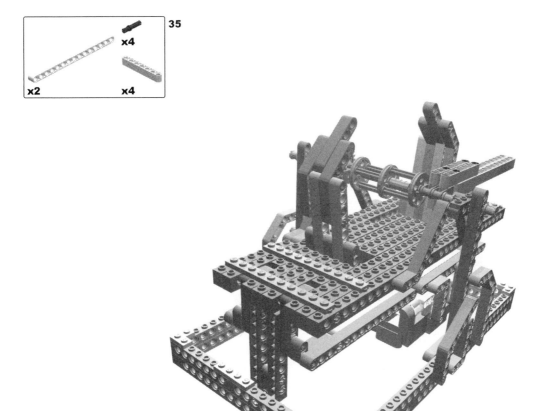

Figure 4-30. *Building the catapult: step 35*

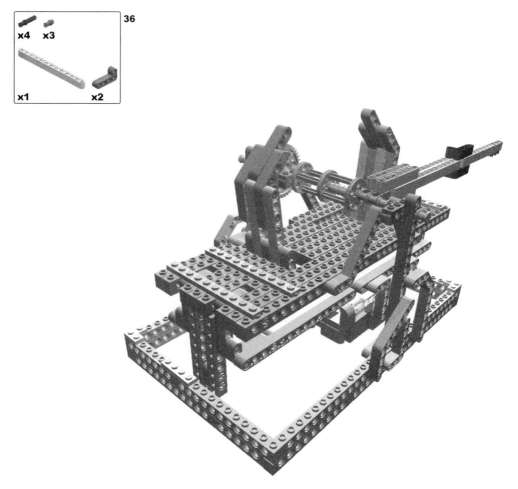

Figure 4-31. *Building the catapult: step 36*

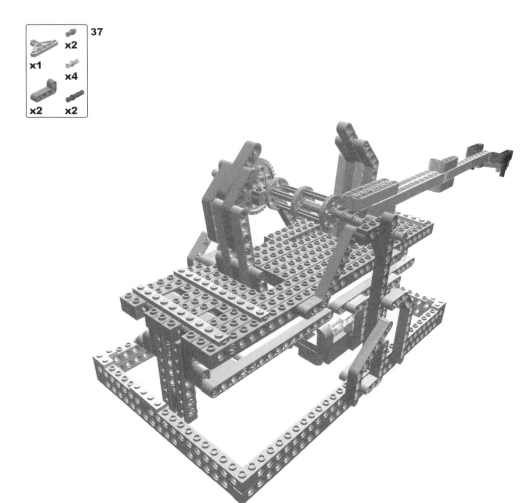

Figure 4-32. *Building the catapult: step 37*

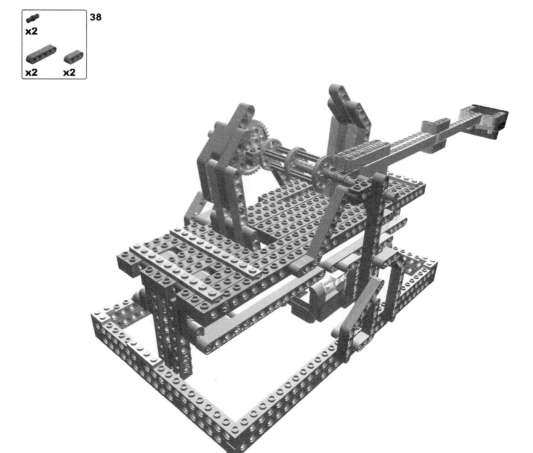

Figure 4-33. *Building the catapult: step 38*

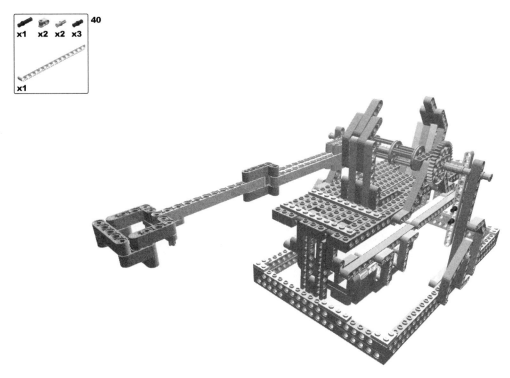

Figure 4-34. *Building the catapult: steps 39 (rotate model) and 40*

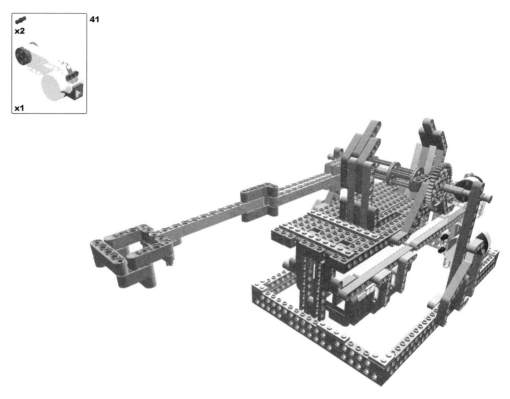

Figure 4-35. *Building the catapult: step 41*

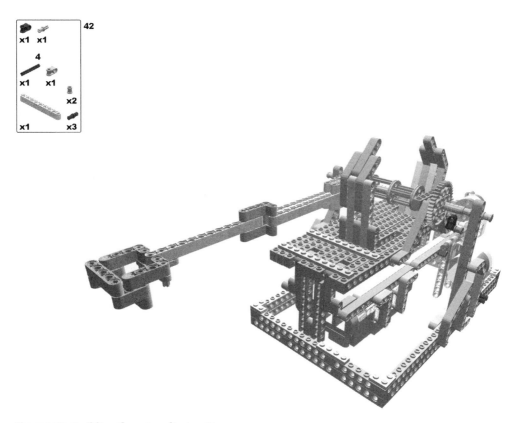

Figure 4-36. *Building the catapult: step 42*

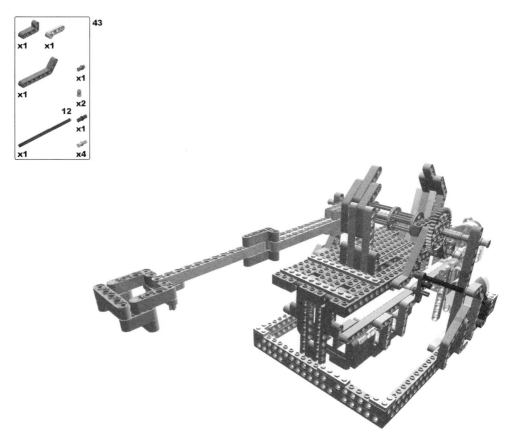

Figure 4-37. *Building the catapult: step 43*

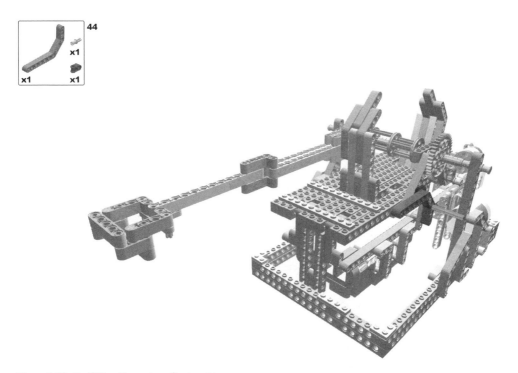

Figure 4-38. *Building the catapult: step 44*

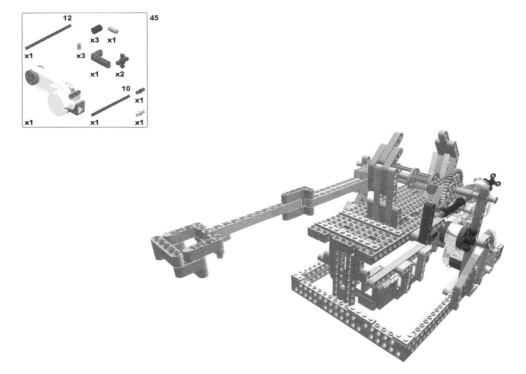

Figure 4-39. *Building the catapult: step 45*

Figure 4-40. *Building the catapult: steps 46 (rotate model) and 47*

As a last step, you have to wire the sensors and the motors to the Brick. Connect each spring leaf's end with a string to a reel: the left one to the left reel, the right one to the right reel. Make sure to connect them in a way that the spring is contracted when the great gear wheel turns in the forward direction.

Figure 4-41 shows the LEGO parts required for the catapult robot.

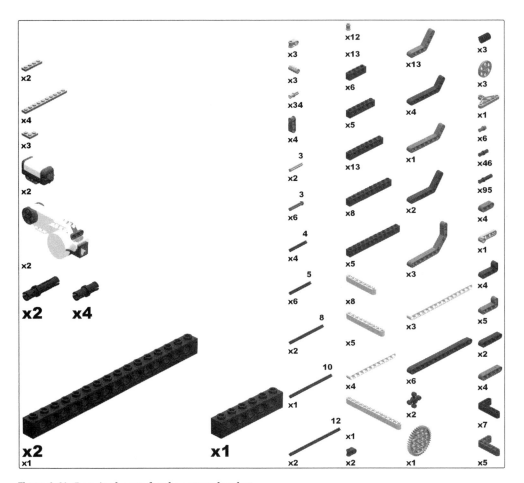

Figure 4-41. *Required parts for the catapult robot*

Programming the Catapult

This section demonstrates how to program the catapult using each of the programming environments introduced in Chapter 2. Just as the operation of a catapult is simple, the general structure of the program is rather simple also, consisting of loading the catapult, waiting for the user to press the trigger, and firing the catapult. Figure 4-42 shows this sequence of program actions.

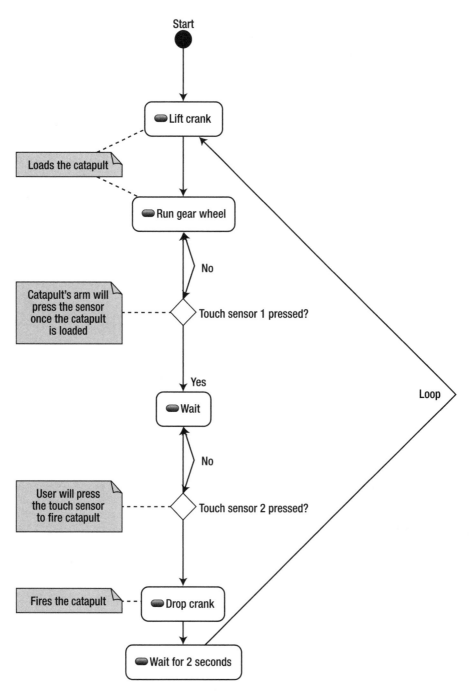

Figure 4-42. *The program's flow for the catapult*

LEGO MINDSTORMS NXT Software

To ensure that the program runs until the user manually switches it off, attach a loop block to the starting point of each NXT program, thus configuring the program to run forever (Figure 4-43).

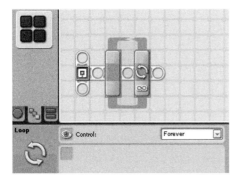

Figure 4-43. *The global forever loop block*

The crank mechanism has to be connected to the great gear wheel by lifting the component appropriately. This is accomplished by running motor A that is in charge of the lifting device by 30 degrees. Hence, you insert a motor block into the forever loop (Figure 4-44).

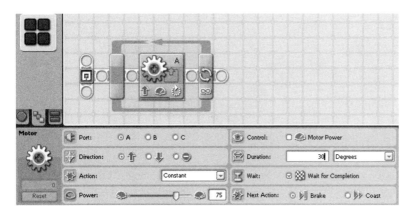

Figure 4-44. *The motor block lifting the crank mechanism*

Now that the crank mechanism is attached to the gear wheel, run the wheel, thus lifting the hurling arm and concurrently contracting the leaves by coiling their strings. Stop it once the arm hits the first touch sensor. Hence, you use a forever loop with the touch sensor's press event as the stop criterion (Figure 4-45) and place a motor block for motor C inside (Figure 4-46).

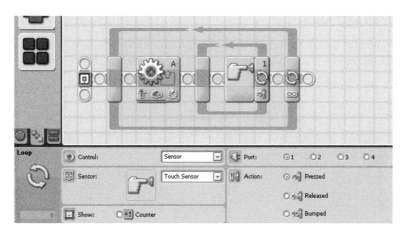

Figure 4-45. *The loop block for loading, controlled by the touch sensor*

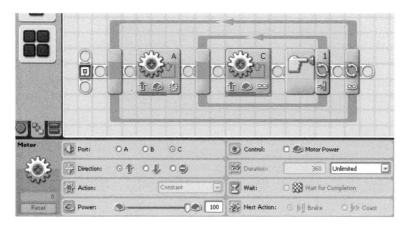

Figure 4-46. *The motor block running the great gear wheel*

Once the catapult is loaded and ready to be fired, stop motor C and wait for the user to press the second touch sensor. Again, you use a loop block controlled by the touch sensor (Figure 4-47).

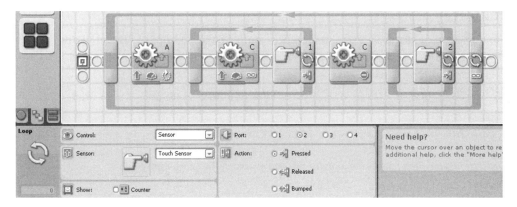

Figure 4-47. *The loop block for firing, controlled by the touch sensor*

Once the user has pressed the button of the sensor, the crank mechanism has to be dropped away from the wheel, thus releasing the kinetic energy stored in the leaves in one blow and tossing the hurling arm. To this end, motor A has to be run by a convenient motor block, this time in the opposite direction. By inserting a wait block, you give the catapult some time to complete the firing process (Figure 4-48).

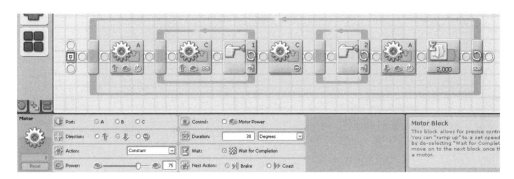

Figure 4-48. *The motor block dropping the crank mechanism and the wait block*

That's it. The main forever loop starts the process again (Figure 4-49).

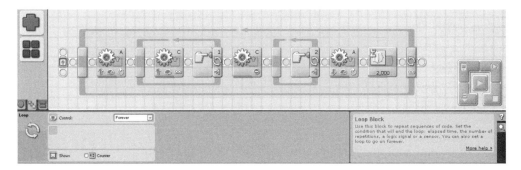

Figure 4-49. *The catapult programmed with NXT-G*

RobotC

For the RobotC program, let's start again with declaring the sensors used. This time, it's two touch sensors:

```
const tSensors touchSensor1 = (tSensors) S1;
const tSensors touchSensor2 = (tSensors) S2;

task main() {

}
```

Again, you need an infinite loop for the endless execution of the program:

```
const tSensors touchSensor1 = (tSensors) S1;
const tSensors touchSensor2 = (tSensors) S2;

task main() {

  // endless loop
  while(true) {
  };
}
```

Rotate the axis of the motor attached to the crank's lifting mechanism by 30 degrees:

```
...
task main() {

. . .
  while(true) {

    // lift crank mechanism
    nMotorEncoder[motorA] = 0;
    while(nMotorEncoder[motorA] <= 30 ) {
      motor[motorA] = 75;
    }
    motor[motorA] = 0;

  };
}
```

To lift the hurling arm and contract the spring's leaves, run the gear wheel until the first touch sensor triggers a "pressed" event. A sensor value of 0 means a logical false:

```
. . .
task main() {

  . . .
  while(true) {
    // lift crank mechanism
    . . .
    motor[motorA] = 0;

    // load catapult
    // run motor until the first
    // touch sensor gets pressed
```

```
    while(SensorValue(touchSensor1) == 0) {
      motor[motorC] = 100;
    };
    motor[motorC] = 0;

  };
}
```

The catapult is now loaded. Wait for the user to press the second touch sensor to fire:

```
. . .
task main() {

. . .
  while(true) {
    . . .
    motor[motorC] = 0;

    // wait for the user to press the second touch sensor
    while(SensorValue(touchSensor2) == 0) {
      // do nothing
    };

  };
}
```

If the user presses the second touch sensor, you have to drop the crank mechanism by running motor A's axle by 30 degrees in the opposite direction:

```
. . .
task main() {

  . . .
  while(true) {
    . . .
    // wait for the user to press the second touch sensor
    while(SensorValue(touchSensor2) == 0) {
      // do nothing
    };

    // drop crank mechanism
    nMotorEncoder[motorA] = 0;
    while(nMotorEncoder[motorA] >= -30 ) {
      motor[motorA] = -75;
    }
    motor[motorA] = 0;

  };
}
```

Finally, wait for the catapult to complete firing:

```
. . .
task main() {
. . .
```

```
  while(true) {
    . . .
    motor[motorA] = 0;

    // wait for two seconds
    wait10Msec(200);

  };
}
```

And you're done! Here's the complete program:

```
const tSensors touchSensor1 = (tSensors) S1;
const tSensors touchSensor2 = (tSensors) S2;

task main() {

  // endless loop
  while(true) {

    // lift crank mechanism
    nMotorEncoder[motorA] = 0;
    while(nMotorEncoder[motorA] <= 30 ) {
      motor[motorA] = 75;
    }
    motor[motorA] = 0;

    // load catapult
    // run motor until until the first
    // touch sensor gets pressed
    while(SensorValue(touchSensor1) == 0) {
      motor[motorC] = 100;
    };
    motor[motorC] = 0;

    // wait for the user to press the second touch sensor
    while(SensorValue(touchSensor2) == 0) {
      // do nothing
    };

    // drop crank mechanism
    nMotorEncoder[motorA] = 0;
    while(nMotorEncoder[motorA] >= -30 ) {
      motor[motorA] = -75;
    }
    motor[motorA] = 0;

    // wait for two seconds
    wait10Msec(200);

  };
}
```

NXC

For the NXC program, start with declaring the two touch sensors:

```
// enable NXC
#include "NXCDefs.h"

// main
task main() {

  // define sensors at port 1 and 2 to be touch sensors
  SetSensorType(IN_1,IN_TYPE_SWITCH);
  SetSensorType(IN_2,IN_TYPE_SWITCH);

}
```

The infinite loop looks very similar to the one in RobotC, so proceed to the lifting of the crank mechanism:

```
. . .
task main() {

  . . .
  SetSensorType(IN_2,IN_TYPE_SWITCH);

  // endless loop
  while(1) {

    // lift crank mechanism
    RotateMotor(OUT_A, 75, 30);
  }
}
```

Running the gear wheel until the first touch sensor triggers a "pressed" event loads the catapult:

```
. . .
task main() {

  . . .
  while(1) {

    . . .
    RotateMotor(OUT_A, 75, 30);

    // load catapult
    // run motor until the first
    // touch sensor gets pressed
    OnFwd (OUT_C, 100);
    while(Sensor(IN_1) == 0) {
      // do nothing
    }
    Off(OUT_C);
  }
}
```

Waiting for the user to press the second touch sensor is done as follows:

```
. . .
task main() {

  . . .
  while(1) {
    . . .
    Off(OUT_C);

    // wait for the user to press the second touch sensor
    while(Sensor(IN_2) == 0) {
      // do nothing
    }

  }
}
```

Now drop the crank:

```
. . .
task main() {

  . . .
  while(1) {

    . . .
    while(Sensor(IN_2) == 0) {
      // do nothing
    }

    // drop crank mechanism
    RotateMotor(OUT_A, -75, 30);
  }
}
```

And wait:

```
. . .
task main() {

  . . .
  while(1) {

    . . .
    // drop crank mechanism
    RotateMotor(OUT_A, -75, 30);

    // wait for two seconds
    Wait(2000);
  }
}
```

Here's the complete NXC program for the catapult:

```
// enable NXC
#include "NXCDefs.h"

// main
task main() {

  // define sensors at ports 1 and 2 to be touch sensors
  SetSensorType(IN_1,IN_TYPE_SWITCH);
  SetSensorType(IN_2,IN_TYPE_SWITCH);

  // endless loop
  while(1) {

    // lift crank mechanism
    RotateMotor(OUT_A, 75, 30);

    // load catapult
    // run motor until the first
    // touch sensor gets pressed
    OnFwd (OUT_C, 100);
    while(Sensor(IN_1) == 0) {
      // do nothing
    }
    Off(OUT_C);

    // wait for the user to press the second touch sensor
    while(Sensor(IN_2) == 0) {
      // do nothing
    }

    // drop crank mechanism
    RotateMotor(OUT_A, -75, 30);

    // wait two seconds
    Wait(2000);
  }
}
```

pbLua

As a start, define the Catapult function and configure the touch sensors at ports 1 and 2 and the motors A and C:

```
-- function Catapult
function Catapult()

  -- configure the touch sensors on input ports 1 and 2
  nxt.InputSetDigi0(1)
  nxt.InputSetDirOutDigi0(1)
  nxt.InputSetDigi0(2)
  nxt.InputSetDirOutDigi0(2)
```

```
-- configure motors A  and C to run in "brake" mode
nxt.OutputSetMode(1,2)
nxt.OutputSetMode(3,2)

end
```

After that, the infinite loop for the endless execution of the program is run:

```
. . .
function Catapult()

    . . .
    -- configure motors A  and C to run in "brake" mode
    nxt.OutputSetMode(1,2)
    nxt.OutputSetMode(3,2)

    -- loop forever
    while 1 do

    end

end
```

This time, define a second function that rotates a motor by a given amount of degrees and use it for lifting the crank mechanism:

```
. . .
function Catapult()

    . . .
    -- loop forever
    while 1 do
        -- lift crank mechanism
        -- rotate motor A by 30 degrees
        rotate(1,30)

    end

end

-- function to rotate a motor by a given number of degrees
function rotate(motor,degrees)

    nxt.OutputEnableRegulation(motor,1)
    nxt.OutputSetMode(motor,2)
    nxt.OutputSetSpeed(motor,32,75,0)
    nxt.OutputSetTachoLimit(motor,degrees)

end
```

Run the gear wheel until the first touch sensor triggers a "pressed" event to load the catapult:

```
. . .
```

```
function Catapult()

  . . .
  -- loop forever
  while 1 do
    . . .
    rotate(1,30)

    -- load catapult
    -- run motor C until the first
    -- touch sensor gets pressed by the liftarm
    nxt.outputSetSpeed(3, 32, 100, 0)
    while nxt.InputGetRawAd(1) == 0
      -- do nothing
    end

    nxt.OutputSetSpeed(3,0,0,0)

  end

end
. . .
```

Wait for the user to press the second touch sensor now:

```
. . .
function Catapult()

  . . .
  -- loop forever
  while 1 do
    . . .
    nxt.OutputSetSpeed(3,0,0,0)

    -- wait for the user to press the second touch sensor
    while nxt.InputGetRawAd(2) == 0
      -- do nothing
    end

  end

end
. . .
```

And the loaded catapult gets fired:

```
. . .
function Catapult()

  . . .
  -- loop forever
  while 1 do
    . . .
    -- wait for the user to press the second touch sensor
    while nxt.InputGetRawAd(2) == 0
      -- do nothing
    end
```

```
      -- drop crank mechanism
      rotate(1,-30)

   end

end
. . .
```

Wait for two seconds:

```
. . .
function Catapult()

   . . .
   -- loop forever
   while 1 do
      . . .
      -- drop crank mechanism
      rotate(1,-30)

      -- wait for 2 seconds
      local endOfWait = nxt.TimerRead() + 2000
      while nxt.TimerRead() < endOfWait
        -- do nothing
      end

   end

end
. . .
```

With calling the Catapult function, the pbLua program for the catapult is finished:

```
-- function Catapult
function Catapult()

   -- configure the touch sensors on input ports 1 and 2
   nxt.InputSetDigi0(1)
   nxt.InputSetDirOutDigi0(1)
   nxt.InputSetDigi0(2)
   nxt.InputSetDirOutDigi0(2)

   -- configure motors A  and C to run in "brake" mode
   nxt.OutputSetMode(1,2)
   nxt.OutputSetMode(3,2)

   -- loop forever
   while 1 do

      -- lift crank mechanism
      -- rotate motor A by 30 degrees
      rotate(1,30)

      -- load catapult
      -- run motor C until until the first
      -- touch sensor gets pressed by the liftarm
```

```
    nxt.outputSetSpeed(3, 32, 100, 0)
    while nxt.InputGetRawAd(1) == 0
      -- do nothing
    end

    nxt.OutputSetSpeed(3,0,0,0)

    -- wait for the user to press the second touch sensor
    while nxt.InputGetRawAd(2) == 0
      -- do nothing
    end

    -- drop crank mechanism
    rotate(1,-30)

    -- wait for 2 seconds
    local endOfWait = nxt.TimerRead() + 2000
    while nxt.TimerRead() < endOfWait
      -- do nothing
    end

  end

end

-- function to rotate a motor by a given number of degrees
function rotate(motor,degrees)

  nxt.OutputEnableRegulation(motor,1)
  nxt.OutputSetMode(motor,2)
  nxt.OutputSetSpeed(motor,32,75,0)
  nxt.OutputSetTachoLimit(motor,degrees)

end

-- now run the Catapult function
Catapult()
```

LeJOS NXJ

Start with defining the Catapult class containing a main() method and importing the lejos.nxt package:

```
package org.nxtdavinci.catapult;

import lejos.nxt.*;

public class Catapult {

  public static void main(String[] args) throws Exception {
  }
}
```

Configure the two touch sensors and the motors' power:

```
. . .
public class Catapult {

  public static void main(String[] args) throws Exception {

    // configure the touch sensors on input ports 1 and 2
    TouchSensor touchSensor1 = new TouchSensor(Port.S1);
    TouchSensor touchSensor2 = new TouchSensor(Port.S2);

    // configure the motors' speed
    Motor.A.setSpeed(600);
    Motor.C.setSpeed(900);
  }
}
```

To lift the crank mechanism as a start, rotate motor A by 30 degrees. Note the enclosing endless loop:

```
. . .
public class Catapult {

  public static void main(String[] args) throws Exception {

    . . .
    Motor.C.setSpeed(900);

    // endless loop
    while(true) {

      // lift crank mechanism
      Motor.A.rotateTo(30);
    }
  }
}
```

Load the catapult now by running the motor attached to the gear until the first touch sensor triggers an event:

```
. . .
public class Catapult {

  public static void main(String[] args) throws Exception {

    . . .
    while(true) {

      // lift crank mechanism
      Motor.A.rotateTo(30);

      // load catapult
      // run gear wheel's motor until the liftarm
      // presses the first touch sensor
      while(!touchSensor1.isPressed()) {
        Motor.C.forward();
      };
```

```
      Motor.C.stop();
    }
  }
}
```

Wait for the user to fire the catapult:

```
. . .
public class Catapult {

  public static void main(String[] args) throws Exception {

    . . .
    while(true) {

      . . .
      while(!touchSensor1.isPressed()) {
        Motor.C.forward();
      };
      Motor.C.stop();

      // wait for the user to fire the catapult
      while(!touchSensor2.isPressed()) {
        // do nothing
      };
    }
  }
}
```

When the user triggers firing, drop the crank mechanism to release the gear wheel:

```
. . .
public class Catapult {

  public static void main(String[] args) throws Exception {

    . . .
    while(true) {

      . . .
      // wait for the user to fire the catapult
      while(!touchSensor2.isPressed()) {
        // do nothing
      };

      // drop crank mechanism
      Motor.A.rotateTo(-30);
    }
  }
}
```

Wait a bit:

```
. . .
public class Catapult {

  public static void main(String[] args) throws Exception {

    . . .
    while(true) {

      . . .
      // drop crank mechanism
      Motor.A.rotateTo(-30);

      // wait for two seconds
      Thread.sleep(2000);

    }
  }
}
```

Now you are finished:

```
package org.nxtdavinci.catapult;

import lejos.nxt.*;

public class Catapult {

  publsic static void main(String[] args) throws Exception {

    // configure the touch sensors on input ports 1 and 2
    TouchSensor touchSensor1 = new TouchSensor(Port.S1);
    TouchSensor touchSensor2 = new TouchSensor(Port.S2);

    // configure the motors' speed
    Motor.A.setSpeed(600);
    Motor.C.setSpeed(900);

    // endless loop
    while(true) {

      // lift crank mechanism
      Motor.A.rotateTo(30);

      // load catapult
      // run gear wheel's motor until the liftarm
      // presses the first touch sensor
      while(!touchSensor1.isPressed()) {
        Motor.C.forward();
      };
      Motor.C.stop();
```

```
    // wait for the user to fire the catapult
    while(!touchSensor2.isPressed()) {
      // do nothing
    };

    // drop crank mechanism
    Motor.A.rotateTo(-30);

    // wait for two seconds
    Thread.sleep(2000);

  }
 }
}
```

Summary

In this chapter you built another military device designed by Leonardo, resulting in a rather complex NXT robot: the catapult. You learned how to make use of the motors for different tasks and became familiar with the first type of sensor, the touch sensor.

On the software side, accessing that sensor and its state is now transparent to you. In addition to that, you learned about implementing more complex control structures and program flow with the different programming languages.

In the next chapter you will learn about another type of sensor, the ultrasonic sensor, when you build Leonardo's invention of the revolving bridge.

■■■

CHAPTER 5

The Revolving Bridge

Water is the driving force of all nature.

—Leonardo da Vinci

In this chapter, you will build Leonardo's revolving bridge. This robot makes use of the ultrasonic sensor, and you will learn how to access it in five different NXT programming languages. This chapter also covers how to synchronize motors and how to use strings to transfer motor control to remote hardware components.

Historical Background

With an interest in hydrodynamic topics and an occupation as a military engineer, it's small wonder that Leonardo undertook the task of devising concepts for bridges for military and economical reasons. During his life, he came up with a lot of concepts for structures over rivers. Most were intended to be flexible and easy to build, so were made of wood rather than stone. Aside from his 720-foot wood bridge meant to span the Golden Horn at the mouth of the Bosporus, other well-known designs include a pontoon bridge, a double-deck bridge that allowed both pedestrians and carriages to cross the river at the same time, and a self-supporting bridge made from wooden balks that did not require nails.

Leonardo drew the revolving bridge in Milan in the 1580s, and the drawing is today contained in the Codex Atlanticus (Figure 5-1). In his letter to Duke Ludovico, he talks of "plans for very light yet stable bridges."

Bridges have always been important to human societies as a means to cross obstacles such as rivers, lakes, or abysses. Stable and reliable bridges have made the transportation of people and goods possible, establishing long-range economical connections on a large scale. In particular, in the medieval ages, with roads and rivers providing the major means of inland transportation, bridges were crucial.

Bridges were also important for military reasons. They could form a bottleneck that hampered enemy troops laden with heavy artillery. Bridges were of paramount importance in military strategies because they formed a point of defense against advancing enemies, as well as represented primary targets for those very adversaries.

In his design of the revolving bridge, Leonardo relies on an antique pretext but solves the problem of defending the structure against the peril of enemies in a fancy way: with hostile troops advancing, the bridge could swing around a pylon, separating it from the shore. The enemy could then no longer cross the river. Simple, but completely efficient.

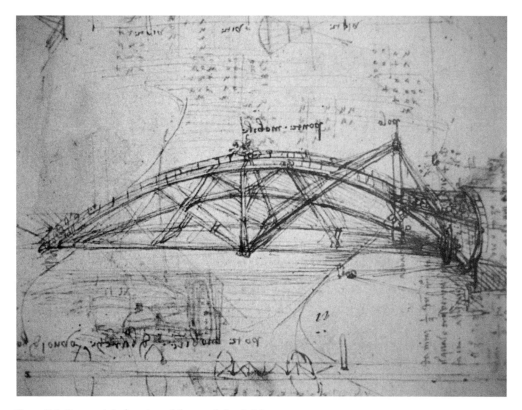

Figure 5-1. *Leonardo's drawing of the revolving bridge*

It must not be forgotten that the revolving mechanism imposed an important economical advantage as well. The bridge's ability to move made it possible for large ships to pass on their (mostly economical) journeys.

Hardware Challenges

Generally speaking, building a bridge with LEGO is not the most complex thing in the world. With Leonardo's revolving bridge, however, the fulcrum it swings around poses a particular challenge. The fulcrum is the only point from which the whole structure is suspended. This means everything must be in balance and stable while allowing for movement.

For the implementation of the fulcrum with LEGO, I use a turntable that is fixed to a base plate. This provides both the required stability and flexibility needed (Figure 5-2).

Figure 5-2. *Implementation of the fulcrum*

Building the Revolving Bridge

Figure 5-3 shows the completed revolving bridge robot. Note that I have added an ultrasonic sensor to Leonardo's original design on the far-side base of the bridge. It is used to automatically swing the bridge away when the sensor spots approaching enemies—a contraption Leonardo certainly would have liked.

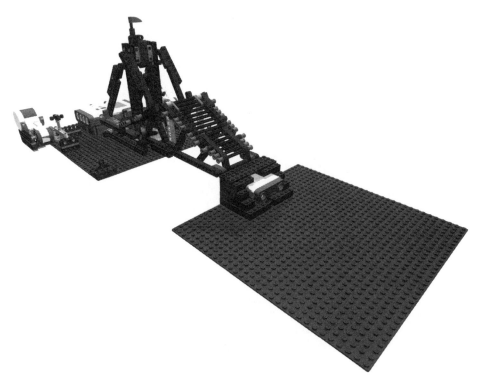

Figure 5-3. *The completed revolving bridge robot*

The following images (Figures 5-4 through 5-42) show step-by-step instructions on how to build the revolving bridge.

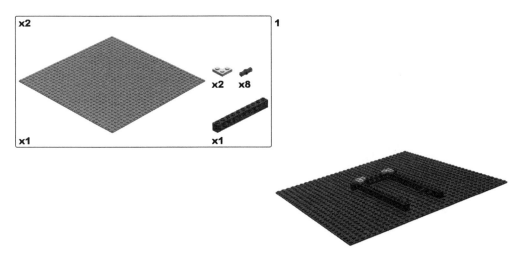

Figure 5-4. *Building the revolving bridge: step 1*

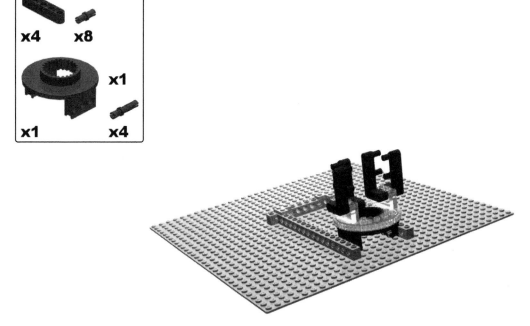

Figure 5-5. *Building the revolving bridge: steps 2 (rotate model) and 3*

Figure 5-6. *Building the revolving bridge: step 4*

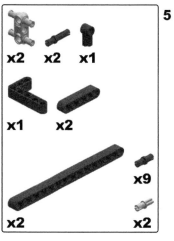

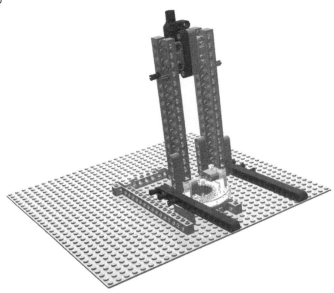

Figure 5-7. *Building the revolving bridge: step 5*

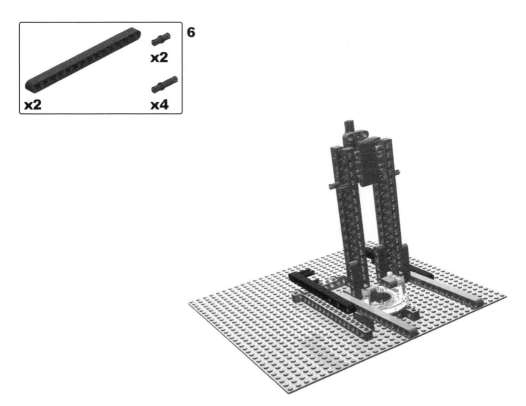

Figure 5-8. *Building the revolving bridge: step 6*

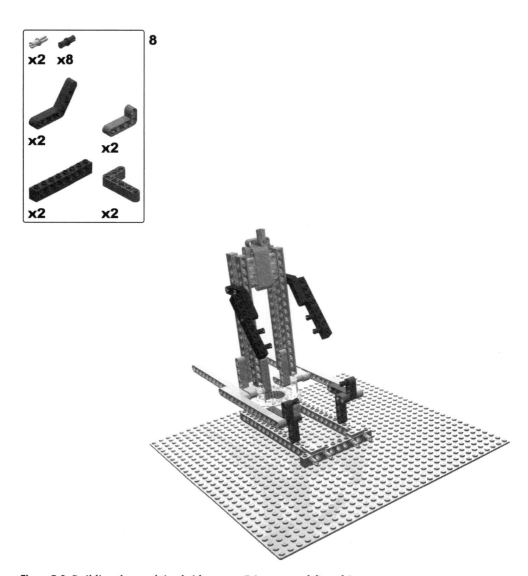

Figure 5-9. *Building the revolving bridge: steps 7 (rotate model) and 8*

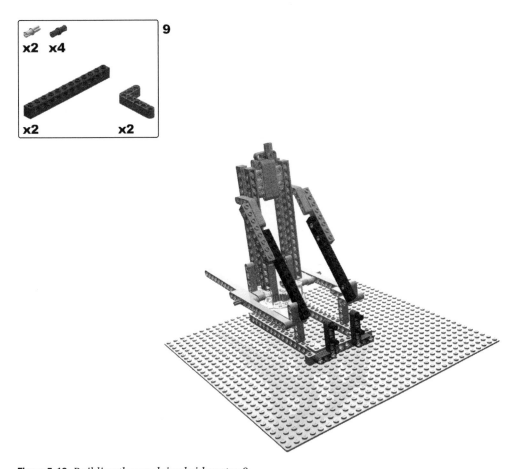

Figure 5-10. *Building the revolving bridge: step 9*

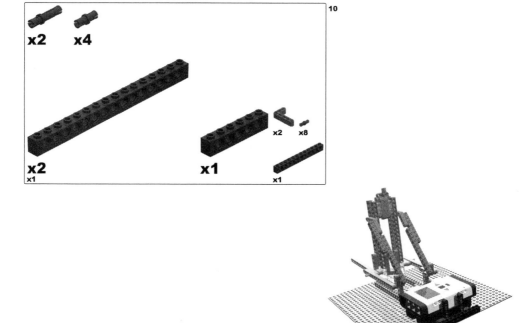

Figure 5-11. *Building the revolving bridge: step 10*

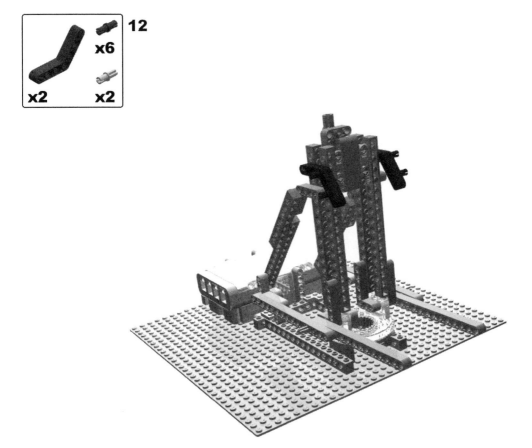

Figure 5-12. *Building the revolving bridge: steps 11 (rotate model) and 12*

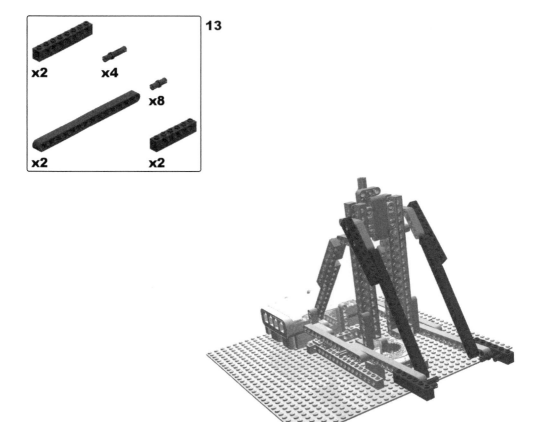

Figure 5-13. *Building the revolving bridge: step 13*

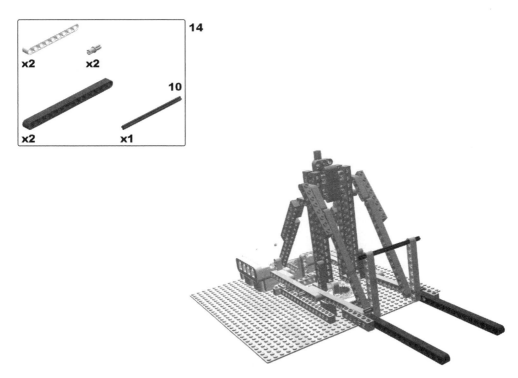

Figure 5-14. *Building the revolving bridge: step 14*

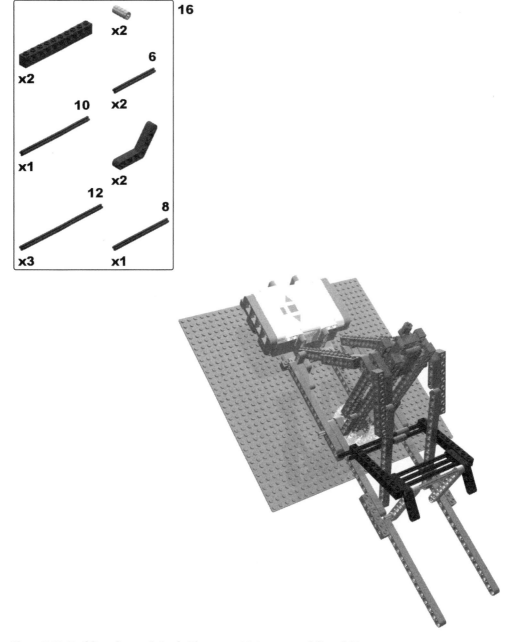

Figure 5-15. *Building the revolving bridge: steps 15 (rotate model) and 16*

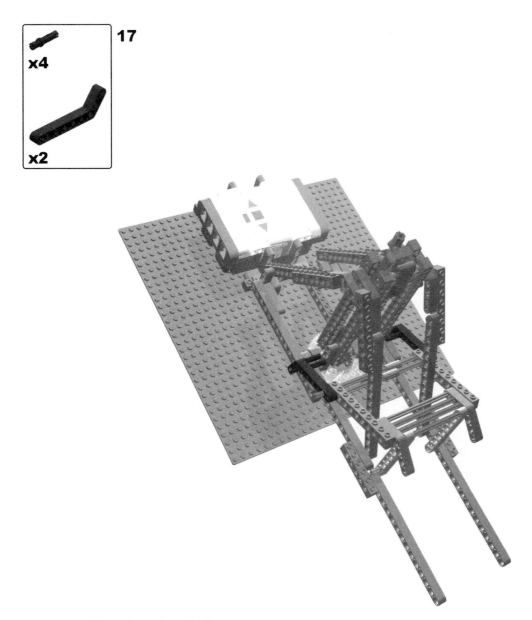

Figure 5-16. *Building the revolving bridge: step 17*

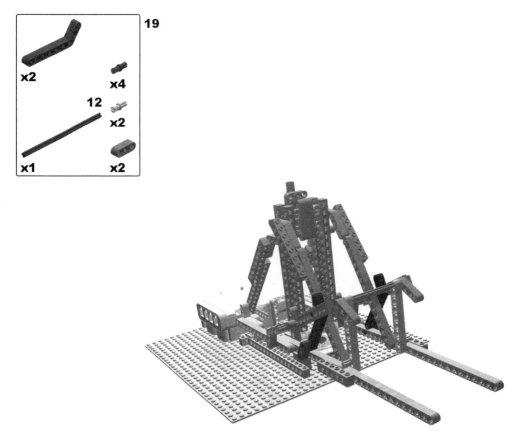

Figure 5-17. *Building the revolving bridge: steps 18 (rotate model) and 19*

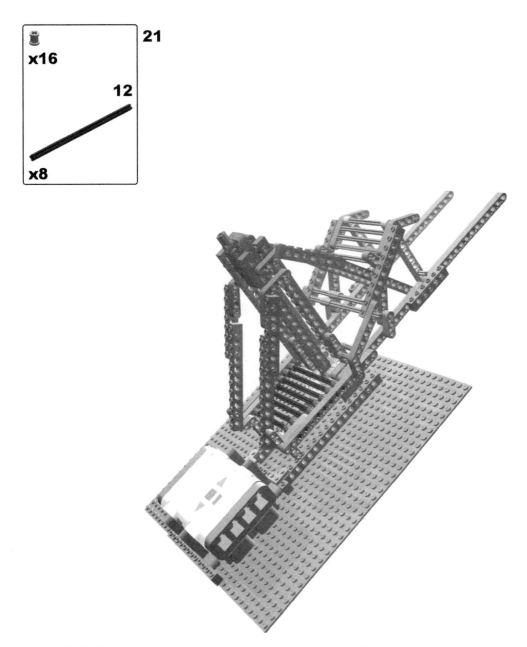

Figure 5-18. *Building the revolving bridge: steps 20 (rotate model) and 21*

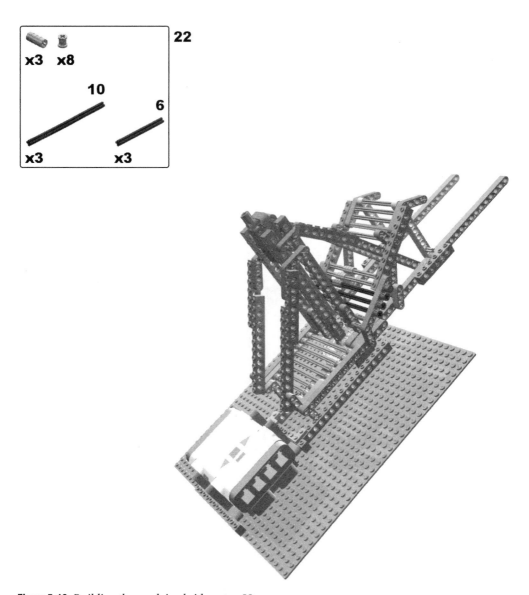

Figure 5-19. *Building the revolving bridge: step 22*

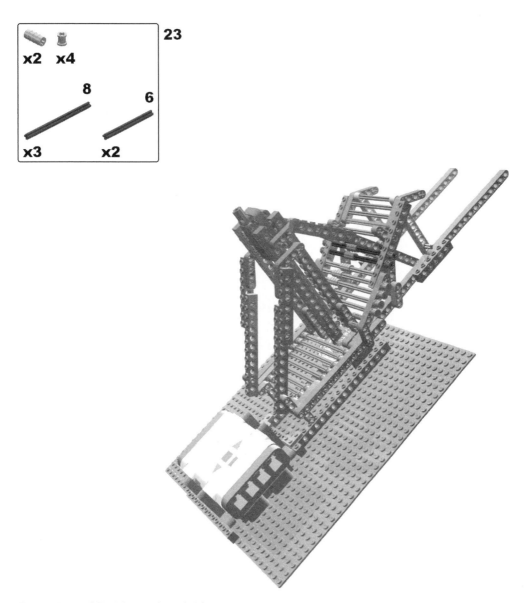

Figure 5-20. *Building the revolving bridge: step 23*

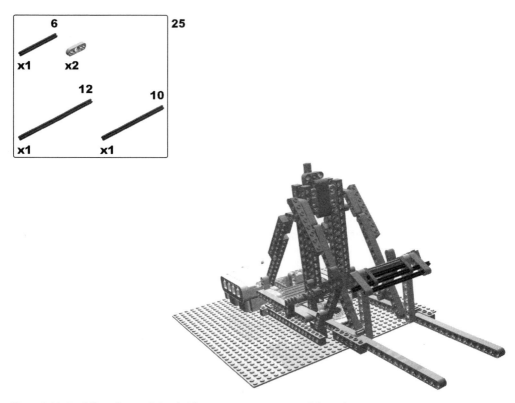

Figure 5-21. *Building the revolving bridge: steps 24 (rotate model) and 25*

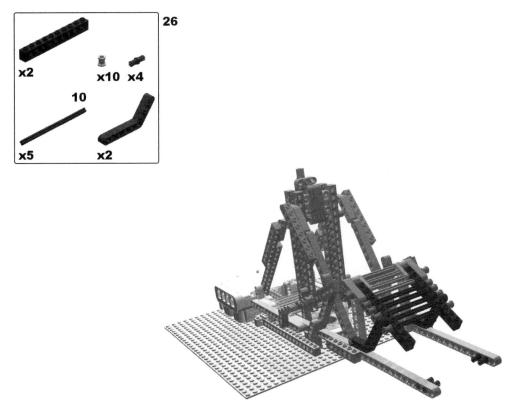

Figure 5-22. *Building the revolving bridge: step 26*

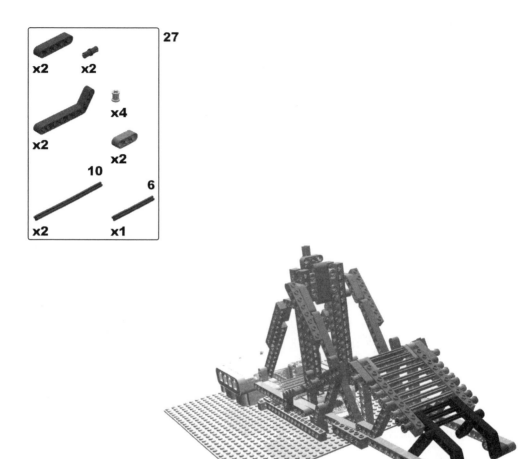

Figure 5-23. *Building the revolving bridge: step 27*

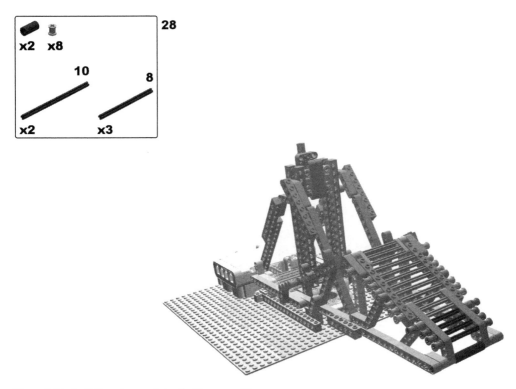

Figure 5-24. *Building the revolving bridge: step 28*

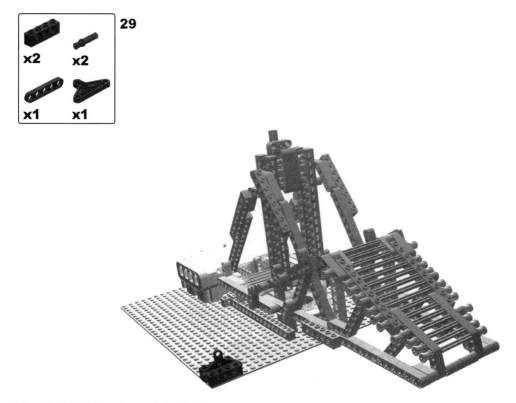

Figure 5-25. *Building the revolving bridge: step 29*

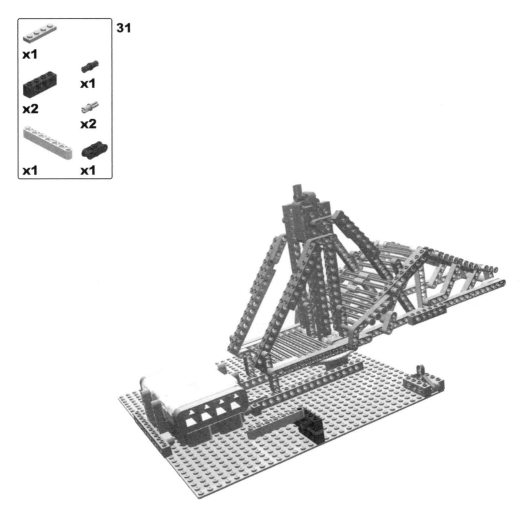

Figure 5-26. *Building the revolving bridge: steps 30 (rotate model) and 31*

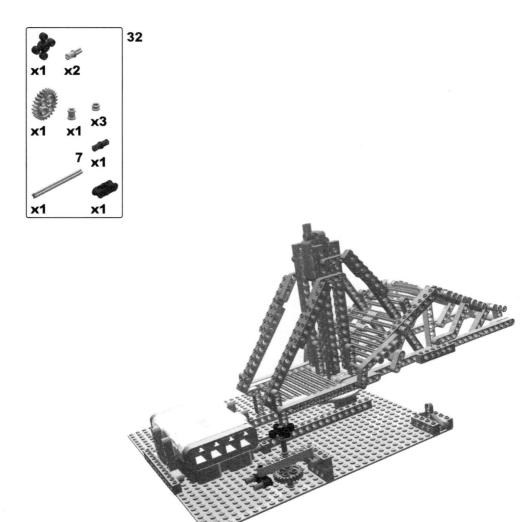

Figure 5-27. *Building the revolving bridge: step 32*

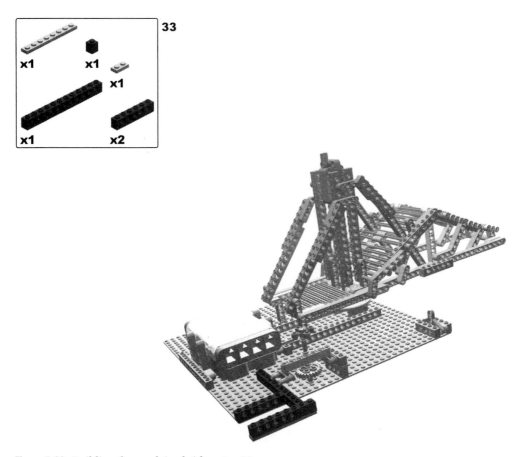

Figure 5-28. *Building the revolving bridge: step 33*

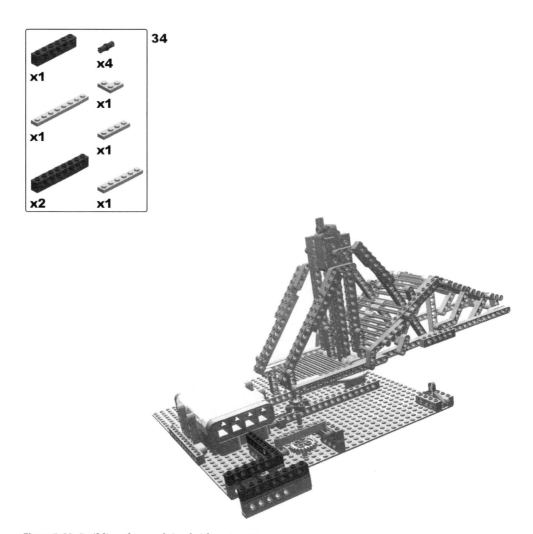

Figure 5-29. *Building the revolving bridge: step 34*

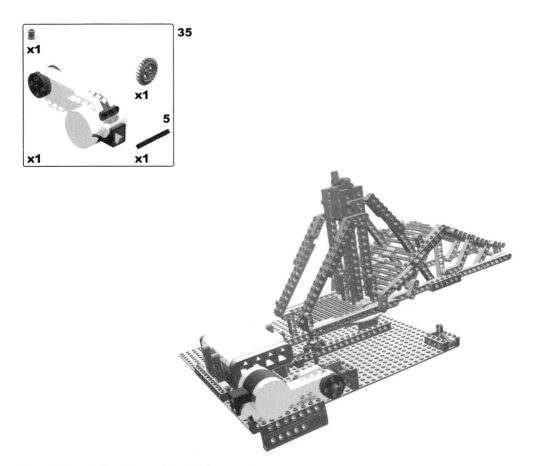

Figure 5-30. *Building the revolving bridge: step 35*

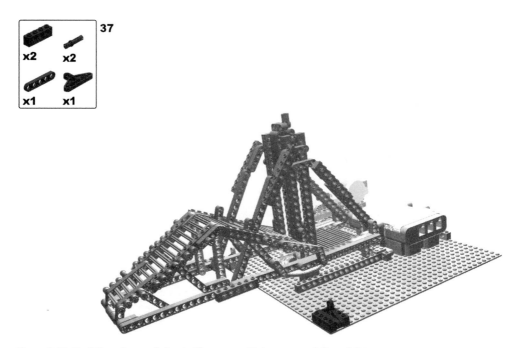

Figure 5-31. *Building the revolving bridge: steps 36 (rotate model) and 37*

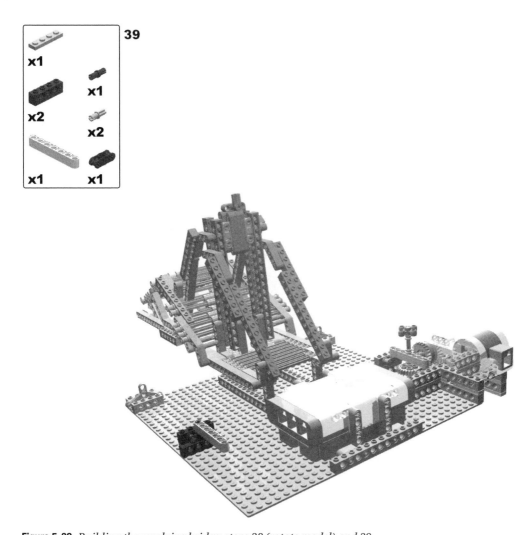

Figure 5-32. *Building the revolving bridge: steps 38 (rotate model) and 39*

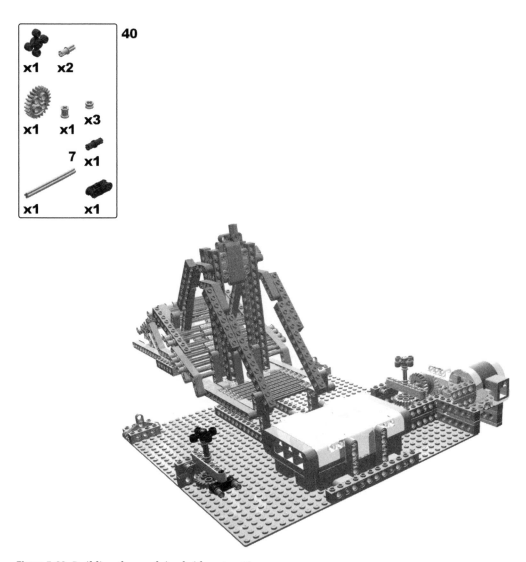

Figure 5-33. *Building the revolving bridge: step 40*

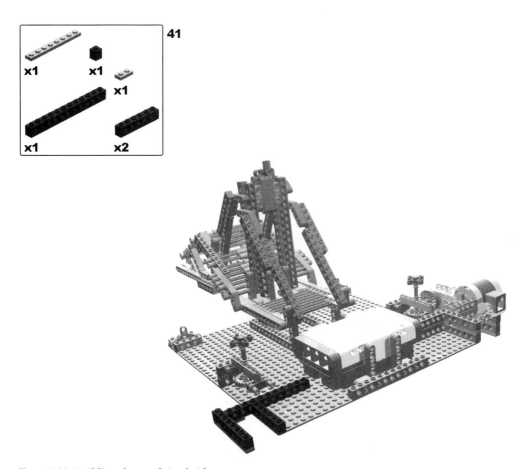

Figure 5-34. *Building the revolving bridge: step 41*

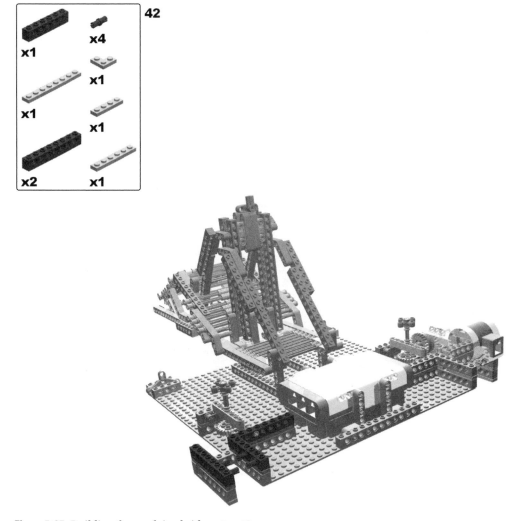

Figure 5-35. *Building the revolving bridge: step 42*

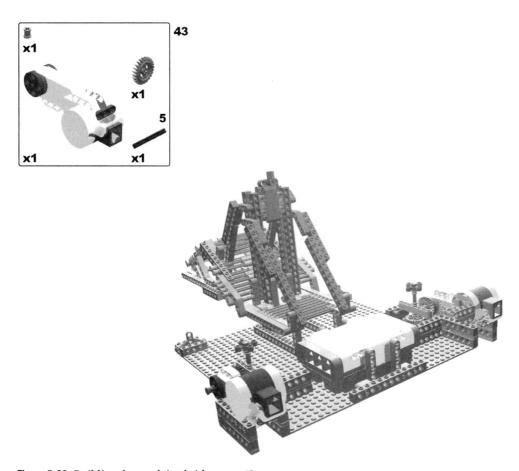

Figure 5-36. *Building the revolving bridge: step 43*

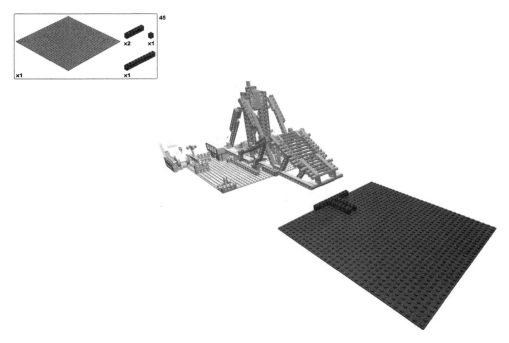

Figure 5-37. *Building the revolving bridge: steps 44 (rotate model) and 45*

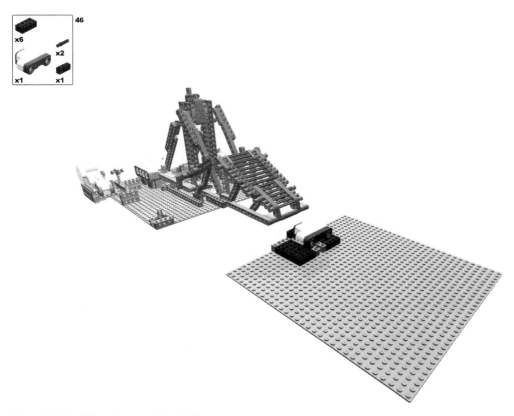

Figure 5-38. *Building the revolving bridge: step 46*

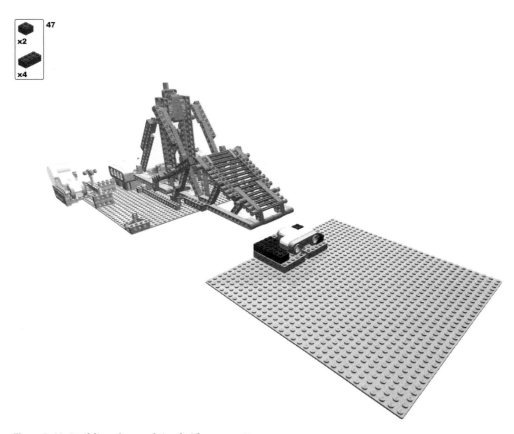

Figure 5-39. *Building the revolving bridge: step 47*

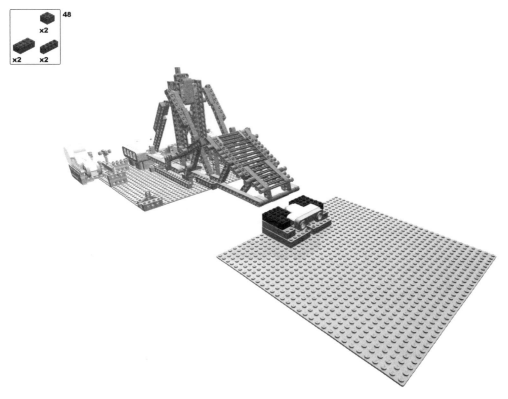

Figure 5-40. *Building the revolving bridge: step 48*

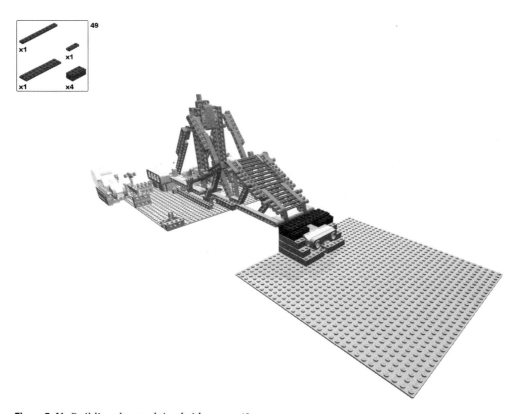

Figure 5-41. *Building the revolving bridge: step 49*

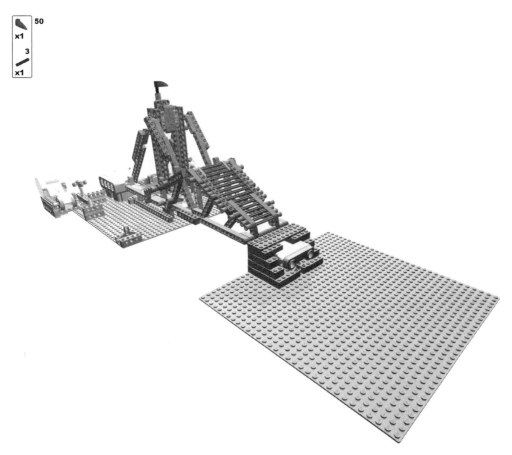

Figure 5-42. *Building the revolving bridge: step 50*

The building of the bridge concludes with wiring the motors and the sensors to the Brick. Finally, you connect the winches with the L-shaped beams at the end of the bridge by strings (e.g., strong sewing threads). Do not forget to pass each thread through the hole of the triangular structure at its corner of the base plate.

Figure 5-43 shows the LEGO parts required for the revolving bridge robot.

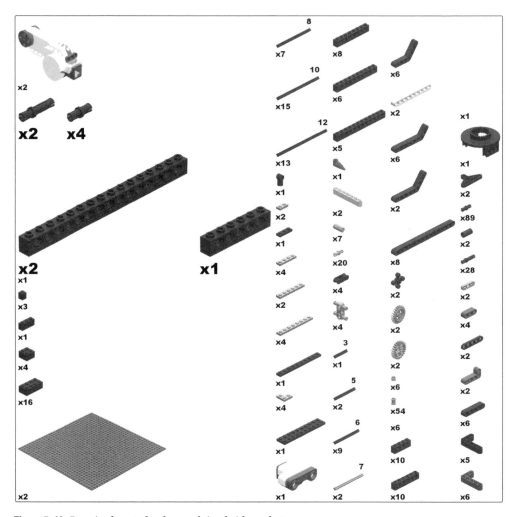

Figure 5-43. *Required parts for the revolving bridge robot*

Programming the Revolving Bridge

Not surprisingly, the general flow of the program for the bridge is not very complex (Figure 5-44):

1. Wait for an object to approach the structure.

2. Once the ultrasonic sensor has detected something, move the bridge to the side by running the two motors.

3. Wait until the sensor does not detect anything anymore.

4. Reset the bridge to its original state.

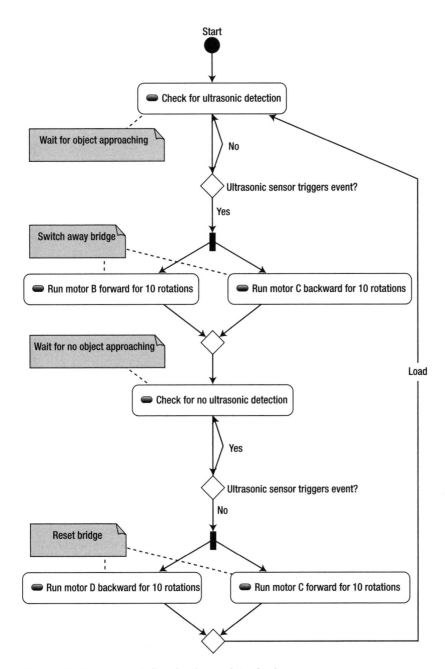

Figure 5-44. *The program's flow for the revolving bridge*

LEGO MINDSTORMS NXT Software

Again, you start with a loop block that runs forever (Figure 5-45).

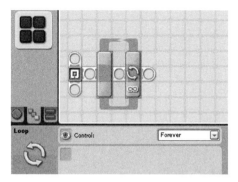

Figure 5-45. *The revolving bridge programmed with NXT-G: the global forever loop block*

Now you wait until the ultrasonic sensor detects an approaching object. Therefore, you insert a loop block again, this time appropriately configured by the ultrasonic sensor (Figure 5-46).

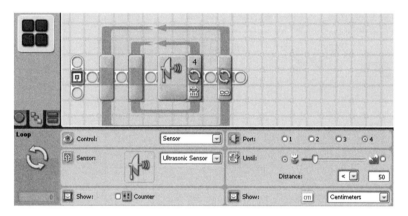

Figure 5-46. *The ultrasonic sensor loop block for detection*

Once an object is detected, switch the bridge away by running the two motors that operate the winches. For synchronizing these two motors, use a Move block that is configured to run them in opposite directions (Figure 5-47).

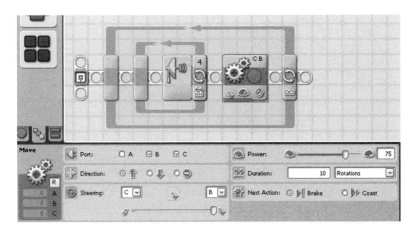

Figure 5-47. *The Move block switching the bridge away*

Now that the bridge is switched away, wait for the ultrasonic sensor to detect that there is no object, which means that the possible enemies have retreated. As before, use a loop block configured by the ultrasonic sensor; this time, though, the stop criterion is vice versa (Figure 5-48).

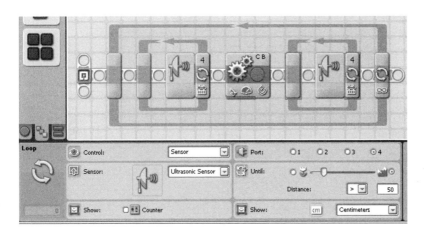

Figure 5-48. *The ultrasonic sensor loop block for no detection*

Once no object can be detected any longer, the bridge is switched back by an appropriately configured Move block (Figure 5-49).

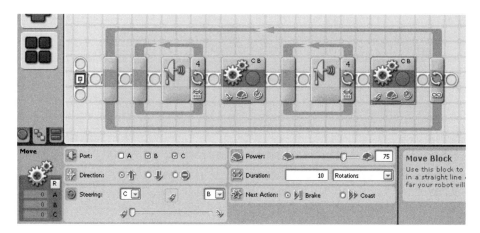

Figure 5-49. *The Move block resetting the bridge*

And you're done. Figure 5-50 shows the complete NXT-G program.

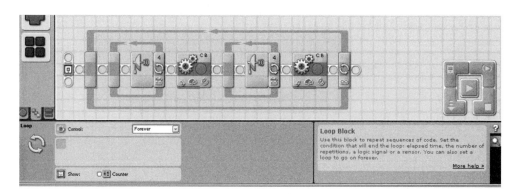

Figure 5-50. *The complete revolving bridge NXT-G program*

RobotC

To program with RobotC, use the ultrasonic sensor attached to port 4:

```
const tSensors sonarSensor = (tSensors) S4;
task main() {

}
```

Again, you need an infinite loop for the endless execution of the program and an inner loop that runs until the ultrasonic sensor detects something:

```
const tSensors ultrasonicSensor = (tSensors) S1;
task main() {

  // endless loop
  while(true) {
```

```
    // wait until ultrasonic sensor detects something
    do {
      // do nothing until ultrasonic sensor detects
      // an object nearer than 50 inches
    } while(SensorValue(ultrasonicSensor) > 50);
  }
}
```

To switch the bridge, run motors B and C in opposite directions for ten rotations. Since you want to synchronize the motors, you should appropriately set the variable nSyncedMotors that is predefined by RobotC to synchBC, which means that motor C is synchronized to motor B. Moreover, set the predefined variable nSyncedTurnRatio to -100, which means that the synchronizing is performed in the opposite turning direction. Note that due to the synchronization, you have to adjust the power of the master motor only:

```
const tSensors ultrasonicSensor = (tSensors) S1;
task main() {

  // endless loop
  while(true) {

    // wait until ultrasonic sensor detects something
    do {
      . . .
    } while(SensorValue(ultrasonicSensor) > 50);

    // synchronize motors B and C in opposite directions
    nSyncedMotors = synchBC;
    nSyncedTurnRatio = -100;

    // run motors for 10 rotations which is 3600 degrees
    nMotorEncoder[motorB] = 0;
    nMotorEncoderTarget[motorB] = 3600;
    motor[motorB] = 75;

  }
}
```

A further loop that runs until the ultrasonic sensor does not detect anything any longer follows:

```
const tSensors ultrasonicSensor = (tSensors) S1;
task main() {
  // endless loop
  while(true) {

    ...
    motor[motorB] = 75;

    // wait until ultrasonic sensor does not detect anything any longer
    while(SensorValue(ultrasonicSensor) < 50) {
      // do nothing until ultrasonic sensor does not detect
      // an object nearer than 50 inches
    }

  };
}
```

Switch the bridge back by running the synchronized motors in the opposite direction:

```
const tSensors ultrasonicSensor = (tSensors) S1;
task main() {

  // endless loop
  while(true) {

    . . .
    while(SensorValue(ultrasonicSensor) < 50) {
     ...
    }

    // run motors back for 10 rotations which is -3600 degrees
    nMotorEncoder[motorB] = 0;
    nMotorEncoderTarget[motorB] = -3600;
    motor[motorB] = 75;

  }
}
```

That's all. The complete program looks like this:

```
const tSensors ultrasonicSensor = (tSensors) S1;
task main() {

  // endless loop
  while(true) {

    // wait until ultrasonic sensor detects something
    do {
      // do nothing until ultrasonic sensor detects
      // an object nearer than 50 inches
    } while(SensorValue(ultrasonicSensor) > 50);

    // synchronize motors B and C in opposite directions
    nSyncedMotors = synchBC;
    nSyncedTurnRatio = -100;

    // run motors for 10 rotations which is 3600 degrees
    nMotorEncoder[motorB] = 0;
    nMotorEncoderTarget[motorB] = 3600;
    motor[motorC] = 75;

    // wait until ultrasonic sensor does not detect anything any longer
    while(SensorValue(ultrasonicSensor) < 50) {
     // do nothing until ultrasonic sensor does not detect
     // an object nearer than 50 inches
    }

    // run motors back for 10 rotations which is -3600 degrees
    nMotorEncoder[motorB] = 0;
    nMotorEncoderTarget[motorB] = -3600;
    motor[motorB] = 75;

  }
}
```

NXC

The NXC program flow starts with the definition of the ultrasonic sensor at port 1:

```
// enable NXC
#include "NXCDefs.h"

// main
task main() {

  // we use an ultrasonic sensor at port 1
  SetSensorType(IN_1,IN_TYPE_REFLECTION);
}
```

The infinite loop for the endless execution of the program contains an inner loop with detection statements for the ultrasonic sensor:

```
. . .
task main() {

  // we use an ultrasonic sensor at port 1
  SetSensorType(IN_1,IN_TYPE_REFLECTION);

  // endless loop
  while(1) {

    // wait until ultrasonic sensor detects something
    do {
      // do nothing until ultrasonic sensor detects
      // an object nearer than 50 inches
    } while(Sensor(IN_1) > 50);
  }
}
```

To switch the bridge, synchronize motors B and C but in opposite directions for 3600 degrees, which is ten rotations:

```
. . .
task main() {

  . . .
  while(1) {

    // wait until ultrasonic sensor detects something
    do {
      // do nothing until ultrasonic sensor detects
      // an object nearer than 50 inches
    } while(Sensor(IN_1) > 50);

    // run motors synchronized for 10 rotations which is 3600 degrees
    // third parameter 100 means: B and C in opposite directions
    RotateMotorEx (OUT_BC, 75, 3600, 100, true);

  }
}
```

Do nothing until the ultrasonic sensor does not detect anything:

```
. . .
task main() {

  . . .
  while(1) {

    . . .
    RotateMotorEx (OUT_BC, 75, 3600, 100, true);

    // wait until ultrasonic sensor does not detect anything any longer
    while(Sensor(IN_1) < 50) {
      // do nothing
    }
  }
}
```

When no approaching enemies are detected, switch the bridge back by running the synchronized motors in the opposite direction, that is, by -3600 degrees:

```
. . .
task main() {

  . . .
  while(1) {

    . . .
    while(Sensor(IN_1) < 50) {
      // do nothing
    }

    // switch back the bridge
    RotateMotorEx (OUT_BC, 75, -3600, 100, true);
  }
}
```

And you are done. The following is the complete NXC program for the revolving bridge:

```
// enable NXC
#include "NXCDefs.h"

// main
task main() {

  // we use an ultrasonic sensor at port 1
  SetSensorType(IN_1,IN_TYPE_REFLECTION);

  // endless loop
  while(1) {

    // wait until ultrasonic sensor detects something
    do {
      // do nothing until ultrasonic sensor detects
      // an object nearer than 50 inches
    } while(Sensor(IN_1) > 50);
```

```
// run motors synchronized for 10 rotations which is 3600 degrees
// third parameter 100 means: B and C in opposite directions
RotateMotorEx (OUT_BC, 75, 3600, 100, true);

// wait until ultrasonic sensor does not detect anything any longer
while(Sensor(IN_1) < 50) {
  // do nothing
}

// switch back the bridge
RotateMotorEx (OUT_BC, 75, -3600, 100, true);

}
}
```

pbLua

Define the RevolvingBridge function and add configurations for the ultrasonic sensor on port 1 and the motors B and C:

```
-- function RevolvingBridge
function RevolvingBridge()

  -- configure the ultrasonic sensor on input port 1
  nxt.InputSetDigi0(1)
  nxt.InputSetDirOutDigi0(1)

  -- configure motors B and C to run in "brake" mode
  -- enable regulation
  nxt.OutputSetMode(2,2)
  nxt.OutputSetMode(3,2)
  nxt.OutputEnableRegulation(2,1)
  nxt.OutputEnableRegulation(3,1)

end
```

The first statement in the infinite loop is another loop that waits until the ultrasonic sensor detects something approaching:

```
-- function RevolvingBridge
function RevolvingBridge()

  . . .
  nxt.OutputEnableRegulation(3,1)

  -- loop forever
  while 1 do

    -- wait for the ultrasonic sensor to detect something nearer than 50 inches
    while nxt.InputGetRawAd(1) > 50
      -- do nothing
    end
  end
end
```

Synchronizing motors B and C in opposite directions and running them for ten rotations switches the bridge away:

```
-- function RevolvingBridge
function RevolvingBridge()

  . . .
  while 1 do

    -- wait for the ultrasonic sensor to detect something nearer than 50 inches
    while nxt.InputGetRawAd(1) > 50
      -- do nothing
    end

    -- run motors B and C synchronized in opposite directions for 10 rotations
    -- first synchronize motor B and C
    nxt.OutputSetRegulation(2,2,1)
    nxt.OutputSetRegulation(3,2,1)
    -- now run motors for 10 rotations (= 3600 degrees)
    nxt.OutputSetSpeed(2, 32, 100, 0)
    nxt.OutputSetSpeed(3, 32, -100, 0)
    nxt.OutputSetTachoLimit(2, 3600)
    nxt.OutputSetTachoLimit(3, 3600)

  end
end
```

Again, you wait, this time until the ultrasonic sensor no longer detects anything in proximity:

```
-- function RevolvingBridge
function RevolvingBridge()

  . . .
  while 1 do

    . . .
    nxt.OutputSetTachoLimit(3, 3600)

    -- wait for the ultrasonic sensor no longer detecting
    -- something nearer than 50 inches
    while nxt.InputGetRawAd(1) < 50
      -- do nothing
    end
  end
end
```

Switch the bridge back:

```
-- function RevolvingBridge
function RevolvingBridge()

  . . .
  while 1 do

    . . .
```

```
    while nxt.InputGetRawAd(1) < 50
      -- do nothing
    end

    -- switch back the bridge
    -- run motors in opposite direction for 10 rotations (= 3600 degrees)
    -- note that each motor runs in the reverse direction than before
    nxt.OutputSetSpeed(2, 32, -100, 0)
    nxt.OutputSetSpeed(3, 32, 100, 0)
    nxt.OutputSetTachoLimit(2, 3600)
    nxt.OutputSetTachoLimit(3, 3600)

  end
end
```

Finally, call the RevolvingBridge function:

```
-- function RevolvingBridge
function RevolvingBridge()

  . . .
  while 1 do

    . . .
  end
end

-- now run the RevolvingBridge function
RevolvingBridge()
```

This is the complete pbLua program for the revolving bridge:

```
-- function RevolvingBridge
function RevolvingBridge()

  -- configure the ultrasonic sensor on input port 1
  nxt.InputSetDigi0(1)
  nxt.InputSetDirOutDigi0(1)

  -- configure motors B and C to run in "brake" mode
  -- enable regulation
  nxt.OutputSetMode(2,2)
  nxt.OutputSetMode(3,2)
  nxt.OutputEnableRegulation(2,1)
  nxt.OutputEnableRegulation(3,1)

  -- loop forever
  while 1 do

    -- wait for the ultrasonic sensor to detect something nearer than 50 inches
    while nxt.InputGetRawAd(1) > 50
      -- do nothing
    end
```

```
    -- run motors B and C synchronized in opposite directions for 10 rotations
    -- first synchronize motor B and C
    nxt.OutputSetRegulation(2,2,1)
    nxt.OutputSetRegulation(3,2,1)
    -- now run motors for 10 rotations (= 3600 degrees)
    nxt.OutputSetSpeed(2, 32, 100, 0)
    nxt.OutputSetSpeed(3, 32, -100, 0)
    nxt.OutputSetTachoLimit(2, 3600)
    nxt.OutputSetTachoLimit(3, 3600)

    -- wait for the ultrasonic sensor no longer detecting
    -- something nearer than 50 inches
    while nxt.InputGetRawAd(1) < 50
      -- do nothing
    end

    -- switch back the bridge
    -- run motors in opposite direction for 10 rotations (= 3600 degrees)
    -- note that each motor runs in the reverse direction than before
    nxt.OutputSetSpeed(2, 32, -100, 0)
    nxt.OutputSetSpeed(3, 32, 100, 0)
    nxt.OutputSetTachoLimit(2, 3600)
    nxt.OutputSetTachoLimit(3, 3600)

  end
end

-- now run the RevolvingBridge function
RevolvingBridge()
```

leJOS NXJ

Again, you start with defining the RevolvingBridge class containing a main() method and importing the lejos.nxt package:

```
package org.davincinxt.revolvingbridge;

import lejos.nxt.Motor;
import lejos.nxt.SensorPort;
import lejos.nxt.UltrasonicSensor;

public class RevolvingBridge {

    public static void main(String[] args) throws Exception {

    }

}
```

Configure the motors' power and the ultrasonic sensor and start an endless loop:

```
. . .
public class RevolvingBridge {

    public static void main(String[] args) throws Exception {

        // speed
        Motor.B.setSpeed(600);
        Motor.C.setSpeed(600);

        // sonar sensor at port 1
        UltrasonicSensor us = new UltrasonicSensor(SensorPort.S1);

        // endless loop
        while(true) {

        }
    }

}
```

Wait until the ultrasonic sensor detects an object nearer than 50 centimeters:

```
. . .
public class RevolvingBridge {

    public static void main(String[] args) throws Exception {

        . . .
        // endless loop
        while(true) {

            // check for detection
            // we do nothing as long as nothing is detected
            int distanceToNearestObject = 1000;
            while((distanceToNearestObject = us.getDistance())>=50) {
                // do nothing
            }

        }
    }

}
```

There's something approaching, so you swing the bridge away. Note that leJOS NXJ did not provide an explicit feature for motor synchronization at the time of this writing:

```
. . .
public class RevolvingBridge {

    public static void main(String[] args) throws Exception {

        . . .
```

```
    // endless loop
    while(true) {

        . . .
        while((distanceToNearestObject = us.getDistance())>=50) {
            // do nothing
        }

        // switch bridge away
        // note that leJOS NXJ did not provide an explicit feature
        // for motor synchronization at the time of this writing
        Motor.B.rotateTo(3600);
        Motor.C.rotateTo(-3600);
    }
}

}
```

Wait until no object nearby can be detected any longer:

```
. . .
public class RevolvingBridge {
    public static void main(String[] args) throws Exception {

        . . .
        // endless loop
        while(true) {

            . . .
            Motor.C.rotateTo(-3600);

            // check for detection
            // we do nothing as long as something is detected
            while((distanceToNearestObject = us.getDistance())<50) {
                // do nothing
            }

        }
    }

}
```

If nothing can be detected any longer, swing the bridge back:

```
. . .
public class RevolvingBridge {
    public static void main(String[] args) throws Exception {
        . . .
        // endless loop
        while(true) {

            . . .
            while((distanceToNearestObject = us.getDistance())<50) {
                // do nothing
            }
```

```
        // reset bridge
        // note that leJOS NXJ did not provide an explicit feature
        // for motor synchronization at the date of this writing
        Motor.B.rotateTo(-3600);
        Motor.C.rotateTo(3600);

        }
    }

}
```

And that's it. Here's the complete leJOS NXJ program for the revolving bridge:

```
package org.davincinxt.revolvingbridge;

import lejos.nxt.Motor;
import lejos.nxt.SensorPort;
import lejos.nxt.UltrasonicSensor;

public class RevolvingBridge {
    public static void main(String[] args) throws Exception {
        // speed
        Motor.B.setSpeed(600);
        Motor.C.setSpeed(600);

        // sonar sensor at port 1
        UltrasonicSensor us = new UltrasonicSensor(SensorPort.S1);

        // endless loop
        while(true) {

            // check for detection
            // we do nothing as long as nothing is detected
            int distanceToNearestObject = 1000;
            while((distanceToNearestObject = us.getDistance())>=50) {
                // do nothing
            }

            // switch bridge away
            // note that leJOS NXJ did not provide an explicit feature
            // synchronization at the date of this writing
            Motor.B.rotateTo(3600);
            Motor.C.rotateTo(-3600);


            // check for detection
            // we do nothing as long as something is detected
            while((distanceToNearestObject = us.getDistance())<50) {
                // do nothing
            }
```

```
        // reset bridge
        // note that leJOS NXJ did not provide an explicit feature
        // for motor synchronization at the date of this writing
        Motor.B.rotateTo(-3600);
        Motor.C.rotateTo(3600);

    }
}

}
```

Summary

In this chapter, you were acquainted with another type of NXT sensor: the ultrasonic sensor. You now know what to use it for, how to use it, and how to access it programmatically in five different NXT programming languages. Furthermore, you also know about synchronizing motors and have seen how to use strings to transfer motor control to remote hardware components.

The next chapter deals with the first of Leonardo's two flying devices addressed in this book: the aerial screw. I will revise the subject of implementing curved structures with LEGO and look at another type of NXT standard sensor, the light sensor.

■ ■ ■

CHAPTER 6

The Aerial Screw

For once you have tasted flight you will walk the earth with your eyes turned skywards, for there you have been and there you will long to return.

—Leonardo da Vinci

In this chapter you will build the first of Leonardo's two flying machines. You will learn how to make curved structures with LEGO parts and use turntables, gear wheels, and axles for creating a stable hub. The light sensor is also introduced in this chapter.

Historical Background

Leonardo was deeply convinced of man's ability to fly by his own muscular power. You might even say he was obsessed by this idea and never gave it up all throughout his life. He clung to the theory that all living beings—humans and animals alike—were mechanically similar. The fact that birds and insects could fly led him to believe that the obvious inability of humans to fly was not a fundamental one and could be overcome by engineering means. Following, as usual, a pragmatic rather than a theoretical approach, Leonardo believed the matter boiled down to creating enough power to overcome the resistance that fixed the human body to the ground. The main challenge was to find a way to sufficiently amplify the muscular powers by mechanical aids.

The draft of Leonardo's aerial screw, drawn around 1490, is part of the so-called "Manuscript B," a notebook comprising 50 double folios, or 100 pages, with an additional 5 loose sheets (Figure 6-1). It's the earliest of Leonardo's bound manuscripts and is now kept in Paris.

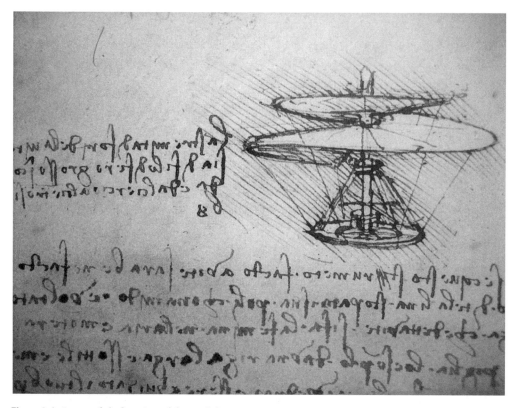

Figure 6-1. *Leonardo's drawing of the aerial screw*

Although the design resembles a modern helicopter, its concept is essentially different from the one a helicopter uses to lift into the air. The aerial screw is based on the idea of "screwing into a fluid medium," while a helicopter flies because of *aerodynamic lift*—a force generated by the flow of air around adequately shaped wings.

■**Note** Incidentally, Leonardo actually *did* create another design that may be reasonably labeled as a helicopter. It is also contained in the Manuscript B.

In addition to his belief in the similarities of the mechanical operations of living beings, Leonardo believed in the similarities of substances, in particular water and air. In his view, air was a lightweight kinsman of water and followed the same fluid mechanics. As a result, it was natural to transfer the experiences he gained from his extended studies of hydrodynamics to design devices meant for movement in the air. This is reflected in the general concept of the aerial screw; it is like a screw propelling a ship by pushing water back. The spiral top of the machine was meant to screw itself through the air, thus driving the whole mechanism upward, provided that an effectual rotation speed could be generated by the underlying powering device.

We might ask if the aerial screw would actually have been able to fly. Apart from the fact that the whole concept of "screwing into the air" couldn't work because air is too thin, the planned power of four men would have been far to low to lift the heavy weight of the 45-foot diameter construction. At most, the screw might have fallen over onto its top.

In contrast to other branches of Leonardo's research, dealing with flight was something he never seems to have presented to potential employers or customers but kept as some kind of private investigation. We do not know if he hoped to exploit his results economically in the end, as they never manifested during his lifetime. After all, this field of research most likely was viewed as too obscure by Renaissance investors, who were mainly interested in tangible and practical applications.

Rising from the ground and flying through the air is one of the oldest dreams of mankind. Many myths tell of godlike beings that are able to fly, either by their sheer will or aided by wings. The legendary Greek story of inventor Daedalus and his son Icarus who flew from Crete using wings Daedalus made is well-known, though it has a tragic outcome: Icarus rises too high, and the wax that keeps the feathers together melts near the sun and he falls to his death.

It is said that like many things, the Chinese were the first to actually bring the idea of humans rising from the soil into the air into reality. In the 14th century, Marco Polo reported that kites in China carried men to scout military troops, noting that this kind of flying has allegedly been used for many centuries there.

We also know of some attempts to fly in medieval Europe, performed by singular people who mostly jumped from elevated locations and tried to mimic birds, often with a tragic end. In general, though, the mainly metaphysically minded people of this era were averse to the general possibility of men flying at all. Consequently, up to the Renaissance, no real progress was made in this matter. It took almost another 300 years after Leonardo's days before human beings could be lifted into the air with the balloons of the Montgolfiere brothers, and another 100 years until the glider and plane experiments of Otto Lilienthal (Figure 6-2) and the Wright brothers were successful.

Figure 6-2. *Otto Lilienthal's glider*

Hardware Challenges

The challenging part of the aerial screw arguably is the twisted upper wing helix. Since LEGO does not provide these types of plates, I use beams of different length attached to a central hub made of turntables and axles (Figure 6-3).

Figure 6-3. *The aerial screw's helix*

You will have to add strings to interconnect the end of the beams with each other and with the central hub. At your leisure, you could optimize the aerial screw's appearance by attaching appropriate sheets of fabric between the beams.

Building the Aerial Screw

Figure 6-4 shows the completed aerial screw robot. To make the program for the aerial screw more instructive, I decided to integrate a light sensor into the base plate to count the number of rotations.

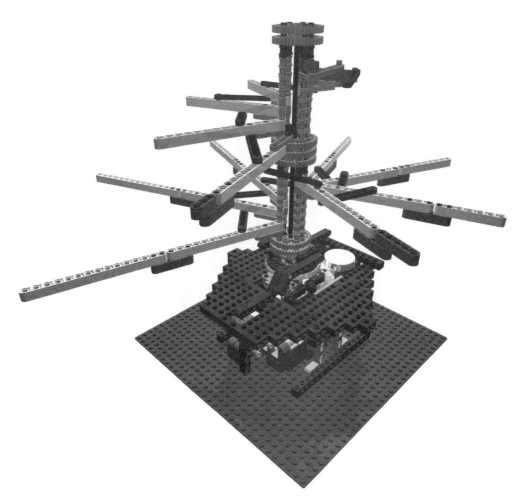

Figure 6-4. *The complete aerial screw robot*

The following images (Figures 6-5 through 6-37) show show step-by-step instructions on how to build the aerial screw.

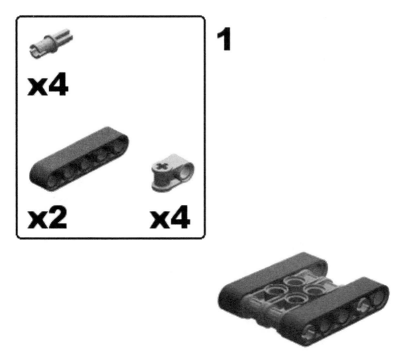

Figure 6-5. *Building the aerial screw: step 1*

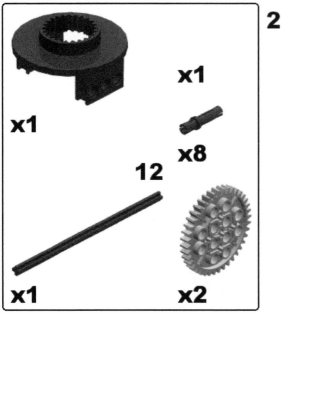

Figure 6-6. *Building the aerial screw: step 2*

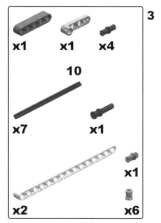

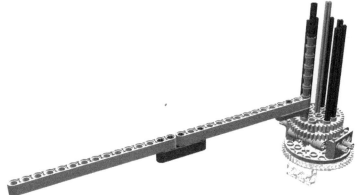

Figure 6-7. *Building the aerial screw: step 3*

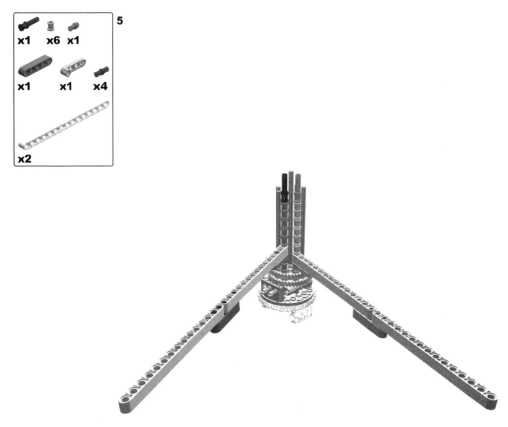

Figure 6-8. *Building the aerial screw: steps 4 (rotate model) and 5*

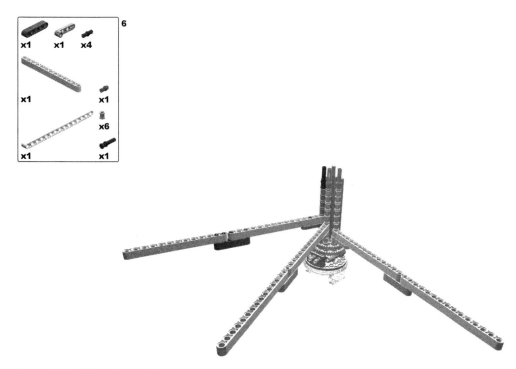

Figure 6-9. *Building the aerial screw: step 6*

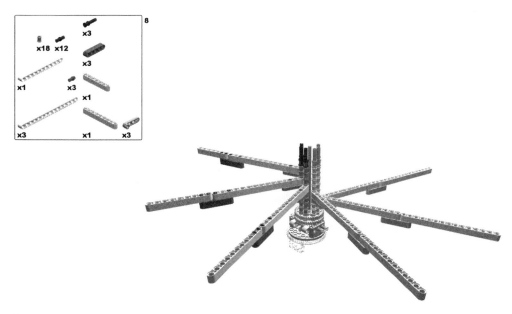

Figure 6-10. *Building the aerial screw: steps 7 (rotate model) and 8*

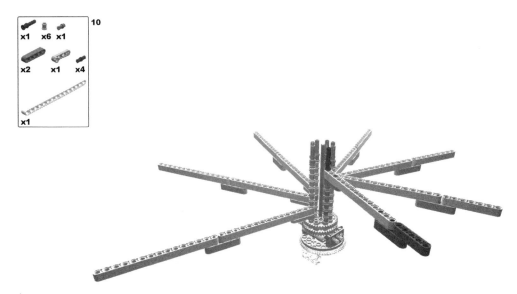

Figure 6-11. *Building the aerial screw: steps 9 (rotate model) and 10*

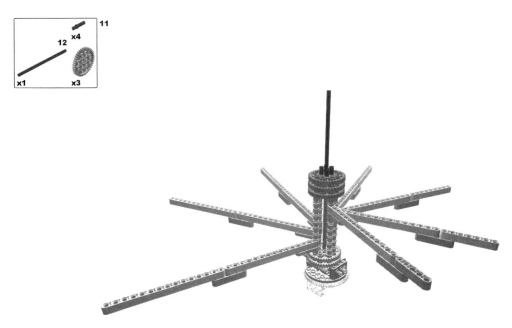

Figure 6-12. *Building the aerial screw: step 11*

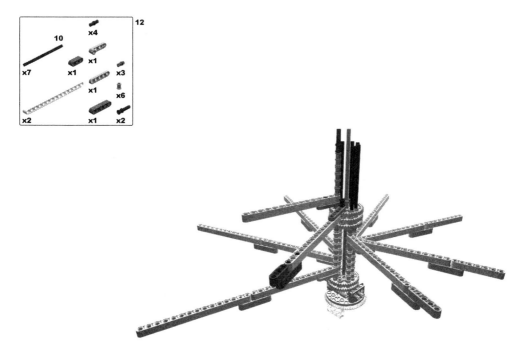

Figure 6-13. *Building the aerial screw: step 12*

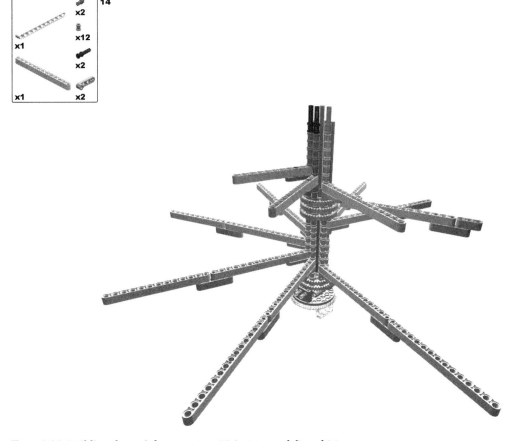

Figure 6-14. *Building the aerial screw: steps 13 (rotate model) and 14*

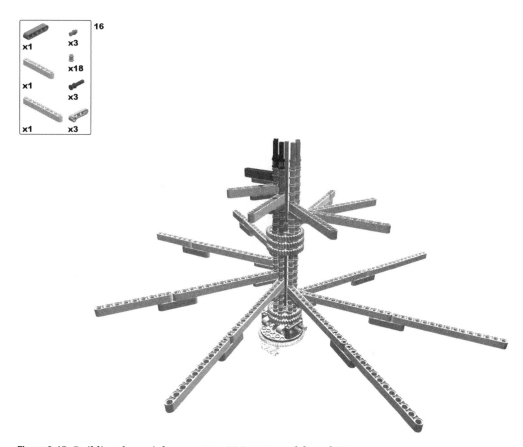

Figure 6-15. *Building the aerial screw: steps 15 (rotate model) and 16*

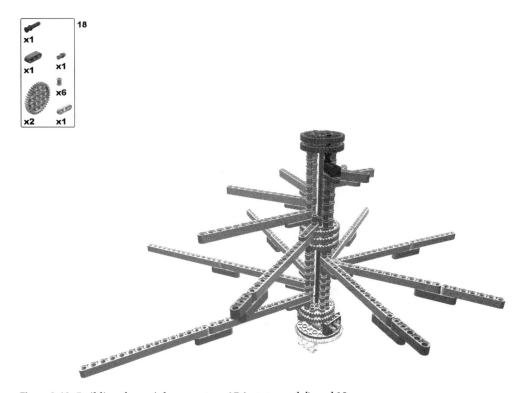

Figure 6-16. *Building the aerial screw: steps 17 (rotate model) and 18*

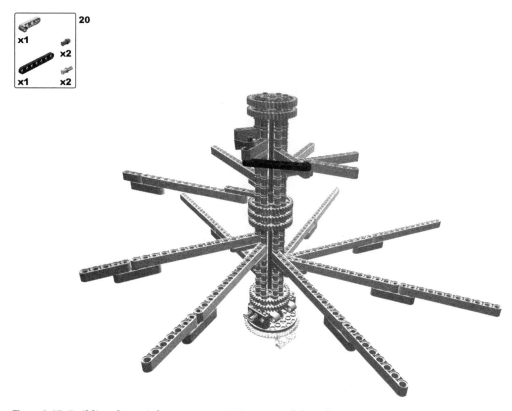

Figure 6-17. *Building the aerial screw: step s 19 (rotate model) and 20*

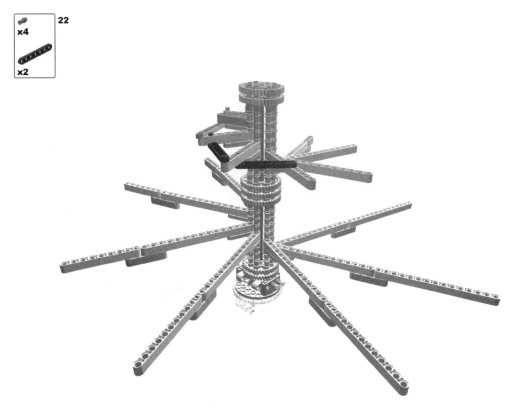

Figure 6-18. *Building the aerial screw: steps 21 (rotate model) and 22*

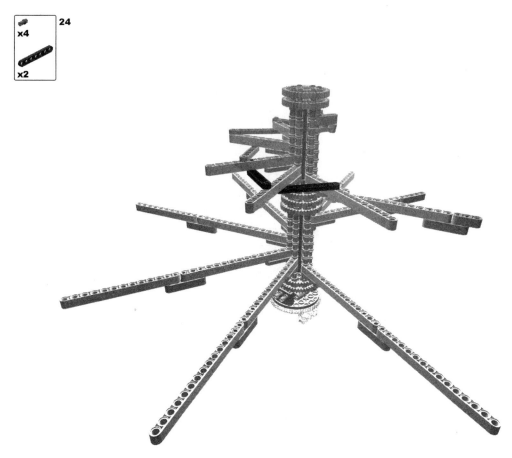

Figure 6-19. *Building the aerial screw: steps 23 (rotate model) and 24*

Figure 6-20. *Building the aerial screw: steps 25 (rotate model) and 26*

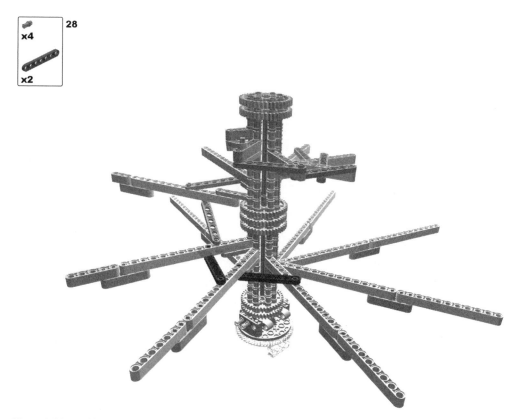

Figure 6-21. *Building the aerial screw: steps 27 (rotate model) and 28*

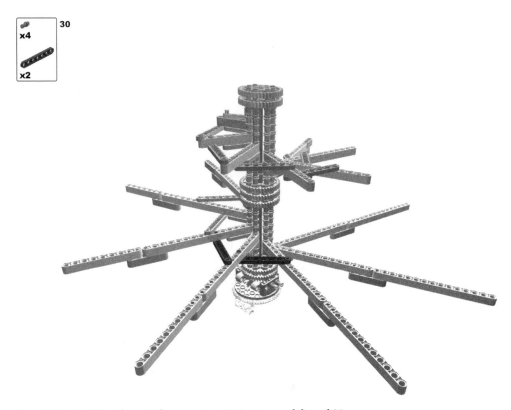

Figure 6-22. *Building the aerial screw: steps 29 (rotate model) and 30*

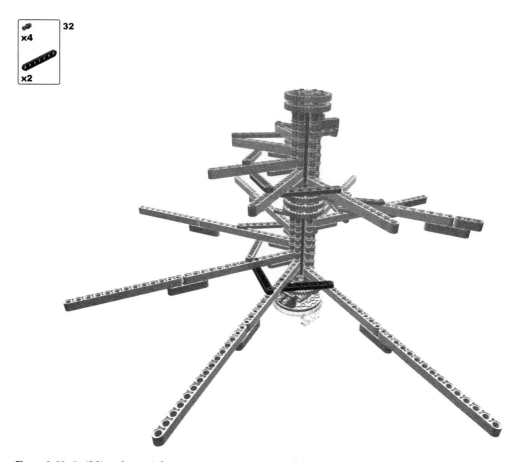

Figure 6-23. *Building the aerial screw: steps 31 (rotate model) and 32*

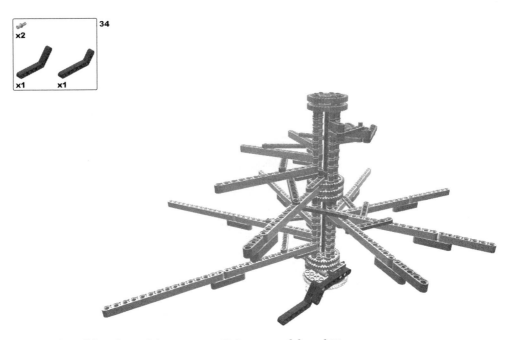

Figure 6-24. *Building the aerial screw: steps 33 (rotate model) and 34*

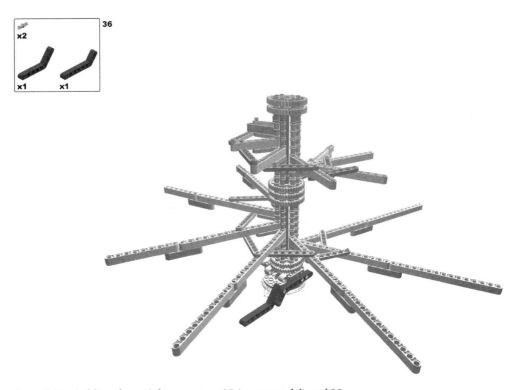

Figure 6-25. *Building the aerial screw: steps 35 (rotate model) and 36*

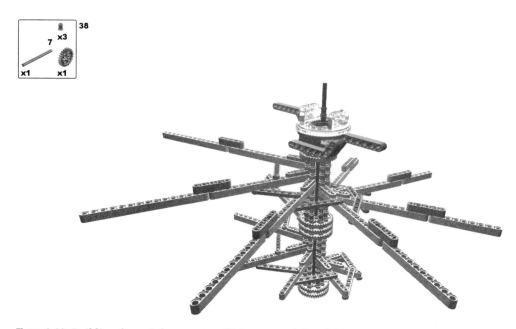

Figure 6-26. *Building the aerial screw: steps 37 (rotate model) and 38*

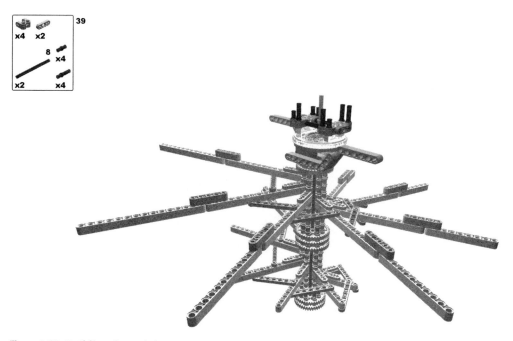

Figure 6-27. *Building the aerial screw: step 39*

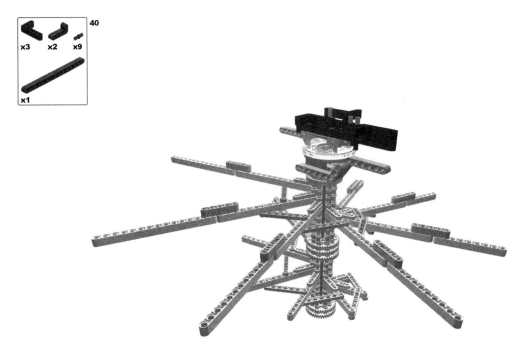

Figure 6-28. *Building the aerial screw: step 40*

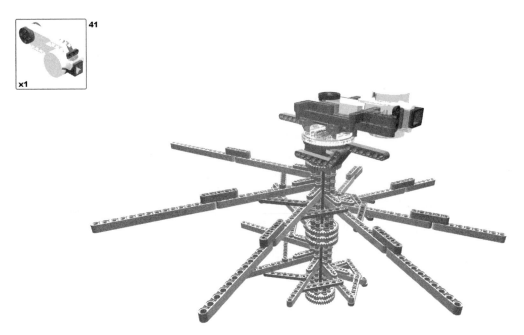

Figure 6-29. *Building the aerial screw: step 41*

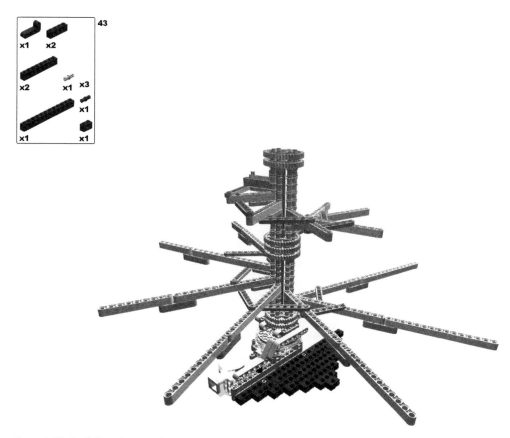

Figure 6-30. *Building the aerial screw: step s 42 (rotate model) and 43*

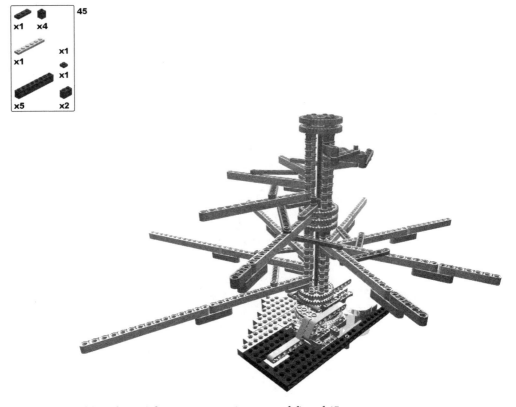

Figure 6-31. *Building the aerial screw: steps 44 (rotate model) and 45*

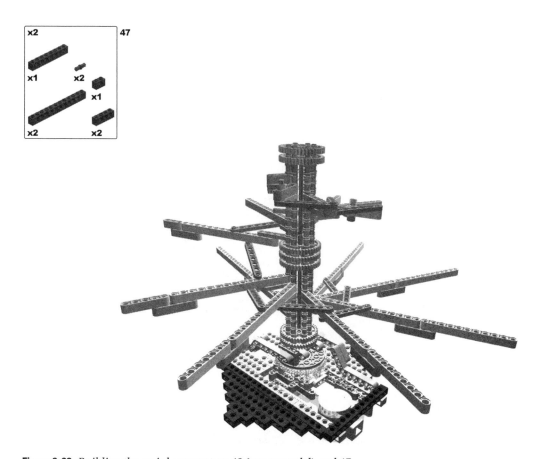

Figure 6-32. *Building the aerial screw: steps 46 (rotate model) and 47*

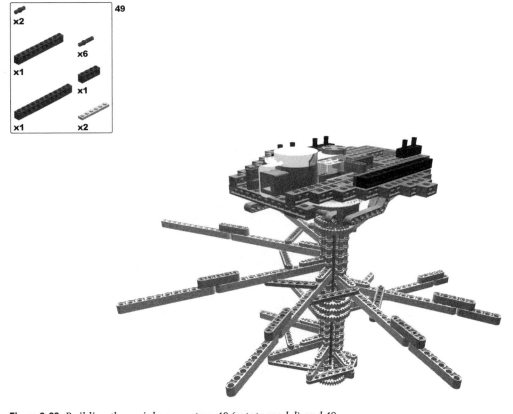

Figure 6-33. *Building the aerial screw: steps 48 (rotate model) and 49*

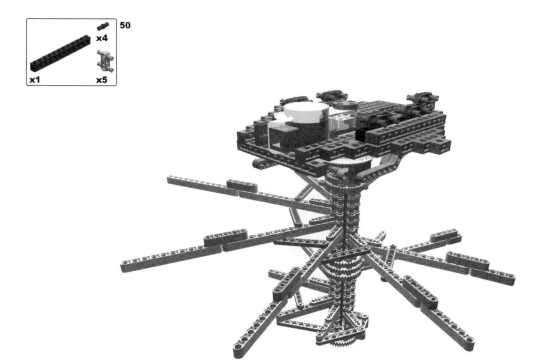

Figure 6-34. *Building the aerial screw: step 50*

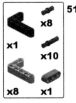

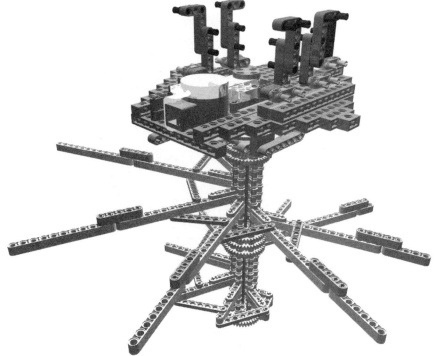

Figure 6-35. *Building the aerial screw: step 51*

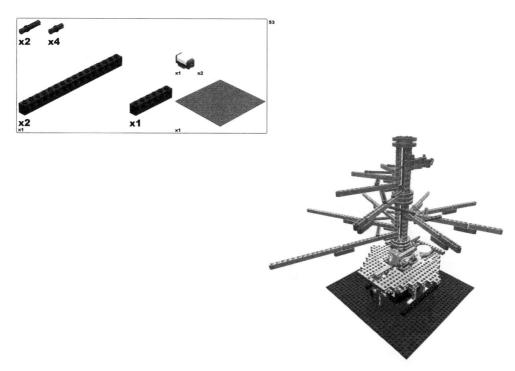

Figure 6-36. *Building the aerial screw: steps 52 (rotate model) and 53*

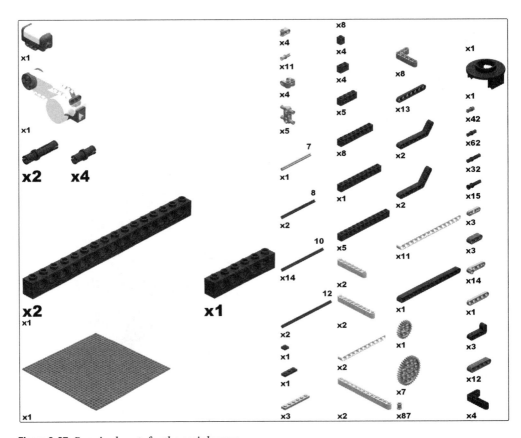

Figure 6-37. *Required parts for the aerial screw*

Programming the Aerial Screw

With the aerial screw's program, you want to simulate the men driving the helix by gripping the levers attached to the central hub and running around it. As the helix's rotation gains speed once the initial inertia is overpowered, the program has to increase the power of the associated motor in the course of time. You use the number of rotations as a factor.

For illustration reasons, the rotations are not counted by the motor's built-in counter but by a light sensor that is countersunk in the platform; each time the spill's grip passes the light sensor, it triggers an event. When the rotation speed is at maximum, you keep on rotating until the user stops the program (Figure 6-38).

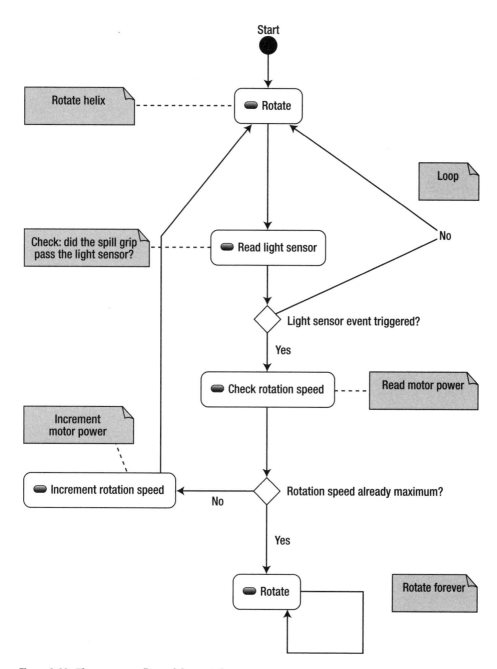

Figure 6-38. *The program flow of the aerial screw*

LEGO MINDSTORMS NXT Software

For this robot, you will not start with a forever loop, but with a loop that runs until the power of the motor of the helix is at 100%. For that, you do the following:

- Define a numeric variable that will hold the motor power (called motorPower) and initialize it with a value of 20.

- Run the helix's motor with an according initial power of 20%.

- Insert a loop block with a logical stop criterion (Figure 6-39).

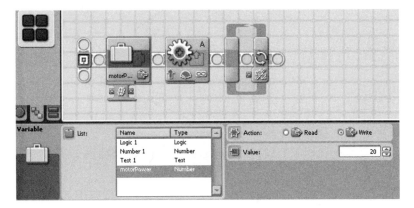

Figure 6-39. *The motor power variable*

Next, you do the following:

- Attach the stop criterion of the loop with a logical comparison block that checks the input against a value of 100.

- Connect the output of the hub's power property with the input A of the logical comparison block.

- Connect the input of the hub's power property with the motorPower variable (Figure 6-40).

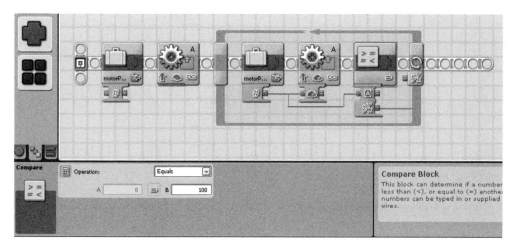

Figure 6-40. *The logical loop block*

In each iteration of the loop, you need a subroutine that checks the light sensor for detection. This is done by inserting a loop block that stops when the light sensor triggers an event (Figure 6-41).

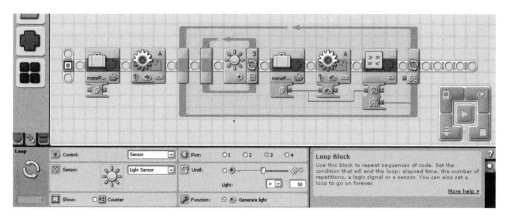

Figure 6-41. *The loop block checking the light sensor*

Note that depending on the ambient light of the particular location you are running the robot in, you might have to adjust the limiting value of the light sensor (I have chosen 50).

When the light sensor recognizes a rotation of the helix, increment the motor power by adding 1 to the motorPower variable. As the variable's output is connected to the motor block's power input port, the motor will run with the incremented power from then on (Figure 6-42).

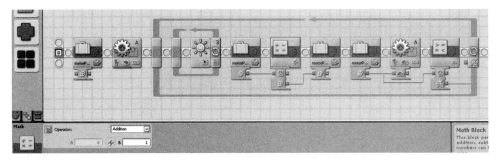

Figure 6-42. *Incrementing the motor power*

When the motor power is at its maximum of 100%, you need to run the motor forever. As you know, this is achieved by adding a forever loop with a contained motor block at the end of the program. And you are done. Figure 6-43 shows the complete NXT-G program for the aerial screw.

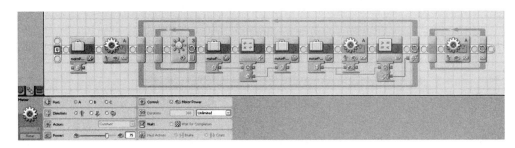

Figure 6-43. *The complete NXT-G program for the aerial screw*

RobotC

To program the aerial screw with RobotC, you use the light sensor attached to port 3:

```
// use the light sensor connected to port 3
const tSensors lightSensor = (tSensors) S3;

// main
task main() {
}
```

Define a variable that holds the present rotation speed (i.e., the present motor power):

```
. . .
// main
task main() {

  // define a variable that holds the present rotation speed
  // initial value is 20
  int rotationSpeed = 20;
}
```

Now rotate until the rotation speed is at its maximum:

```
. . .
```

```
task main() {

  . . .
  int rotationSpeed = 20;

  // loop until rotation speed is maximum (100)
  while(rotationSpeed < 100) {

  }
}
```

Run the motor with the actual power (which determines the rotation speed of the helix) until the light sensor detects the passing grip of the spill:

```
. . .
task main() {

  . . .
  while(rotationSpeed < 100) {

    // loop until light sensor detects the passing spill grip
    do {

      // run the helix's motor with constant speed
      motor[motorA] = rotationSpeed;

      // check light sensor
    } while(SensorValue(lightSensor) >= 50);
  }
}
```

Upon detection by the light sensor, you increment the rotation speed:

```
. . .
task main() {

  . . .
  while(rotationSpeed < 100) {

    // loop until light sensor detects the passing spill grip
    do {
      . . .
    } while(SensorValue(lightSensor) >= 50);

    // the grip has passed the light sensor
    // hence we increment the rotation speed
    rotationSpeed = rotationSpeed + 1;
  }
}
```

At the end of the outer loop, the rotation speed will be at its maximum, so you run the motor with constant maximum power henceforth:

. . .

```
task main() {

  . . .
  while(rotationSpeed < 100) {
    . . .
  }

    // rotation speed is maximum now
    // so we run the helix with constant motor power
    // until user stops the program manually
    while(true) {
      motor[motorA] = 100;
    }
}
```

Here's the complete RobotC program for the aerial screw:

```
// use the light sensor connected to port 3
const tSensors lightSensor = (tSensors) S3;

// main
task main() {

  // define a variable that holds the present rotation speed
  // initial value is 20
  int rotationSpeed = 20;

  // loop until rotation speed is maximum (100)
  while(rotationSpeed < 100) {

    // loop until light sensor detects the passing spill grip
    do {

      // run the helix's motor with constant speed
      motor[motorA] = rotationSpeed;

      // check light sensor
    } while(SensorValue(lightSensor) >= 50);

    // the grip has passed the light sensor
    // hence we increment the rotation speed
    rotationSpeed = rotationSpeed + 1;

  }

  // rotation speed is maximum now
  // so we run the helix with constant motor power
  // until the user stops the program manually
  while(true) {
    motor[motorA] = 100;
  }
}
```

NXC

The program code for NXC and for RobotC do not differ very much. The differences are shown here.

The light sensor attached to port 3 is configured using the following statement:

```
// enable NXC
#include "NXCDefs.h"

// main
task main(){

  // define sensor at port 3 to be a light sensor with active light
  SetSensorType(IN_3,IN_TYPE_LIGHT_ACTIVE);
}
```

Running the motor with the actual power (which determines the rotation speed of the helix) until the light sensor detects the passing grip of the spill looks like this in NXC:

```
. . .
task main() {

  . . .
  while(rotationSpeed < 100) {
    // loop until light sensor detects the passing spill grip
    do {

      // run the helix's motor with constant speed
      OnFwd (OUT_A, rotationSpeed);

      // check light sensor
    } while (Sensor(IN_3) >= 50);
  }
}
```

And here's the final loop for running the motor with constant maximum power:

```
. . .
task main() {

  . . .
  while(rotationSpeed < 100) {
    . . .
  }

  // rotation speed is maximum now
  // so we run the helix with constant motor power
  // until user stops the program manually
  while(1) {
    OnFwd (OUT_A, 100);
  }
}
```

The complete NXC program for the aerial screw is as follows:

```
// enable NXC
#include "NXCDefs.h"
```

```
// main
task main(){

  // define sensor at port 1 to be a light sensor with active light
  SetSensorType(IN_3,IN_TYPE_LIGHT_ACTIVE);

  // define a variable that holds the present rotation speed
  // initial value is 20
  int rotationSpeed = 20;

  // loop until rotation speed is maximum (100)
  while (rotationSpeed < 100) {
    // loop until light sensor detects the passing spill grip
    do {
      // run the helix's motor with constant speed
      OnFwd (OUT_A, rotationSpeed);
      // check light sensor
    } while(Sensor(IN_3) >= 50);

    // the grip has passed the light sensor
    // hence we increment the rotation speed
    rotationSpeed = rotationSpeed + 1;
  }

  // rotation speed is maximum now
  // so we run the helix with constant motor power
  // until the user stops the program manually
  while(1) {
    OnFwd (OUT_A, 100);
  }
}
```

leJOS NXJ

As usual, start with a class AerialScrew that has a main() method and imports the lejos.nxt package:

```
package org.nxtdavinci.aerialscrew;
```

```
import lejos.nxt.*;
```

```
public class AerialScrew {

  public static void main(String[] args) throws Exception {

  }
}
```

Configure the light sensor:

. . .

```
public class AerialScrew {

  public static void main(String[] args) throws Exception {
```

```
    // configure the light sensor on input port 3
    LightSensor lightSensor = new LightSensor(Port.S3);

  }
}
```

and define the variable for the rotation speed, setting it to an initial value of 20:

. . .

```
public class AerialScrew {

  public static void main(String[] args) throws Exception {

    // configure the light sensor on input port 3
    LightSensor lightSensor = new LightSensor(Port.S3);

    // define a variable that holds the present rotation speed
    // initial value is 20
    int rotationSpeed = 20;

  }
}
```

Next, you loop until the rotation speed is at maximum:

. . .

```
public class AerialScrew {

  public static void main(String[] args) throws Exception {

    . . .
    int rotationSpeed = 20;

    // loop until rotation speed is maximum (100)
    while (rotationSpeed < 100) {

    }
  }
}
```

Inside the loop, run the motor with the actual rotation until the light sensor detects the passing grip of the spill:

. . .

```
public class AerialScrew {

  public static void main(String[] args) throws Exception {

    . . .
    while (rotationSpeed < 100) {

      // set the power of the helix's motor to the rotation speed
      Motor.A.setSpeed(rotationSpeed);
```

```
        // loop until light sensor detects the passing spill grip
        do {

          // run the motor forward
          Motor.A.forward();

          // check the light sensor
        } while(lightSensor.readValue() >= 50);

      }
    }
}
```

Upon detection by the light sensor, you increment the rotation speed:

. . .

```
public class AerialScrew {

  public static void main(String[] args) throws Exception {

    . . .
    while (rotationSpeed < 100) {

      . . .
      do {

        // run the motor forward
        Motor.A.forward();

        // check the light sensor
      } while(lightSensor.readValue() >= 50);

      // increment the rotation speed
      rotationSpeed++;

    }
  }
}
```

When the rotation speed is at its maximum, run the motor with constant maximum power forever:

. . .

```
public class AerialScrew {

  public static void main(String[] args) throws Exception {

    . . .
    while (rotationSpeed < 100) {

      . . .
      // increment the rotation speed
      rotationSpeed++;
```

```
      // run the motor with maximum power
      Motor.A.setSpeed(100);

      while(true) {
        Motor.A.forward();
      }
    }
  }
}
}
```

This is the complete leJOS NXJ program for the aerial screw:

```
package org.nxtdavinci.aerialscrew;

import lejos.nxt.*;

public class AerialScrew {

  public static void main(String[] args) {

    // configure the light sensor on input port 3
    LightSensor lightSensor = new LightSensor(Port.S3);

    // define a variable that holds the present rotation speed
    // initial value is 20
    int rotationSpeed = 20;

    // loop until rotation speed is maximum (100)
    while(rotationSpeed < 100) {

      // set the power of the helix's motor to the rotation speed
      Motor.A.setSpeed(rotationSpeed);

      // loop until light sensor detects the passing spill grip
      do {

        // run the motor forward
        Motor.A.forward();

        // check the light sensor
      } while(lightSensor.readValue() >= 50);

      // increment the rotation speed
      rotationSpeed++;

      // run the motor with maximum power
      Motor.A.setSpeed(100);

      while(true) {
        Motor.A.forward();
      }

    }
  }
}
```

pbLua

The first thing to do for the pbLua program is to define the AerialScrew function:

```
-- function AerialScrew
function AerialScrew()

end
```

Next, configure the light sensor and the motor running the helix:

```
. . .
function AerialScrew()

  -- configure the light sensor on input port 3
  nxt.InputSetDigiO(3)
  nxt.InputSetDirOutDigiO(3)

  -- configure motor A to run in "brake" mode
  nxt.OutputSetMode(1,2)

end
```

You need to set the variable for the rotation speed to an initial value of 20:

```
. . .
function AerialScrew()

  . . .
  -- configure motor A to run in "brake" mode
  nxt.OutputSetMode(1,2)

  -- define a variable that holds the present rotation speed
  -- initial value is 20
  local rotationSpeed = 20

end
```

Now loop until the rotation speed is at maximum:

```
. . .
function AerialScrew()

  . . .
  local rotationSpeed = 20

  -- loop until rotation speed is maximum (100)
  while rotationSpeed < 100 do

  end
end
```

Inside the loop, run the motor with the actual rotation until the light sensor detects the passing grip of the spill:

```
. . .
function AerialScrew()
```

```
. . .
-- loop until rotation speed is maximum (100)
while rotationSpeed < 100 do

  -- set the power of the helix's motor to the rotation speed
  -- 32 means "run mode"
  nxt.outputSetSpeed(1, 32, rotationSpeed, 0)

  -- loop until light sensor detects the passing spill grip
  while nxt.InputGetRawAd(3) >= 50
    -- do nothing
  end
  end
end
```

Upon detection by the light sensor, you increment the rotation speed:

```
. . .
function AerialScrew()

  . . .
  -- loop until rotation speed is maximum (100)
  while rotationSpeed < 100 do

    . . .
    -- loop until light sensor detects the passing spill grip
    while nxt.InputGetRawAd(3) >= 50
      -- do nothing
    end

    -- increment the rotation speed
    rotationSpeed = rotationSpeed + 1

  end
end
```

Now the rotation speed is at its maximum and you may run the motor with constant maximum power until the user turns the program off:

```
. . .
function AerialScrew()

  . . .
  -- loop until rotation speed is maximum (100)
  while rotationSpeed < 100 do

    . . .

  end

  -- run the motor with maximum power
  nxt.outputSetSpeed(1, 32, 100, 0)

end
```

Last but not least, you call the AerialScrew function in the program:

```
. . .
function AerialScrew()


   . . .


end
```

```
-- Now run the AerialScrew function
AerialScrew()
```

The complete pbLua program for the aerial screw looks like this:

```
-- function AerialScrew
function AerialScrew()

  -- configure the light sensor on input port 3
  nxt.InputSetDigi0(3)
  nxt.InputSetDirOutDigi0(3)

  -- configure motor A to run in "brake" mode
  nxt.OutputSetMode(1,2)

  -- define a variable that holds the present rotation speed
  -- initial value is 20
  local rotationSpeed = 20

  -- loop until rotation speed is maximum (100)
  while rotationSpeed < 100 do

    -- set the power of the helix's motor to the rotation speed
    -- 32 means "run mode"
    nxt.outputSetSpeed(1, 32, rotationSpeed, 0)

    -- loop until light sensor detects the passing spill grip
    while nxt.InputGetRawAd(3) >= 50
      -- do nothing
    end

    -- increment the rotation speed
    rotationSpeed = rotationSpeed + 1

  end

  -- run the motor with maximum power
  nxt.outputSetSpeed(1, 32, 100, 0)

end
```

```
-- Now run the AerialScrew function
AerialScrew()
```

Summary

In this chapter, I introduced the first of this book's two flying machines invented by Leonardo. If you completed the building instructions, you saw a possible way to mimic curved structures with LEGO parts and how to use turntables, great gear wheels, and axles for creating a stable hub. You also learned how to use and program the light sensor for detection.

In the next chapter, you will implement Leonardo's second flying device, the renowned flying machine. You will also examine another topic that is of particular interest to the NXT robot builder: remote control.

CHAPTER 7

The Flying Machine

There shall be wings! If the accomplishment be not for me, 'tis for some other.

—Leonardo da Vinci

In this chapter you will build another one of Leonardo's inventions intended for lifting man into the air: the flying machine. The subject of controlling a LEGO NXT robot with strings is revisited and you will learn about integrating the Brick with a rather fragile structure. Last but not least, this chapter deals with one of the most intriguing NXT topics: remote communication via Bluetooth.

Historical Background

Leonardo's flying machine certainly is one of his most famous and most frequently displayed inventions. It illustrates his approach toward human flight, using his studies on birds and insects. While his aerial screw, which you built in the previous chapter, follows the movement of objects in water, the flying machine mimics a bird's way of flying.

Leonardo's studies of flight were most likely the most scientific up to that point in time. Flying was a lifelong dream of Leonardo; in 1505, he reported that a bird visiting him in his cradle was one of his first childhood memories.

The draft for the flying machine was produced around the same time as the aerial screw at the end of the 1480s and is contained in the same Manuscript B codex. It's basically an *ornithopter*, a flying contraption driven by birdlike flexible wings; indeed, Leonardo often referred to it as "the great bird" (Figure 7-1).

One of the interesting things about the flying machine is the fact that the pilot does not use his arms for powering it; instead, the wings are moved by a man's feet, which push two pedals connected to the wings by a sophisticated system of cables. There is a complete lack of steering devices, which was also true of the armored car. It is conceivable that Leonardo meant to tackle that issue once the challenge of making the machinery fly was resolved.

But the flying machine would have been much too heavy to actually lift into the air. It seems Leonardo may not have been aware of this problem; he even considered a test flight over a lake. To prevent the pilot from drowning, though, he intended to supply the contraption with inflated skins. Maybe he was deterred by the fate of his contemporary Giovanni Battista Danti who reportedly tried to fly in a similar device over the Umbrian Lake Trasimeno and died when he crashed into the roof of a church.

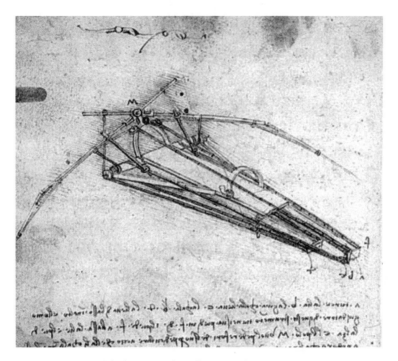

Figure 7-1. *Leonardo's drawing of the flying machine*

As noted in Chapter 6, Leonardo was convinced of the fundamental similarity of the mechanical basics of man and animal and the ability of humans to reproduce a bird's way of flying. "A bird is an instrument according to mathematical law, which instrument it is within the capacity of man to reproduce with all its movements," he stated. Hence, the idea of building an "artificial bird" powered by a man's extremities was clearly on track.

Hardware Challenges

No doubt the central issue when building the flying machine with LEGO parts is the wings. In particular, the elastic connections Leonardo used to allow the wings to rotate and bend impose special challenges to the LEGO designer. The LEGO replacements have to not only be flexible and stable, but also must not hinder the complex overall movement of the wing.

For this challenge, I use a turntable for the rotational movement (Figure 7-2).

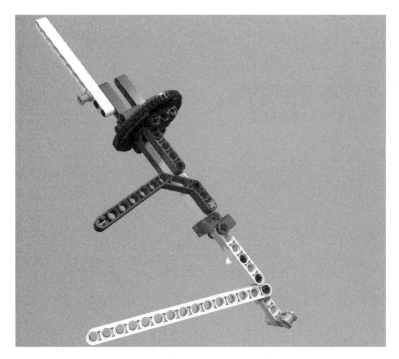

Figure 7-2. *The wing implemented with LEGO*

Another critical point is the propulsion of the wings. Originally, Leonardo designed two pedals stepped on alternately by the pilot. Over a sophisticated system of attached wires the wings were set into a complex movement. I've kept the wires but replaced the pedals with two winches that are each driven by a motor (Figure 7-3).

Figure 7-3. *The propulsion of the wings implemented with LEGO parts*

However, I have not abandoned the pedals. You will create a remote control by which you will be able to drive the wings with your feet, thus adopting the place of the pilot. This is explained later in the section on building the remote control.

Building the Flying Machine

Figure 7-4 shows the completed flying machine robot.

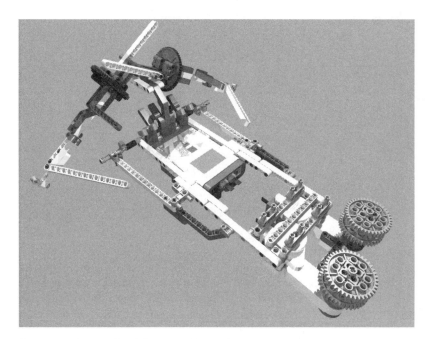

Figure 7-4. *The completed flying machine robot*

The following images show step-by-step instructions on how to build the flying machine.

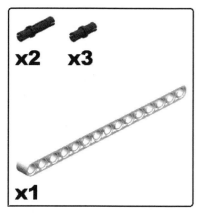

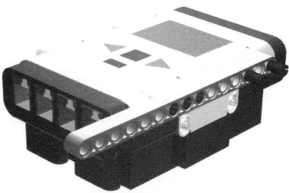

Figure 7-5. *Building the flying machine: step 1*

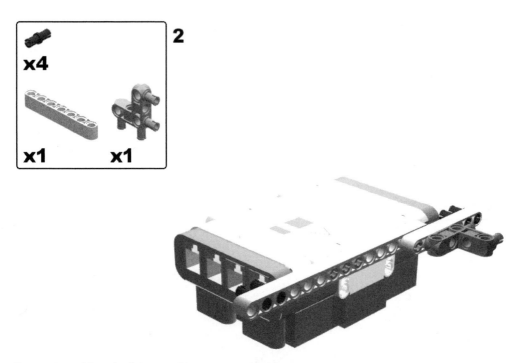

Figure 7-6. *Building the flying machine: step 2*

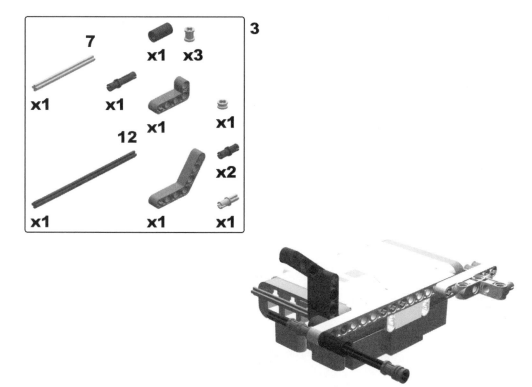

Figure 7-7. *Building the flying machine: step 3*

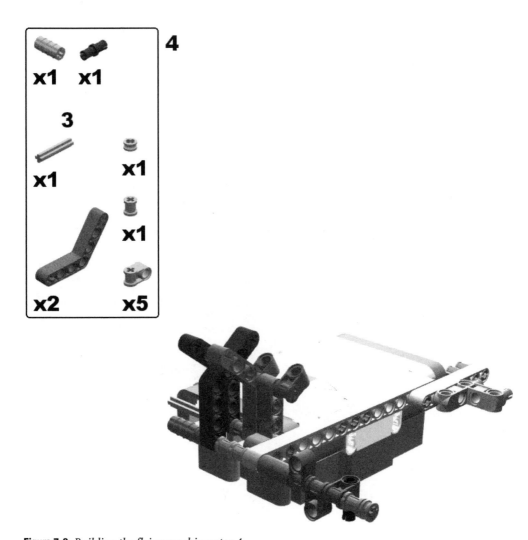

Figure 7-8. *Building the flying machine: step 4*

☐ **5**

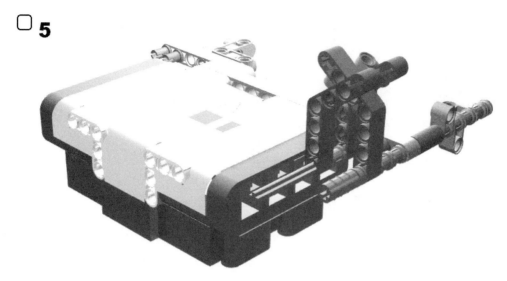

Figure 7-9. *Building the flying machine: step 5 (rotate model)*

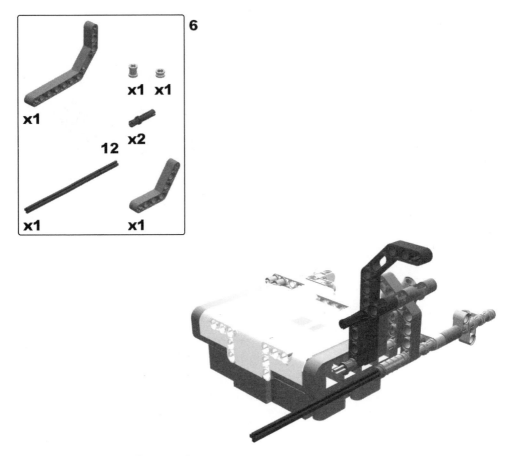

Figure 7-10. *Building the flying machine: step 6*

Figure 7-11. *Building the flying machine: step 7*

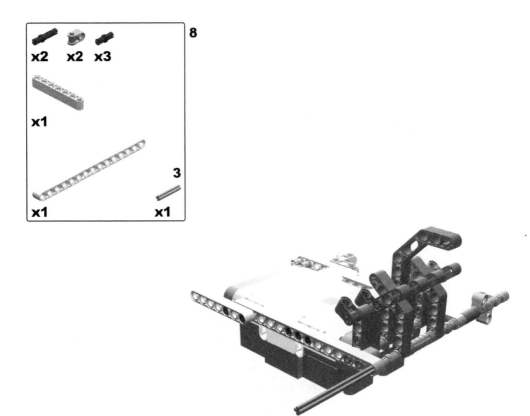

Figure 7-12. *Building the flying machine: step 8*

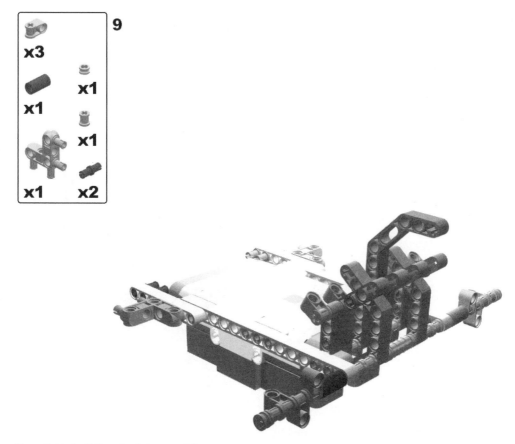

Figure 7-13. *Building the flying machine: step 9*

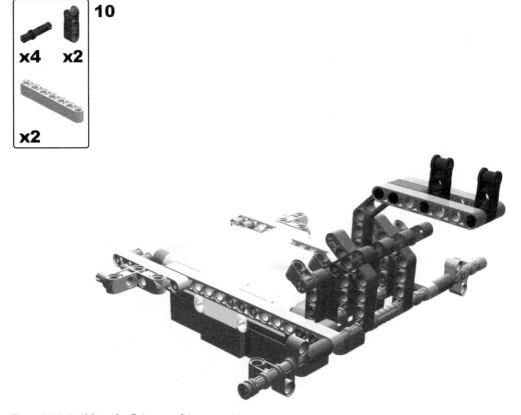

Figure 7-14. *Building the flying machine: step 10*

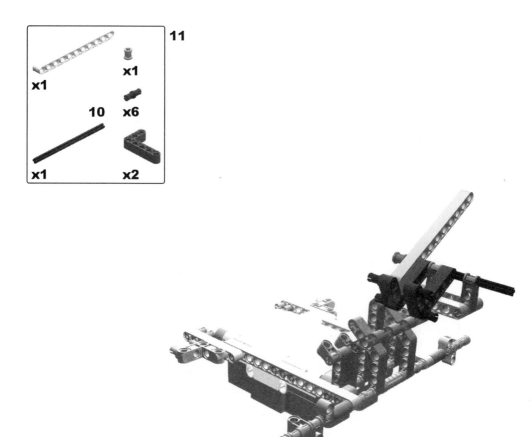

Figure 7-15. *Building the flying machine: step 11*

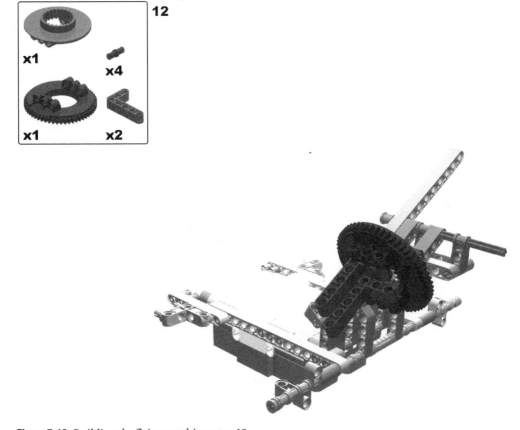

Figure 7-16. *Building the flying machine: step 12*

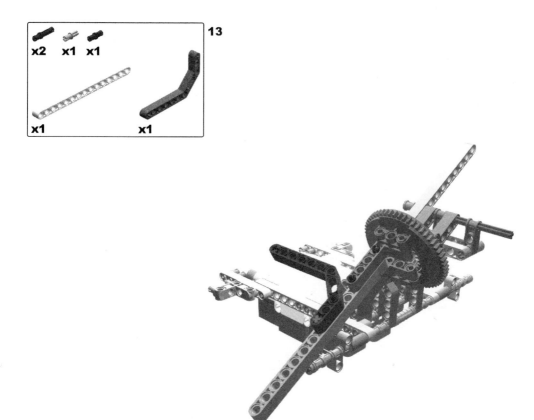

Figure 7-17. *Building the flying machine: step 13*

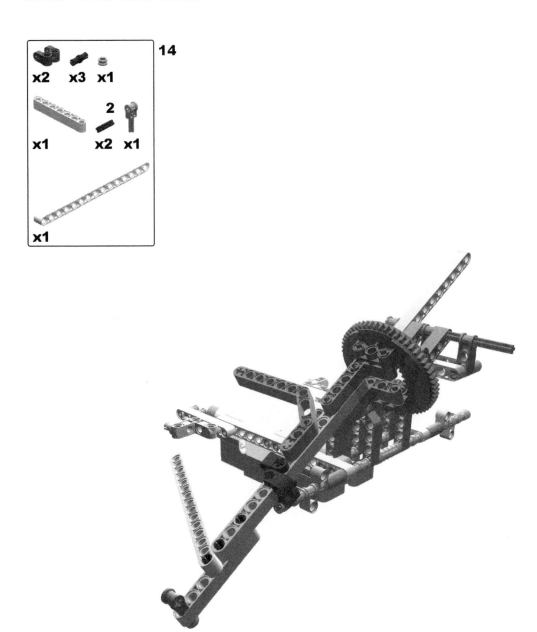

Figure 7-18. *Building the flying machine: step 14*

15

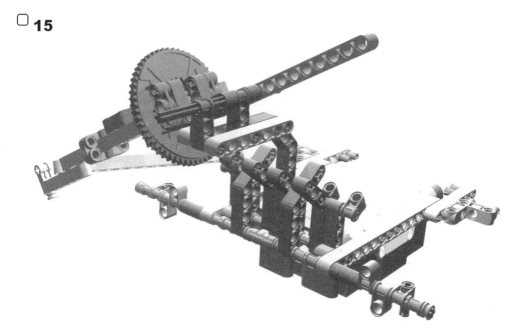

Figure 7-19. *Building the flying machine: step 15 (rotate model)*

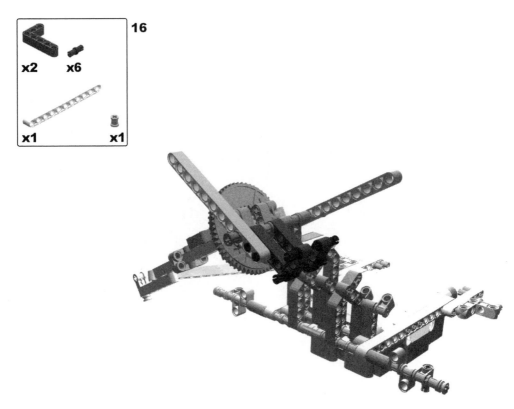

Figure 7-20. *Building the flying machine: step 16*

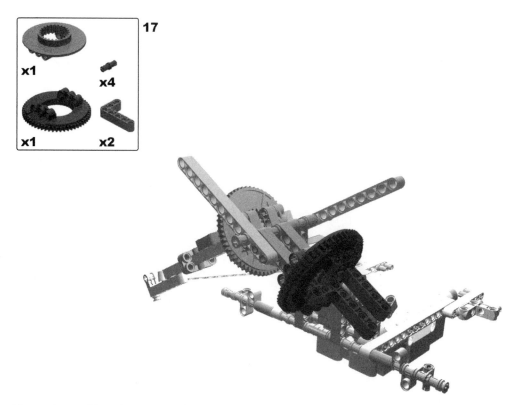

Figure 7-21. *Building the flying machine: step 17*

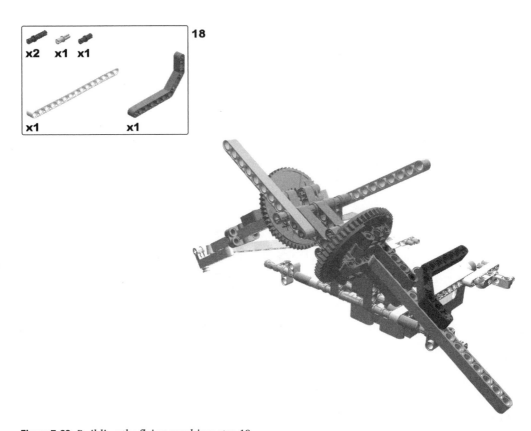

Figure 7-22. *Building the flying machine: step 18*

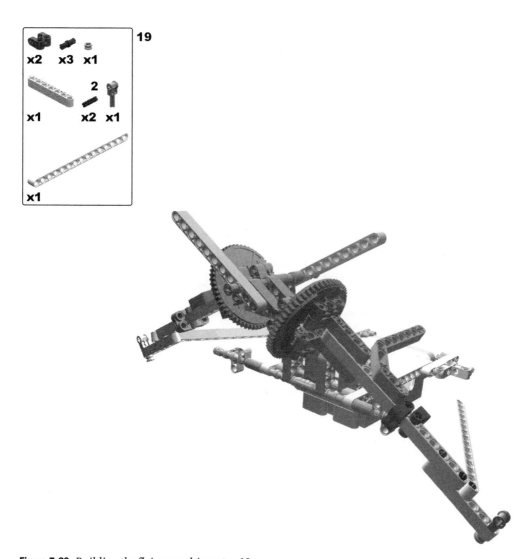

Figure 7-23. *Building the flying machine: step 19*

20

Figure 7-24. *Building the flying machine: step 20 (rotate model)*

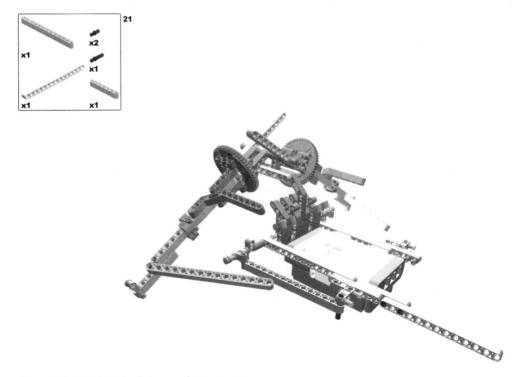

Figure 7-25. *Building the flying machine: step 21*

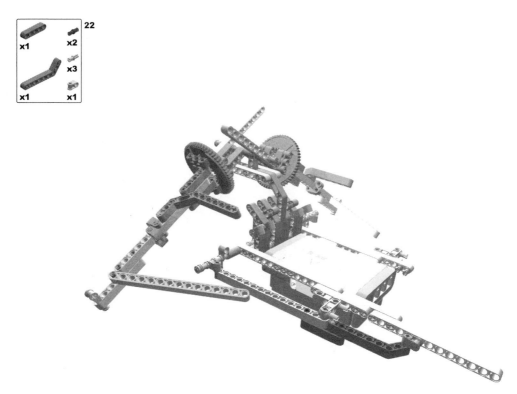

Figure 7-26. *Building the flying machine: step 22*

Figure 7-27. *Building the flying machine: step 23 (rotate model)*

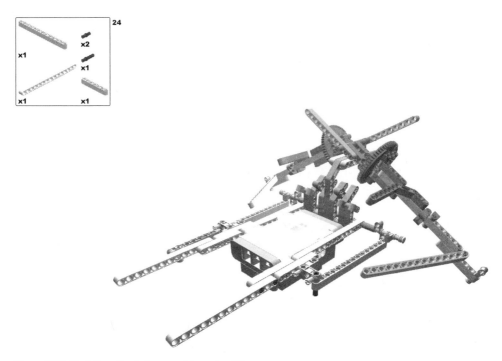

Figure 7-28. *Building the flying machine: step 24*

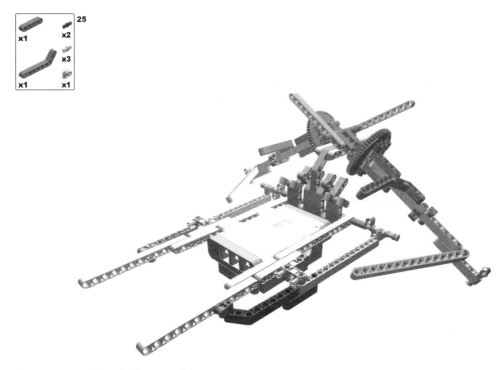

Figure 7-29. *Building the flying machine: step 25*

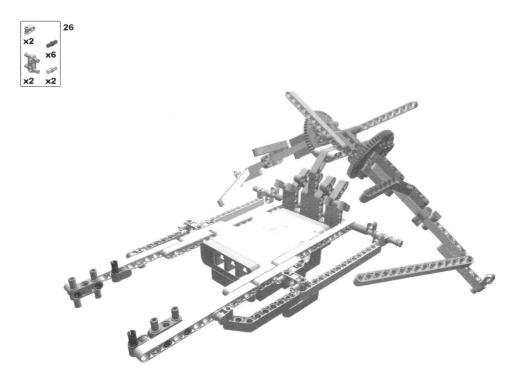

Figure 7-30. *Building the flying machine: step 26*

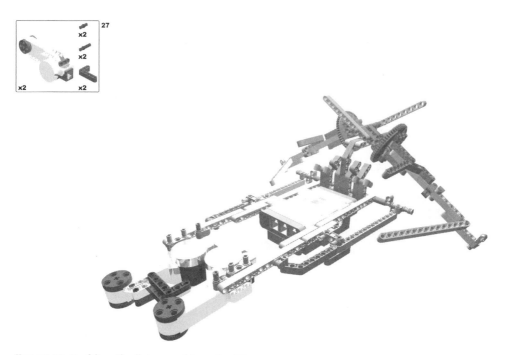

Figure 7-31. *Building the flying machine: step 27*

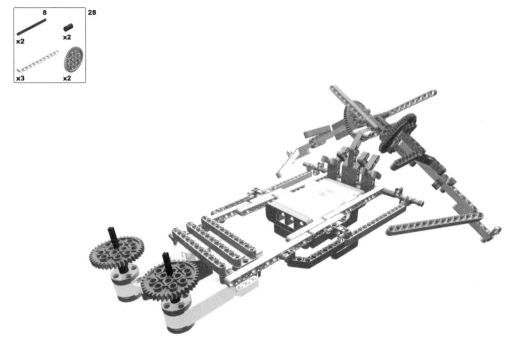

Figure 7-32. *Building the flying machine: step 28*

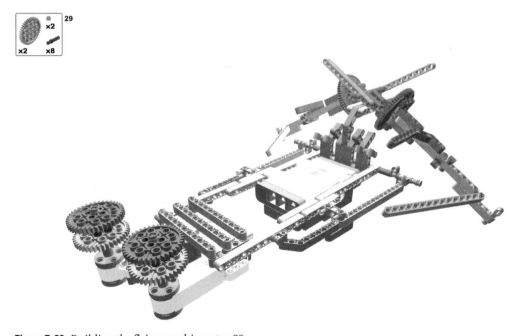

Figure 7-33. *Building the flying machine: step 29*

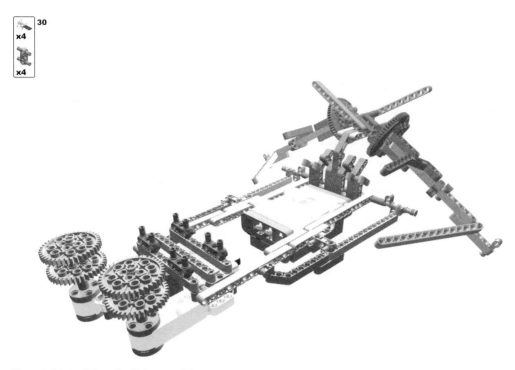

Figure 7-34. *Building the flying machine: step 30*

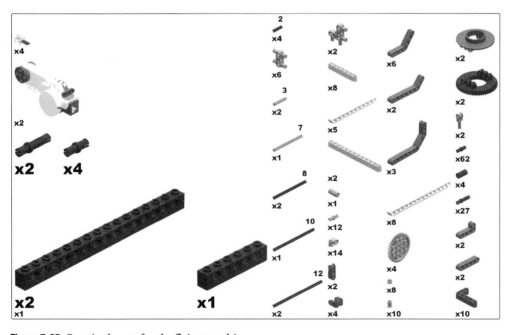

Figure 7-35. *Required parts for the flying machine*

The Wires That Lower the Wings

The following steps show how to wire the wings to the winches in order to lower them. Note that you will have to repeat these steps for each wing:

1. Take a strong sewing thread and tie it to the middle of the outer beam of the wing. Pass it through the double split axle joiner, then through the inner hole of the turntable, and finally through the axle joiner at the wing's apron. Next, pass that wire through the two four-pinned axle joiners at the end of the pilot's seat and tie it to the outer rim of the lower right gear at the stern of the flying machine. This wire folds the wing and is illustrated by the thick black line in Figure 7-36.

2. Take a second thread and fix it to the 15-holed beam of the wing, between the L-shaped beams that connect it to the turntable and the double bent lift arm. Pass it through the down-pointing axle joiner below, through the two four-pinned axle joiners at the end of the pilot's seat, and tie it to the outer rim of the lower right gear at the stern of the flying machine. This wire lowers the wing and is illustrated by the dotted and slashed line in Figure 7-36.

3. Finally, take another thread and tie it to the end of the double-bent lift arm that is pointing down from the wing. Pass it straight through the two four-pinned axle joiners at the end of the pilot's seat and fix it at the outer rim of the lower right gear at the stern of the flying machine. This wire rotates the wing in an upward direction and is illustrated by the dotted black line in Figure 7-36.

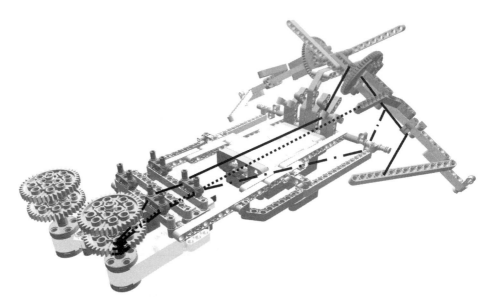

Figure 7-36. *The wires that lower the wings*

Be sure to align the wires' length so that they are completely taut when the wings are fully lowered (Figure 7-37). They are taut when the right winch (when viewing the flying machine from behind) has coiled the wires for two complete rotations, turning in a clockwise direction.

Figure 7-37. *The position of the wires when the wings are completely lowered*

The Wires That Lift the Wings

The following steps show how to place the wires to lift the wings. Again, the steps have to be performed for each wing:

1. Take a strong sewing thread and tie it to the outer end of the 11-holed opposite beam of the wing. Pass it through the up-pointing axle joiner below, and through the two four-pinned axle joiners at the end of the pilot's seat, and tie it to the outer rim of the lower left gear at the stern of the flying machine. This wire lifts the wing and is illustrated by the thick black line in Figure 7-38.

2. Take a second thread and fix it to the end of the outer beam of the wing. Pass it through the pole located at the end of the 7-holed beam, through the double split axle joiner, and through the inner hole of the turntable. Finish that wire by threading it through the axle joiner at the wing's apron and through the two four-pinned axle joiners at the end of the pilot's seat, and tie it to the outer rim of the lower left gear at the stern of the flying machine. This wire unfolds the wing and is illustrated by the dotted black line in Figure 7-38.

3. Finally, tie a third thread to the end of the double-bent lift arm that is pointing down from the wing. Pass it through the up-pointing axle joiner below, and through the two four-pinned axle joiners at the end of the pilot's seat, and tie it to the outer rim of the lower left gear at the stern of the flying machine. This wire rotates the wing in a downward direction and is illustrated by the dotted and slashed line in Figure 7-38.

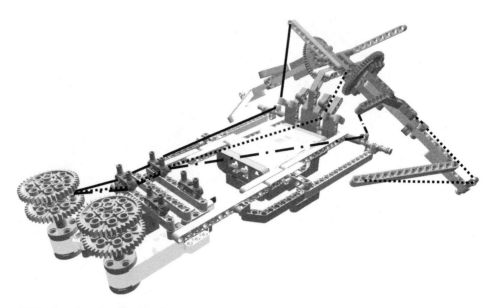

Figure 7-38. *The wires that lift the wings*

Be sure to align the wires' length so that they are completely taut when the wings are fully lifted (Figure 7-39). They are taut when the left winch (when viewing the flying machine from behind) has coiled the wires for two complete rotations, turning in a counterclockwise direction.

Attach the ends of the wires to the outer rim of the winches as shown in Figure 7-36. Make sure that the wires are long enough to allow for two full rotations of the winches in each direction.

Note that in the previous figures, only the wiring for one wing is displayed. The other wing is wired analogously.

Figure 7-39. *The position of the wires when the wing is completely lifted*

Building the Remote Control

To enable you to take the place of the pilot and actually control the flying machine with your feet as Leonardo intended, you will build a pedal-based remote control for the robot (Figure 7-40). You will also see how to use Bluetooth communication between two NXT Bricks in NXT programs.

Figure 7-40. *The completed remote control for the flying machine*

The images (Figures 7-41 through 7-52) show step-by-step instructions on how to build the remote control for the flying machine.

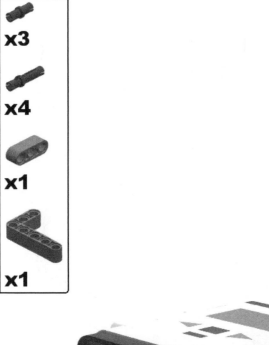

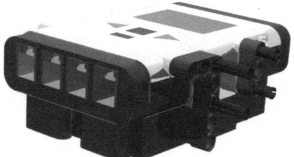

Figure 7-41. *Building the remote control for the flying machine: step 1*

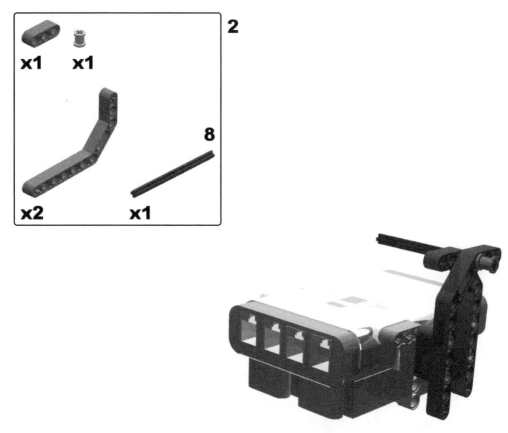

Figure 7-42. *Building the remote control for the flying machine: step 2*

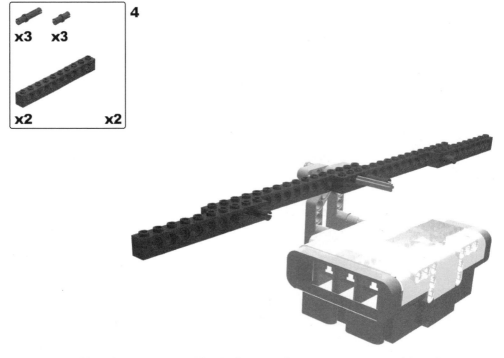

Figure 7-43. *Building the remote control for the flying machine: steps 3 (rotate model) and 4*

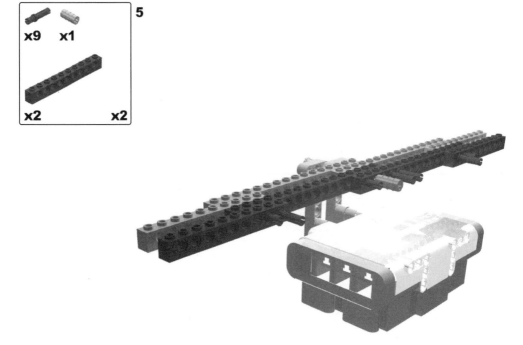

Figure 7-44. *Building the remote control for the flying machine: step 5*

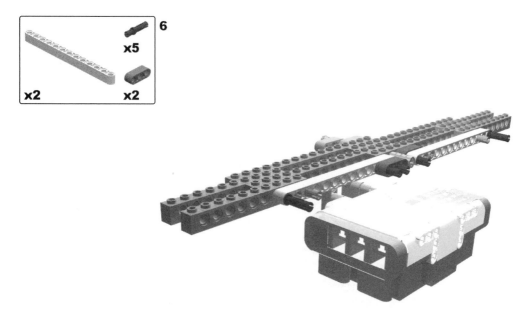

Figure 7-45. *Building the remote control for the flying machine: step 6*

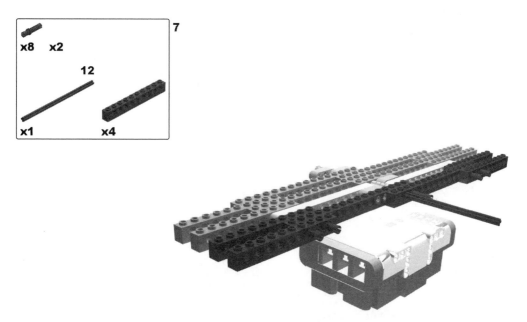

Figure 7-46. *Building the remote control for the flying machine: step 7*

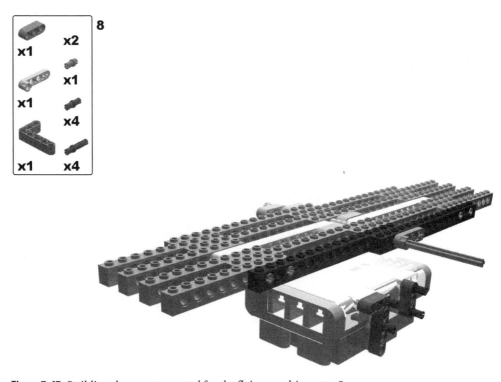

Figure 7-47. *Building the remote control for the flying machine: step 8*

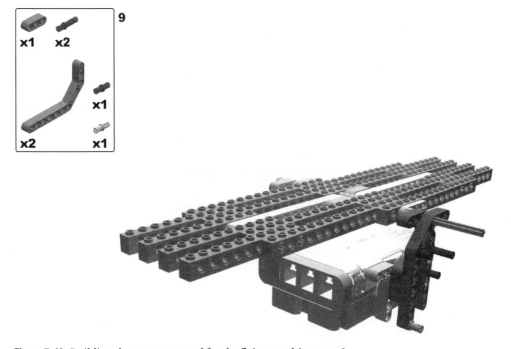

Figure 7-48. *Building the remote control for the flying machine: step 9*

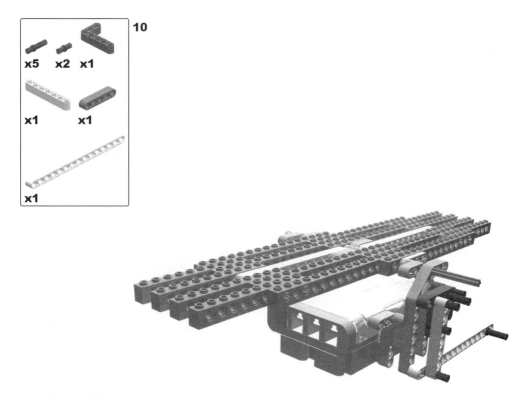

Figure 7-49. *Building the remote control for the flying machine: step 10*

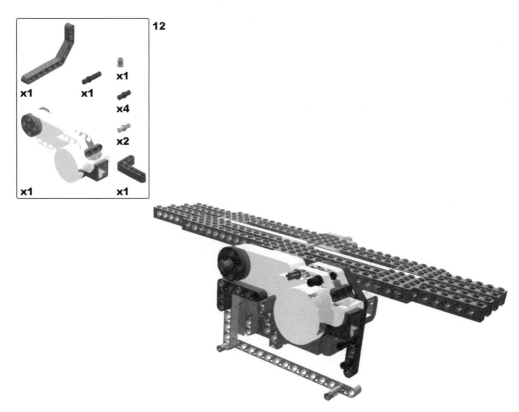

Figure 7-50. *Building the remote control for the flying machine: step s 11 (rotate model) and 12*

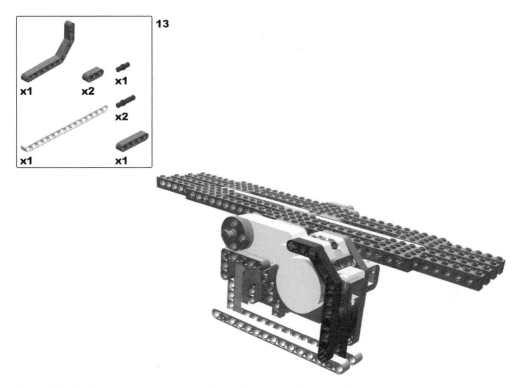

Figure 7-51. *Building the remote control for the flying machine: step 13*

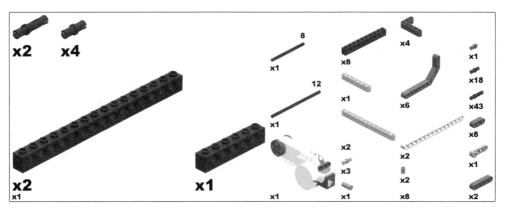

Figure 7-52. *Required parts for the flying machine robot*

The pilot works the remote control by alternately pushing the pedals down with his feet. Attach the motor's cable to port C.

Programming the Flying Machine

To program the flying machine, you need two programs: one running on the flying machine itself and one on the remote control. The program running on the remote control checks the input from the pedals moved by the pilot's feet and sends the information to the flying machine (Figure 7-53).

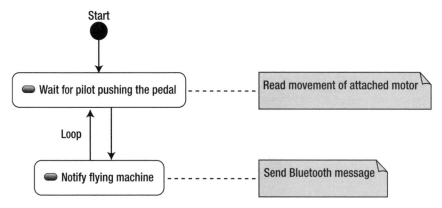

Figure 7-53. *The remote control program's flow*

The program running on the flying machine itself receives the messages and drives the winches appropriately (Figure 7-54).

You will use an internal variable to hold the wings' state. Note that alternatively you could hold this state on the remote control instead; but this is more unreliable since the remote control would not know of any hardware failures that might occur during the wings' movement. Furthermore, it would require sending at least two different types of Bluetooth messages: "lift wings" and "lower wings."

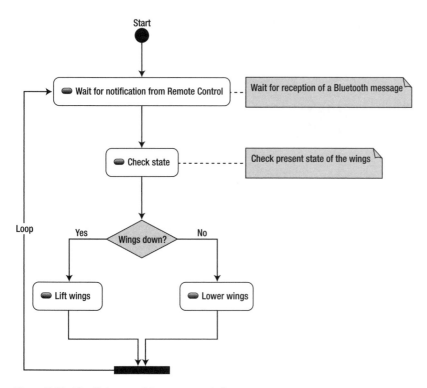

Figure 7-54. *The flying machine program's flow*

LEGO MINDSTORMS NXT Software

In this section, you will program both the flying machine and the remote control with NXT-G. Once the two Bricks are connected via Bluetooth, you will start both programs, lower the wings, and start performing the pilot's job. Happy pedaling!

The Remote Control's Program

The program on the remote control starts with a forever loop and contains logic for waiting for the pilot to move the pedals, which boils down to checking for rotations of the attached motor. For that, you use a wait block configured by the rotation sensor that every motor has built-in (Figure 7-55). The wait block will pause the program until the motor is rotated forward by at least 30 degrees, a value that corresponds to lowering the pedal to the right side.

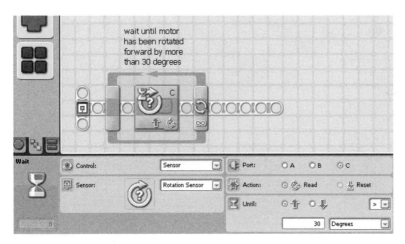

Figure 7-55. *The remote control programmed with NXT-G: waiting for the pedal's motor to be rotated forward*

Next, you simply send the arbitrary numerical value 42 by a Bluetooth message, using a send message block (Figure 7-56).

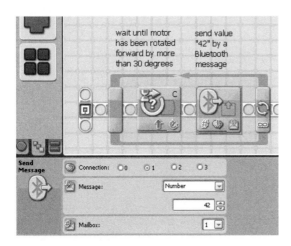

Figure 7-56. *Sending a Bluetooth notification*

The program also has to recognize the lowering of the pedal on the other side. Since the wait block does not allow for logical OR statements, you can't use the one already placed in the program for both directions. Instead, you place a second one after the first notification, configured to wait until the motor has rotated at least 30 degrees backward (Figure 7-57).[1]

---

1. You could use two concurrent threads instead of the sequential logic here, but that topic is not covered in this book.

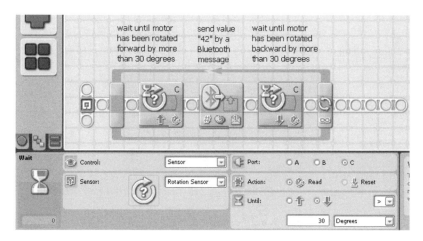

Figure 7-57. *Waiting for the pedal's motor to be rotated backward*

Sending a Bluetooth notification again completes the program (Figure 7-58).

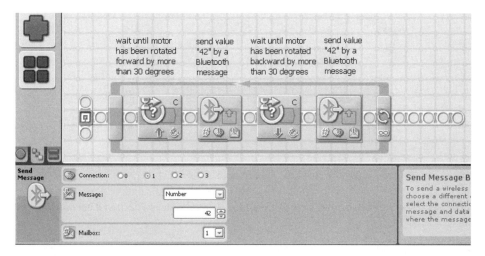

Figure 7-58. *The complete program of the remote control programmed with NXT-G*

The Flying Machine's Program

On the flying machine, start with defining a logical variable called wingsUp and initialize it with False (Figure 7-59).

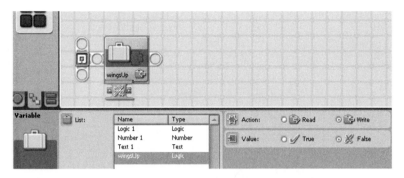

Figure 7-59. *The flying machine programmed with NXT-G: initializing the internal state variable*

Next, using a wait block, wait for Bluetooth notifications from the remote control (Figure 7-60).

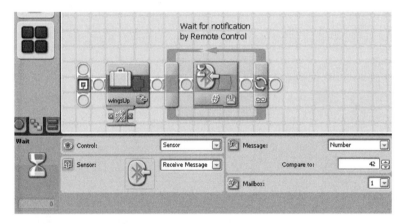

Figure 7-60. *Waiting for a notification from the remote control*

When the message comes in, you have to check the state variable and switch it according to its value (Figure 7-61).

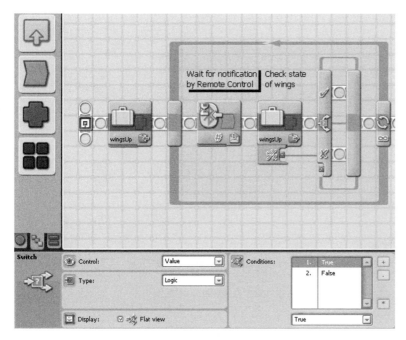

Figure 7-61. *Switching according to the internal state*

If the wings are up, lower them by running the two motors appropriately and setting the internal state variable wingsUp to False (Figure 7-62).

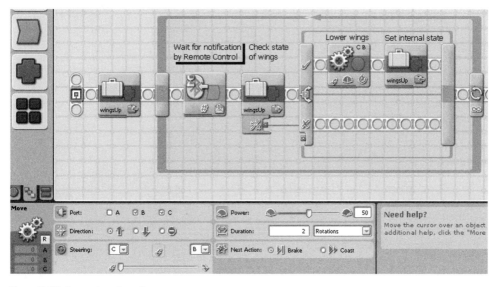

Figure 7-62. *Lowering the wings*

If the wings are down, lift the wings and set the internal state variable to True. Figure 7-63 shows the complete program.

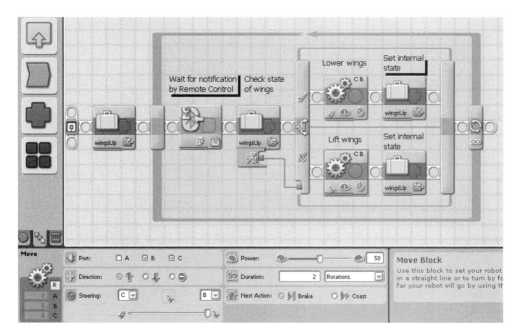

Figure 7-63. *The complete flying machine program with NXT-G*

NXC

At the time of this writing, among the programming environments addressed in this book, only NXT-G and NXC supported inter-Brick Bluetooth communication. Therefore, NXC is the final programming environment described for the remote control and the flying machine.

The Remote Control's Program

At the beginning of the program check whether the NXT Brick on the flying machine is connected via Bluetooth:

```
// enable NXC
#include "NXCDefs.h"

// main
task main() {

  // check connection of the flying machine's NXT Brick
  // on connection 1
  // display error and stop if no connection is available
  if(!(BluetoothStatus(1)!=NO_ERR)) {
    TextOut(5,LCD_LINE2,"no conn");
    Wait(2000);
    Stop(true);
  }
}
```

The first thing to do in the forever loop is to reset the internal rotation sensor:

```
. . .
task main() {

  // check connection of the flying machine's NXT Brick
  . . .

  // program shall run until user turns it off
  while(true) {

    // reset the internal rotation sensor of motor C
    ResetAllTachoCounts(OUT_C);

  }
}
```

Now wait for the user to push down the pedal:

```
. . .
task main() {

  . . .
  while(true) {

    // reset the internal rotation sensor of motor C
    ResetAllTachoCounts(OUT_C);

    // we wait for the user pushing down the pedal
    // corresponds to the motor turning at least 30 degrees
    // in an arbitrary direction
    while(!abs(MotorRotationCount(OUT_C))) {
      // do nothing
    }

  }
}
```

Once the user pushes down the pedal, you send an appropriate Bluetooth message:

```
. . .
task main() {

  . . .
  while(true) {

    . . .
    while(!abs(MotorRotationCount(OUT_C))) {
      // do nothing
    }

    // now we send an appropriate message via Bluetooth
    string message = "42";
    SendRemoteString(1,1,message);

  }
}
```

This is the complete NXC program for the remote control:

```
// enable NXC
#include "NXCDefs.h"

// main
task main() {

  // check connection of the flying machine's NXT Brick
  // on connection 1
  // display error and stop if no connection is available
  if(!(BluetoothStatus(1)!=NO_ERR)) {
    TextOut(5,LCD_LINE2,"no conn");
    Wait(2000);
    Stop(true);
  }

  // program shall run until user turns it off
  while(true) {

    // reset the internal rotation sensor of Motor C
    ResetAllTachoCounts(OUT_C);

    // we wait for the user pushing down the pedal
    // corresponds to the motor turning at least 30 degrees
    // in an arbitrary direction
    while(!abs(MotorRotationCount(OUT_C))) {
      // do nothing
    }

    // now we send an appropriate message via Bluetooth
    string message = "42";
    SendRemoteString(1,1,message);
  }
}
```

The Flying Machine's Program

For the flying machine, start by checking the availability of the Bluetooth connection to the remote NXT Brick and define an internal variable that holds the state of the wings:

```
// enable NXC
#include "NXCDefs.h"

// main
task main() {

  // check connection of the flying machine's NXT Brick
  // on connection 1
  // display error and stop if no connection is available
  if(!(BluetoothStatus(1)!=NO_ERR)) {
    TextOut(5,LCD_LINE2,"no conn");
    Wait(2000);
    Stop(true);
  }
```

CHAPTER 7 ■ THE FLYING MACHINE

```
  // internal state variable
  bool wingsUp = false;
}
```

Run the forever loop and wait for incoming Bluetooth messages from the remote control:

```
. . .
task main() {

  . . .
  // internal state variable
  bool wingsUp = false;

  // program shall run until user turns it off
  while(true) {

    // we wait for an incoming message from the remote control
    // on inbox 1
    string message;
    while(!ReceiveRemoteString(1,true,message)) {
    }

    // we are interested in messages from the remote control only
    if(StrToNum(message)!=42)
      continue;
  }
}
```

Once a message arrives, lower or lift the wings, depending on the value of the internal state variable:

```
. . .
task main() {

  . . .
  while(true) {

    . . .
    if(StrToNum(message)!=42)
      continue;

    // move wings according to the internal state
    if(wingsUp) {
      // lower wings
      moveWings(false);
    } else {
      // lift wings
      moveWings(true);
    }
    // switch state variable
    wingsUp = !wingsUp;

  }
}
```

Note that you have used the moveWings() function. To define it at the beginning of the program, do the following:

```
// enable NXC
#include "NXCDefs.h"

// function for lowering or lifting the wings
sub moveWings(bool lift) {
  // run motors synchronized for 2 rotations (720 degrees)
  if(lift) {
    RotateMotorEx (OUT_BC, 50, 720, 100, true);
  } else {
    RotateMotorEx (OUT_BC, 50, 720, -100, true);
  }
}

// main
task main() {
  . . .
}
```

You have finished the NXC program for the flying machine:

```
// enable NXC
#include "NXCDefs.h"

// function for lowering or lifting the wings
sub moveWings(bool lift) {
  // run motors synchronized for 2 rotations (720 degrees)
  if(lift) {
    RotateMotorEx (OUT_BC, 50, 720, 100, true);
  } else {
    RotateMotorEx (OUT_BC, 50, 720, -100, true);
  }
}

// main
task main() {

  // check connection of the flying machine's NXT Brick
  // on connection 1
  // display error and stop if no connection is available
  if(!(BluetoothStatus(1)!=NO_ERR)) {
    TextOut(5,LCD_LINE2,"no conn");
    Wait(2000);
    Stop(true);
  }

  // internal state variable
  bool wingsUp = false;

  // program shall run until user turns it off
  while(true) {
```

```
// we wait for an incoming message from the remote control
// on inbox 1
string message;
while(!ReceiveRemoteString(1,true,message)) {
}

// we are interested in messages from the remote control only
if(StrToNum(message)!=42)
  continue;

// move wings according to the internal state
if(wingsUp) {
  // lower wings
  moveWings(false);
} else {
  // lift wings
  moveWings(true);
}
// switch state variable
wingsUp = !wingsUp;

  }
}
```

Summary

In this final LEGO NXT robot implementation of an invention of Leonardo da Vinci, you built fragile structures and integrated the NXT Brick into them. You also deepened your knowledge of controlling a robot with strings, implementing a system of wires and counterwires that interact in a rather complex way.

You also made acquaintance with the fascinating topic of the communication of two NXT Bricks via Bluetooth. This enables you to control the robot remotely from another Brick.

With the knowledge you've gained in this and the previous chapters, you will now be able to build and program pretty complex and capable NXT robots. Most likely, you will have also decided which of the programming environments you feel most at home with. If all this has gingered you up to further indulge in more of the hardware and software aspects of the NXT universe, the following chapter presents possible next steps.

CHAPTER 8

■■■

Outlook: What NXT?

Life is pretty simple: you do some stuff. Most fails. Some works. You do more of what works. If it works big, others quickly copy it. Then you do something else. The trick is the doing something else.

—Leonardo da Vinci

Now that you have completed this tour through some of Leonardo's most impressive inventions, built them with LEGO parts, and programmed them using five different environments, you might want to take a break, step back, and admire Leonardo's genius—and perhaps feel some satisfaction for your own creations. However, since you are a member of a community bustling with creative spirit, you may also want to look toward the future and ask yourself "what NXT?" With the robots you've already made, where can you go from here?

Enhancing the Five Robots

The first thing that comes to mind when thinking about further steps is refining and enhancing the creations you have been working on. When building, programming, and testing them, you certainly will not only notice weaknesses and ways to optimize certain features, but you will probably also get ideas on how to accomplish some tasks in a completely different way and think about additional capabilities of the machine in question. Ideally, you will even be able to advance Leonardo's original designs, standing "on the shoulders of a giant and thus seeing farther than him." In the next few sections, I introduce some topics that have occurred to me. You might have also thought of others.

The Armored Car

The most noticeable drawback of the armored car is that it's stone blind: it just rolls forward forever without noticing anything that happens around it. But you can give it the capability to detect things in front of it, that is, in the driving direction.

The means to do so is an ultrasonic sensor, best placed in the turret, looking forward. If you adjust it pointing slightly downward, it can detect objects located ahead pretty reliably. You would change the program so that once the sensor detects something, the armored car would stop and perform some action. For an example on how to implement this, see the programming section of Chapter 5 on the revolving bridge. You could program it to fire a gun pointing forward. That would be rather impressive, wouldn't it?

To accomplish this, a third motor and a device that mimics a gun capable of firing a ball are required. Fortunately, such a device exists in the LEGO universe: the Zamor shooter from the LEGO BIONICLE Piraka series. Brian Davis, a member of the MDP, has already shown how to use it in connection with a NXT; see his DAZLR (Dual Action Zamor Launching Robot) on the official LEGO MINDSTORMS NXT community site (http://mindstorms.lego.com/MeetMDP/BDavis.aspx). However, integrating the shooter and the third motor into the existing armored car's frame without messing up the cover and preserving the elegant symmetric design might prove to be a pretty tough challenge.

Lastly, you could make the armored car capable of moving around in all directions, not just forward. This is something that goes beyond Leonardo's original design, where no means of steering is shown. It could be achieved by attaching the front wheels to some sort of moveable axis and reconfiguring the two drive motors in a way that one drives the rear wheels and the other operates the front axis.

The Catapult

In the catapult, the mechanism that switches the crank to and away from the great gear wheel is not as reliable as it could be. In particular, in the end phase of loading the catapult, that is, when the force on the gear wheel and therefore on the crank mechanism that blocks the wheel is very strong, the worm gear tends to loosen its grip and drop away slightly. As a consequence, you may encounter premature launching of the catapult when it's not fully loaded, resulting in inadequate shooting ranges. To fix this, you could use a device-driven second motor that lowers or lifts the worm gear from above, preventing the worm gear from undesired dropping away.

Another feature that comes to mind for the catapult is some sort of device that automatically provides projectiles once the arm is sufficiently lowered, in other words, a magazine. It should be able to deliver exactly one ball to the arm when the first touch sensor detects the complete loading of the catapult.

The Revolving Bridge

The revolving bridge is programmed to move away once the ultrasonic sensor detects an advancing object, and to move back when the object has passed. Currently, this action depends on dead reckoning; the two motors that drive the winches are run for a certain number of rotations. Yet, dead reckoning is not known to be the best of all strategies in robotics. Because the program does not check the robot's inner (reckoned) state against the actual physical state, small deviations in the motors' performance or other hardware failures will eventually create a noticeably different condition than what the program thinks the robot is in. For instance, imagine if some unforeseen obstacle in the river blocks the bridge's movement, or, even worse, one of the ropes breaks. The program would still assume the bridge is completely swung back when it really isn't. All the subsequent actions would also be inaccurate since there are no fallback mechanisms to detect such failures, let alone to recover from them.

A possible solution is to use two touch sensors mounted at the two endpoints of the bridge's far-side end—one located on the back of the winch, the other at the far-side base on the opposite bank. You would change the program to no longer rely on a fixed number of motor rotations but on touch events from the referring sensors to make sure the bridge completes its swing.

Last but not least, the revolving bridge is not able to distinguish between enemies and friends approaching on the far side; it will swing away in any case. It goes without saying that this is not always the desired action; it's the purpose of a bridge to allow the right people to cross the river. Therefore, a means for the bridge's operator to swing back the bridge when it's reasonable, or to completely disable the swinging mechanism for some time, is required. A touch sensor that could serve as some sort of button for manual activation or deactivation could provide this kind of capability.

The Aerial Screw

In the aerial screw you used a light sensor sunk into its floor to count rotations of the central hub. However, these values are not very reliable, in particular, at higher rotation speeds. Instead you could count the rotation programmatically using the internal tachometer of the NXT motor. You could replace the light sensor with a touch sensor that is coupled to a nipple that projects into the plane of rotation of the hub's grips and gets bent by each revolution.

The Flying Machine

In the flying machine, to hold the information on the internal state of the wings, you use a simple logical variable in the flying machine's program. However, this is error-prone; its value is set after the appropriate function to lift or lower the wings is processed. If some hardware issue occurs that prevents the wings from moving as planned, the program will not notice. Like the dead reckoning of the revolving bridge, this may lead to an inconsistency where the internal representation of the robot in the program does not match the actual state of the flying machine's wings. Hence, it would be advisable to retrieve the information on that state by a more reliable mechanism, for instance, by touch sensors placed appropriately at the endpoints of the wings' movement.

Furthermore, you will notice that Bluetooth messages that are sent from the remote control to the flying machine while the wings are actually moving are simply ignored. This means the pilot might have to repeat his movements.

You might want to enhance the programs and the hardware in a way that either blocks the pedals while the wings are lowered or lifted, or that subsequently queues and processes the movements by the pilot.

Remotely Controlling the Robots

The programs for the first four robots run on the Brick and do not require external control, making the robots autonomous, as robots should be. Yet, as you saw in Chapter 7 on the flying machine, on some occasions it is desirable or even necessary to have the ability to control the robot remotely by a program running somewhere other than on the Brick—for instance, for testing or for outsourcing tasks that can't be accomplished by the Brick due to its memory limitations. This other location might be another Brick or any other Bluetooth-enabled device, including a cell phone or, most common, a computer.

Note that although the logical control flow is run on the external device, both approaches nevertheless require a small program that runs on the Brick and processes the commands it receives from the controller. Such a program is rather simple and is confined to translating the control commands to actuate the hardware periphery appropriately.

Unlike for the RCX, there's currently no ready-made hardware remote control available for the NXT. Yet, implementations of such a device can be built based on a second NXT. While the NXT can run the attached motors on different power levels, it is also able to read the actual state of them, in particular, the number of degrees they have rotated. As you can manually move the axis pulled into a motor, you can use such a motor as some kind of rotation sensor and therefore build a remote control axis on top of it, similar to a joystick. The NXT Brick just serves as an evaluator of this sort of input, and a decent program of yours running on the Brick might take this input, interpret it appropriately, and eventually send the desired commands via Bluetooth to the robot you want to control. Together with touch or light sensors, any complex kind of remote control might be created this way.

Not surprisingly, some people in the community have already done this. The official LEGO MINDSTORMS NXT community site has information on Brian Davis's BTRC (BlueTooth Remote Control). Another pretty advanced one is that of Steve Hassenplug, another prominent member of the MDP. His remote control can also be found on the LEGO MINDSTORMS NXT community site: `http://mindstorms.lego.com/MeetMDP/SteveH.aspx`. Particularly remarkable is the NXT Joystick created by MDP member Philo. The page, `http://philohome.com/nxtjoystick/joystick.htm`, even contains building instructions.

Remote controls based on software open the door to the (virtually) unlimited memory space of today's computers and to a universe of additional programming environments. Any language that is able to support USB or Bluetooth communication may be used to control a NXT robot remotely. With the release of the Bluetooth Developer Kit (BDK) by LEGO in late 2006, implementation of such language support has become even easier. As a result, a multitude of different systems for remotely controlling the NXT Brick exist for a large variety of programming languages, ranging from object-oriented, high-level platforms such as Java and C# to scripting languages such as Perl and Python. The page `http://www.teamhassenplug.org/NXT/NXTSoftware.html` provides a good overview of NXT remote programming software. One of the most promising and already quite powerful candidates is Microsoft's Robotics Studio, based on a sophisticated service-oriented architecture that is decoupled from the actual technical platform the robot is running on. For further reading, see `http://msdn.microsoft.com/robotics/getstarted/default.aspx`.

There are also some applications that target the mobile sector, including the NXT Mobile Application by LEGO that is downloadable at `http://mindstorms.lego.com/Overview/Mobile%20Application.aspx` and enables you to control your NXT robot with cell phones produced by a variety of different vendors.

After you apply this to your da Vinci LEGO robots, a possible next step might be to implement a set of applications that allow you to control them remotely.

Making Other Inventions of Leonardo with LEGO

In addition to refining the five robots introduced in this book, you might want to recreate some of Leonardo's other inventions with LEGO. And indeed, there are an abundance of interesting machines that would be very worthwhile to bring into the LEGO universe. Two that I find appealing are the theater stage for Orpheus (described in Chapter 1) and the canal excavation machine. For other ideas, you can get inspiration from the resources mentioned in the next section.

The Theater Stage for Orpheus

This draft of a theater stage set for the popular myth of Orpheus is made up of two hemispheres that can be opened, closed, and rotated to allow spectators to see the scenes in a circular movement (Figure 8-1).

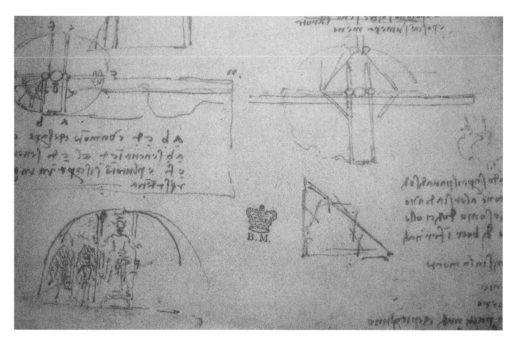

Figure 8-1. *The theater stage set*

The challenges are the revolving spheres and the elevator, and how to add sound and light effects as well as programmatically tune the interaction of all the components.

The Canal Excavation Machine

During the course of his various occupations related to hydraulic engineering, Leonardo invented various devices to facilitate and accelerate his projects. One of these is a very large canal excavation machine (Figure 8-2).It is a sophisticated system of tracks, ropes, and weights intended to work on three different levels concurrently and to be operated by two gangs of workers. Many procedures that this sort of hydraulic work required could be automated with this digger that could easily move forward.

Leonardo's unusually detailed and refined drawing gives rise to the presumption that the draft was intended to be presented to a possible customer.

Figure 8-2. *The canal excavation machine*

Recommended Web Sites

There's a wealth of information available on the Web on Leonardo da Vinci and LEGO MINDSTORMS. This section presents some sites that I find particularly interesting and worthwhile to visit.

Web Sites on Leonardo da Vinci

The number of web sites on Leonardo is legion. The following are some of my favorites.

Universal Leonardo

Universal Leonardo (http://www.universalleonardo.org) is a project that aims to radically extend public understanding and appreciation of the deep unity and extraordinary diversity of Leonardo da Vinci's work in all his fields of endeavor, as the site states. It presents European exhibitions on Leonardo and his works. It also contains many different sections on Leonardo's life, his inventions, and his other works. Among other things, you can inspect his drawings, manuscripts, and paintings; learn about the different occupations of Leonardo's life; play games; and dig through a bibliography. In a nutshell, you can spend hours on this site, which is presented in a very appealing way.

Leonardo3

Leonardo3 (http://www.leonardo3.net) is the official web site of the Leonardo3 exhibition in Milan, a project that is particularly dedicated to the visualization of Leonardo's work in three dimensions. Its intention is to create virtual reconstructions of the environments, objects, instruments, and laboratories in which some of the most significant ideas in the history of technology were conceived and developed, as the site states. Consequently, there's a wealth of magnificent images of Leonardo's inventions on the site, most of them based on computer graphics. Yet, the real experience is visiting the exhibition itself, with all its real models and interactive devices; so if you're in northern Italy, check it out.

Wikipedia

There's a lot of material on Leonardo da Vinci available on Wikipedia, the free online encyclopedia (http://en.wikipedia.org/wiki/Leonardo_da_Vinci). Not surprisingly, the most comprehensive content can be found in the Italian edition, where you can spend days just following the links provided. Yet, for those of us who have not mastered the Italian language, the English version is almost similar in scope and content.

And don't forget: Wikipedia depends on the collaboration of its readers. If you have something worthwhile to contribute, don't hesitate to add it to the site.

Sites on LEGO MINDSTORMS NXT

I already touched on some LEGO sites in Chapter 1, so I list those here without discussing them in depth.

LEGO.com MINDSTORMS NXT

The LEGO.com MINDSTORMS NXT site (http://mindstorms.lego.com) is the official home of MINDSTORMS NXT on the Web. It is published by LEGO and contains everything that's related to NXT, including LEGO's support for it: technical information, software, the NXT-related web communities set up by LEGO, books, videos, and press announcements.

LEGO.com MINDSTORMS NXTLOG

LEGO.com MINDSTORMS NXTLOG (http://mindstorms.lego.com/nxtlog) is the place for you to share and archive your LEGO MINDSTORMS NXT projects and get inspiration from the MINDSTORMS NXT community. The NXTLOG is an administrated repository of NXT robots where anyone can publish their own creations and comment on other creations. At the time of this writing, NXTLOG hosted more than 2,000 different projects. It's a tremendous source of inspiration.

LEGO Education

LEGO Education (http://www.legoeducation.com) is a joint venture between the company Pitsco Inc. and the educational division of the LEGO Group. LEGO is committed to the educational sector, in particular in the United States, and actively endorses the usage of its kits in schools and universities. This squares with the fact that a special educational version of the NXT kit has been developed.

LEGO Education "combines the motivational advantages of LEGO Education sets with award-winning software and standards-based activity packs that integrate math, science, and technology into engaging hands-on classroom projects," as stated in the site's About Us section. The site offers a lot of material for these purposes, such as teaching materials, a blog, and, quite interestingly for noninstructors, a store where you can buy a variety of NXT-related stuff.

The NXT STEP

The NXT STEP (`http://thenxtstep.blogspot.com`) is a blog dedicated to the NXT and related robotics topics that was founded by MCP member James Kelly in summer 2006. Today, around a dozen contributors write for the blog; I have the honor to be one of them.

The NXT STEP certainly has become one of the (if not *the*) most popular LEGO blogs, with more than 30,000 visitors per month. This success is a result of its very active posting and commenting as well as the high level of quality and in-depth knowledge provided there. It's one of the two blogs that are listed on LEGO's official MINDSTORMS NXT site.

nxtasy.org

nxtasy.org (`http://nxtasy.org`) is one of the first online forums for NXT-related topics and most likely is presently the largest one. No doubt its founders Guy Ziv and Eric Salinas, supported by some rather prominent contributing members of the LEGO community, have succeeded in their self-set goal of being "a source of news and knowledge exchange for LEGO MINDSTORMS NXT users all over the world."

Aside from various subsections of the forum with presently almost 1,000 registered members, there's a blog, a repository of NXT robots, and a page of challenges nxtasy.org arranges now and then.

This Author's Site

My NXT-related site (`http://mynxt.matthiaspaulscholz.eu`) has proven to be not the most unpopular one on the Web. You will find on this site a number of robots I've made as well as their building instructions, links to tools, other NXT-related sites and events, and, last but not least, a contact page that allows you to send messages to me. I usually try to respond as soon as possible to any question, suggestion, or wish from my readers. I am particularly obliged to my readers for feedback on this book. You can also find there media related to this book, such as pictures and videos of the robots, updates on the programs, and other materials.

Recommended Books

Although the NXT was released less than one year ago, already books on the topic have been published. I introduce a selection of them in this section. Note that a list that is likely to be updated frequently can be found on the official LEGO MINDSTORMS NXT site at `http://mindstorms.lego.com/Books`.

LEGO MINDSTORMS NXT: The Mayan Adventure

Like the book you are now reading, *LEGO MINDSTORMS NXT: The Mayan Adventure* by Jim Kelly (Apress, 2006) is also from the Technology in Action series by Apress. Kelly is the operator of THE NXT STEP blog mentioned previously. The book is a perfect introduction to the NXT universe, in particular for younger readers since the technical details are clad in a suspenseful story of a young boy who experiences an adventure as part of an expedition into the Guatemalan jungle and solves the problems he encounters by building and refining five NXT robots. The step-by-step instructions and the brainstorming techniques the book uses make it an ideal beginner's guide for becoming familiar with the NXT kit and its programming environment.

The LEGO MINDSTORMS NXT Idea Book

The LEGO MINDSTORMS NXT Idea Book: Design, Invent, and Build by the contributors of the NXT STEP blog (No Starch Press, 2007) contains nine different robots as well as a chapter on different theoretical topics related to the NXT. This book provides the reader with a great overview on the possibilities of the NXT kit, including the usage of NXT-G, the NXT programming language created by LEGO.

Maximum LEGO NXT: Building Robots with Java Brains

Maximum LEGO NXT: Building Robots with Java Brains by Brian Bagnall (Variant Press, 2007) is written by one of the administrators of the leJOS project who has written large parts of the leJOS implementation for the NXT's predecessor, RCX. He is also the author of various other books on LEGO MINDSTORMS.

In this new book, he provides an overview of the NXT, introduces the leJOS Java platform—alongside a crash course in common Java—and applies it to no less than 24 complete NXT projects. It's a must for anyone who's interested in programming the NXT with Java.

Leonardo's Machines: Da Vinci's Inventions Revealed

Leonardo's Machines: Da Vinci's Inventions Revealed by Domenico Laurenza, Mario Tadei, and Edoardo Zanon (David & Charles Publishers, 2006) was of particular help to me in creating the LEGO robots in this book. Written by three Italian engineers, this book is related to the Leonardo3 project mentioned previously and is a prodigious source of in-depth information on Leonardo's inventions. What makes the book so very unique is the 3D computer graphics the authors have created based on Leonardo's sketches: multitudes of high-resolution color artwork, diagrams, and explosion graphics. It's a perfect source for anyone who wants to understand how his inventions were supposed to work, let alone for anyone who wants to recreate them with LEGO or any other materials.

APPENDIX A

■■■

Installation and Configuration of the Programming Environments Used in the Book

This appendix provides an overview of the installation and configuration of the programming environments used in this book. Note that some of them are still in early stages of development and some of the configuration features may have changed or new ones may have been added since the writing of this book. Therefore, it's advisable to check the programming environment's manual for relevant changes.

LEGO MINDSTORMS NXT Software

Installation

The LEGO MINDSTORMS NXT Software comes on a CD that is part of the NXT retail kit. To install the software that runs on Windows and Mac OS X only, insert the CD into your computer's CD drive. The installation routine will autostart, presenting a dialog to choose the installation's language.[1]

Next, the installer will initialize. Don't be disturbed by the (local) web page that is displayed, stating that your Bluetooth driver is not supported. This message always pops up since the installation program does not actually check your driver against the list of drivers known to collaborate flawlessly with the software. If you have doubts about your particular Bluetooth stack, have a look at the list on the official LEGO MINDSTORMS web site: `http://mindstorms.lego.com/Overview/Bluetooth.aspx`.

After a dialog displays the components to be installed and the disk space required by them you can specify the installation's target location on your machine. Then you'll have to accept the license agreement. Once done, a summary window informs you about the actions that will be performed by the installer. This is the last chance to cancel the installation; once you click Next, the installation will actually start. When it finishes, you can optionally register yourself on the LEGO NXT web site.

After a reboot of the computer, you start the LEGO MINDSTORMS NXT Software by clicking the icon the installer has placed on your desktop.

---

1. Though there is a dialog to choose a language, version 1.0 of the LEGO MINDSTORMS NXT Software only supported an English installation at the time this book was written.

Configuration

Getting the Latest Software Versions

Now you need to ensure that you are running the most recent NXT firmware version. To check the version in the software you just installed, start the software and navigate to the Update NXT Firmware dialog via the Tools ➤ Update NXT Firmware menu (Figure A-1).

Figure A-1. *Updating the NXT firmware*

The firmware releases that are available locally on your machine are listed here. To check whether there are more recent ones available on the Web, click the Check button in the right upper corner. Your web browser will open with the official LEGO NXT MINDSTORMS Software update site. Select the latest version (if there is more than one available), download it, and follow the installation instructions.

■**Note** It is recommended to check the Update NXT Firmware page from time to time to make sure you have the most recent version of the software.

Setting Up Profiles

I recommend setting up separate profiles for each of your NXT projects. A *profile* is a user-specific folder where the software saves programs, custom blocks, and other settings. There's already a default profile you could use for all your work with the LEGO MINDSTORMS NXT Software, but I recommend separating your NXT projects into different profiles. This makes it easier to group programs and custom blocks that are logically related.

Setting up a particular profile is easy; just run the Edit ➤ Manage Profiles feature from the menu bar and click Create to make a new profile (Figure A-2).

Figure A-2. *The NXT Manage Profiles page*

Updating the NXT Firmware on the Brick

Now you will upgrade the firmware on the NXT Brick to the one you just downloaded and installed. This is best done using the USB cable to connect the Brick with the computer and switch it on.

In the software, navigate to the Update NXT Firmware dialog again via the Tools ➤ Update NXT Firmware menu. This time, select the most recent version from the list (if you downloaded one, it should appear here; otherwise, something went wrong) and click the Download button (Figure A-3).

Figure A-3. *Updating the NXT firmware on the Brick*

You will notice a clicking sound from the Brick while the firmware is downloaded. This should stop once the download is complete; an appropriate message will be displayed then.

Setting Up a Bluetooth Connection to the Brick

To complete the configuration, you will set up a Bluetooth connection to the NXT Brick, provided that you have a Bluetooth stack at your disposal.[2]

I will assume that you have already successfully installed a working Bluetooth stack on your machine and that this stack is compatible with the LEGO MINDSTORMS NXT Software. For current compatible stacks, see the official list at http://mindstorms.lego.com/Overview/Bluetooth.aspx. To connect the NXT Brick via Bluetooth to the software on your machine, first switch on the Brick to enable Bluetooth, using the settings entry.

Now open a program in the software and navigate to the NXT Window dialog by clicking the Brick symbol on the control panel in the right lower corner of the editor window (Figure A-4).

Figure A-4. *The NXT control panel*

The NXT window will open and you can start scanning for the Brick by pressing the Scan button. After some while, the Brick should appear in the list of communications labeled as Available (Figure A-5).

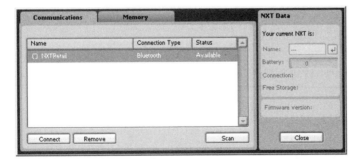

Figure A-5. *Connecting to the Brick via Bluetooth*

---

2. A USB connection is sufficient for programming and remotely controlling the Brick, but for mobile robots, a Bluetooth connection is far more convenient.

When you click the Connect button, a Bluetooth connection will be established between the Brick and the software on your machine. When you close the dialog, installation and configuration of the LEGO MINDSTORMS NXT Software is complete. The control panel is the place where you will download your programs and run them on the Brick.

NXC

Installation

As mentioned in Chapter 2, NXC is best used in connection with the BricxCC environment. The installer for BricxCC can be freely downloaded at http://bricxcc.sourceforge.net and is presently available for Windows only. Make sure to use the most recent version because it is the only one that contains appropriate support for NXC.

Once the download is complete, execute the setup routine. After accepting the license agreement and viewing some configuration steps where usually no changes are required, BricxCC is installed at the selected location.

Configuration

Before you start the BricxCC, make sure your NXT Brick is connected to your machine. The first thing BricxCC does is ask you to configure the referring COM port[3] (in case you want to use Bluetooth) or the USB connection (Figure A-6).

Figure A-6. *Configuring the connection to the Brick*

You may skip this step, but if you do, certain options will be unavailable in the IDE. You can also complete this step later, using the Find Brick feature from the Tools menu.

Once the BricxCC has started successfully, check the connection by running the Diagnostics utility from the Tools entry in the menu bar (Figure A-7).

---

3. On Windows XP, this information may be obtained from the Bluetooth Devices dialog in the system settings of the Control Panel.

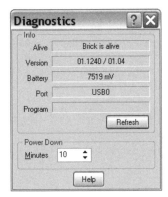

Figure A-7. *Checking the connection to the Brick*

Now that the IDE is installed and configured appropriately, you can start writing NXC programs and downloading them to the Brick. It is advisable at the start to load one of the NXC sample programs that comes with BricxCC. You can compile, download, and run it on the Brick using the items in the menu or the toolbar (Figure A-8).

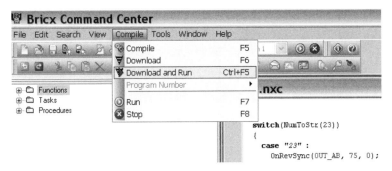

Figure A-8. *Downloading and running an NXC program on the Brick*

Feel free to further experiment with other features of BricxCC, including direct remote control and monitoring of the Brick or downloading new versions of the LEGO NXT firmware.

RobotC

Installation

RobotC is a commercial product produced by the Carnegie Mellon University Robotics Academy that can be purchased at http://www.robotc.net for $49US for a single license[4] on CD-ROM or $30US for an Internet download. You will also find a lot more information at this site, including a Quickstart Guide, tutorials, sample programs, and a user forum. The most interesting thing is a trial version that allows you to evaluate the product for free for 30 days.

Once you download and start the installer, installation is simply performed by clicking through steps that usually do not require any changes except for accepting the license agreement. You can start RobotC from the icon placed on your desktop.

Configuration

On the startup screen you have to choose between two different types of licenses. The product starts with a 30-day trial license. Since RobotC comes with its own separate firmware, you have to replace the original LEGO NXT firmware on the Brick with RobotC's. This is a mandatory step of the configuration.

To do so, connect the Brick to the computer with the USB cable. Switch it on and run the Link Setup feature from the Robot ➤ NXT Brick menu (Figure A-9).

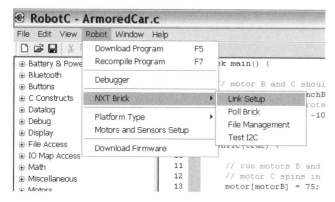

Figure A-9. *Linking to the Brick*

In the NXT Brick Link Selection dialog, click the Refresh Lists button and you should notice your Brick listed as connected (Figure A-10).

---

4.   There's also a classroom license for up to 12 computers available for $265.

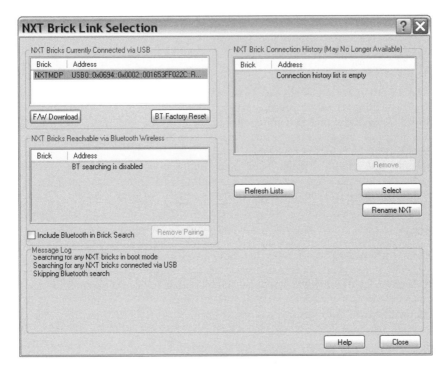

Figure A-10. *Connected Bricks*

When you click the F/W Download button, you trigger the replacement of the Brick's firmware with RobotC's firmware. Select the firmware file that is located in the Firmware folder of your RobotC installation; it is selected by default. The download of the firmware will start and display a set of log messages on the open window (Figure A-11).

Similar to the process of downloading the original LEGO NXT firmware with the LEGO MIND-STORMS NXT software, you will notice a clicking sound until the replacement is finished and RobotC has restarted the Brick.

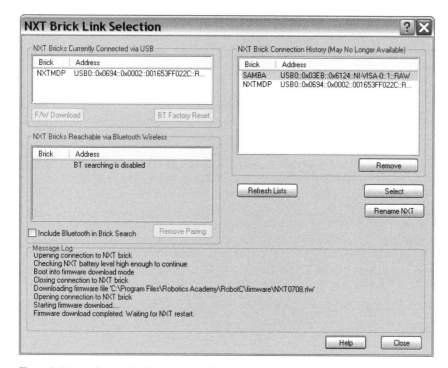

Figure A-11. *Replacing the firmware on the Brick*

RobotC is now ready to be used for writing, compiling, downloading, running, and debugging programs to and on the Brick, using the entries in the Robot menu (Figure A-12).

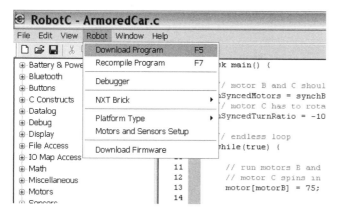

Figure A-12. *Downloading to and running programs on the Brick*

I encourage you to try the various features of RobotC, in particular the debugger.

leJOS NXJ

Installation

Since leJOS NXJ is based on the Java programming language and does not currently come with its own programming environment support, it's advisable to use an existing Java IDE on the market. I recommend Eclipse, a platform that is open source and has undoubtedly become the most popular environment for Java-based applications over the past years, and justifiably so. Eclipse can be downloaded for free at http://www.eclipse.org.

Next, you need to download leJOS NXJ itself, which is open source and can be downloaded for free at http://lejos.sourceforge.net. Unzip the archive that contains the leJOS NXJ distribution into a local folder. Note that unlike the other programming environments previously introduced, leJOS NXJ also supports Linux.

Finally, you need to install the libusb drivers on your operating system. The libusb drivers are packed into an open source USB library and allow applications to access any USB device in a generic way without writing any line of kernel driver code. The API is used by the leJOS NXJ low-level routines.

To install libusb, download it from http://libusb.sourceforge.net (for Linux or Mac OSX) or from http://libusb-win32.sourceforge.net (for Windows) and follow the installation instructions provided there.

Configuration

Since leJOS NXJ is still in a rather early stage of its life cycle, configuration and usage is not as seamless as it will be once it has matured. For instance, in the alpha version available at the time of this writing, programs could not be saved on the Brick but had to be redownloaded for every execution.

Environment variables

You need to set the environment variable LEJOS_HOME to the folder you installed the distribution into and add the distribution's bin folder to the PATH environment variable.

Eclipse

Configuration of Eclipse for use with leJOS NXJ is done on the project level. Since there is currently no particular leJOS NXJ plug-in available—a gap that will certainly be closed by the community in the near future—you will work with the standard features Eclipse provides for Java projects by default. To create a new Java project, open the Project ➤ Properties dialog and assign the libraries contained in the lib folder of your local leJOS NXJ distribution to the libraries on the build path (Figure A-13).

■Note If you are not familiar with the basics of Eclipse, there is an abundance of documentation at http://www.eclipse.org.

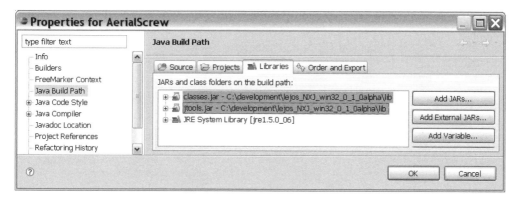

Figure A-13. *Configuring the Java project*

To link and download programs to the Brick, use the External Tools feature of Eclipse. For linking, define an external tool called lejoslink. Open the External Tools Configuration wizard by navigating through the Run ➤ External Tools ➤ External Tools menu and create a new configuration with settings, as displayed in Figure A-14.

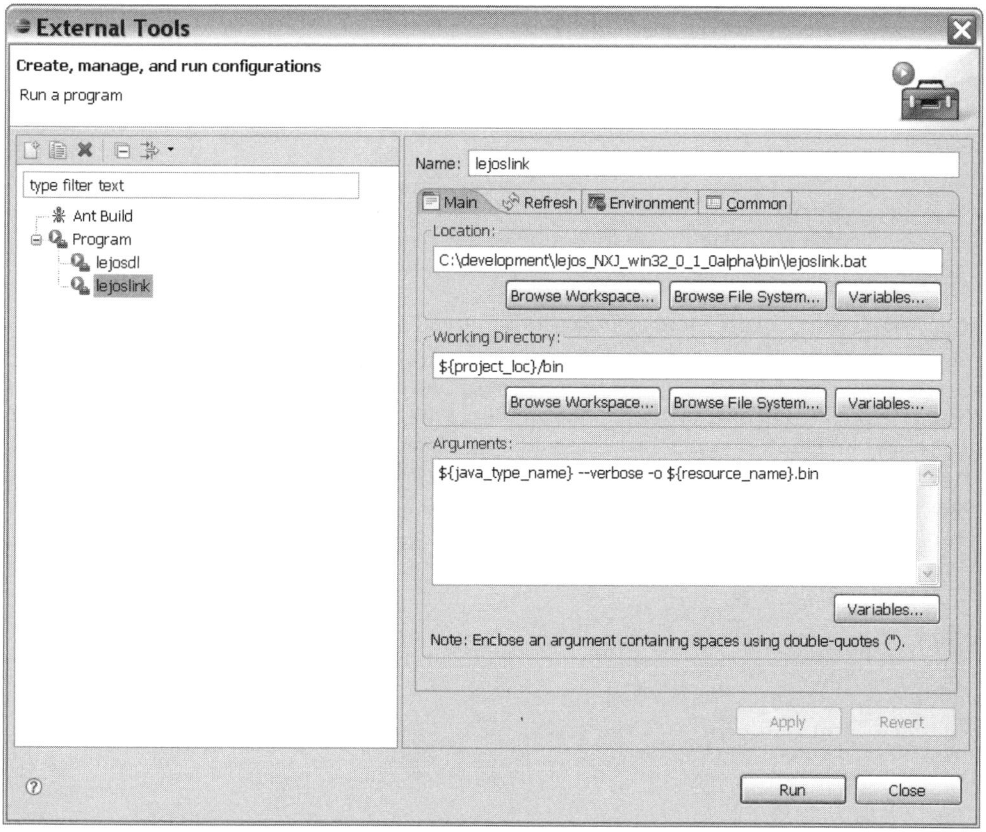

Figure A-14. *Creating an external tool for linking*

You will create another configuration for downloading to and running on the Brick (Figure A-15).

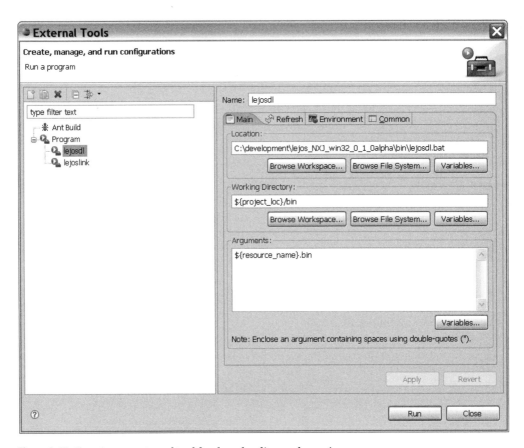

Figure A-15. *Creating an external tool for downloading and running*

To link, download, and run your leJOS NXJ program on the Brick, you simply have to select the file in your project and run the two external tools from the External Tools menu. Note that the NXT Brick must be connected to your machine with the USB cable and set to "firmware update mode." To achieve this, click the reset button for more than four seconds and it will start ticking. Click the orange button and download the program to the Brick. It will start running immediately after the download is complete.

pbLua

Installation

pbLua is freely downloadable from Ralph Hempel's web site at http://www.hempeldesigngroup.com/lego/pbLua. After the download has finished, unpack the downloaded archive, which contains the pbLua interpreter and some samples, into a folder at your leisure. Since pbLua does not currently come with its own programming environment support, it's advisable to use an existing IDE on the market. Again I recommend Eclipse. There is a collection of Lua plug-ins for Eclipse available at http://luaeclipse.luaforge.net.

Install Eclipse and the Lua plug-ins according to the installation instructions.

Configuration

Since pbLua comes with its own firmware, you have to replace the one on the Brick. To do so, take the following steps:

1. Connect the Brick to the computer with the USB cable.

2. Switch on the Brick.

3. Download the pbLua firmware file nxt-lua.rfw that comes with the pbLua distribution, using the firmware download utility of the LEGO MINDSTORMS NXT Software (see the "Updating the NXT Firmware on the Brick" section on the configuration of the LEGO MINDSTORMS NXT Software).

Once the download has started, the Brick will start to click. Wait until the download utility states that the software has been downloaded successfully. The clicking sound will stop and the display of the Brick will show a string starting with pblua <version>.

Unplug the USB cable and plug it in again to make the computer recognize the new USB device. The operating system will ask for the appropriate driver for it. Use the .inf file that is contained in the usbDrivers folder in the pbLua distribution. You may safely ignore the warning that the driver is not signed. If all goes well, you will see a new entry, "pbLua USB Serial Port," in the list of serial ports on your machine (for Windows, this list can be accessed by the Device Manager of your Systems dialog in the Control Panel). Write down the number of the associated COM port; you will need it later.

To communicate with the Brick now, in particular to download programs, you need a telnet client. On Windows XP this client is HyperTerminal, which should be installed by default. You can access it through the Accessories ➤ Communications panel. However, you are free to use any telnet client you like.

Open it and set up a new connection to the new COM port (Figure A-16).

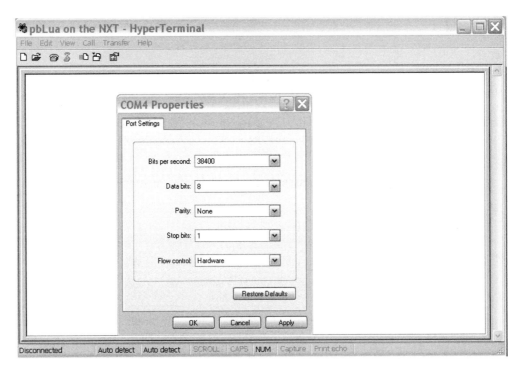

Figure A-16. *Creating a connection to the Brick*

Once the connection is established, hit the Return key a few times until the pbLua prompt (>) appears on the terminal. Now the Brick is able to accept direct input of commands or the download of a program.

To download a program, use the text file download capabilities of your telnet client. With HyperTerminal, for instance, this is done by navigating to Transfer ➤ Send Text File in the menu bar and selecting the pbLua program in question.

If your program has a main call to a function, it will run immediately; otherwise, you can run the function by typing in a call to the terminal and clicking Return. This will call the function on the Brick (Figure A-17).

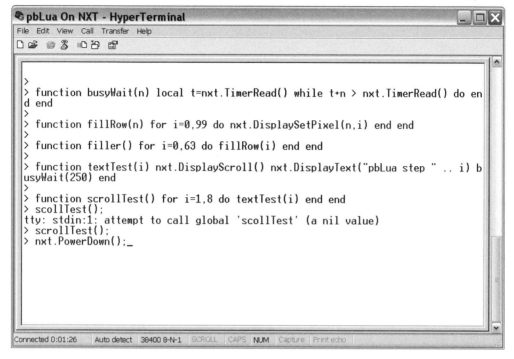

Figure A-17. *Remotely calling a pbLua function on the Brick*

It's advisable to download some of the sample programs that come with the pbLua distribution and run them by calling some of the functions contained there to test the proper working of the firmware on the Brick.

Since the gray button on the Brick with the pbLua firmware is no longer configured to switch off the Brick, you will have to perform this task with the software; simply call the nxt.PowerDown() function in the terminal (Figure A-17).

Keep in mind that you can always put the original LEGO NXT firmware back on the Brick by performing the instructions in the "Updating the NXT Firmware on the Brick" section of this chapter. You might be required to reset the Brick beforehand by pushing the reset button located in one of the holes on the bottom of the Brick for more than four seconds.

Leonardo's Letter of Application to the Duke of Milan

This is a translation of the letter that Leonardo da Vinci wrote to Ludovico Sforza, the duke of Milan, to apply for a position as a military engineer in 1482. Sketches of some of his inventions introduced in this book may have been attached to it.

Having, most illustrious lord, seen and considered the experiments of all those who pose as masters in the art of inventing instruments of war, and finding that their inventions differ in no way from those in common use, I am emboldened, without prejudice to anyone, to solicit an appointment of acquainting your Excellency with certain of my secrets.

1. I can construct bridges which are very light and strong and very portable, with which to pursue and defeat the enemy; and others more solid, which resist fire or assault, yet are easily removed and placed in position; and I can also burn and destroy those of the enemy.

2. In case of a siege I can cut off water from the trenches and make pontoons and scaling ladders and other similar contrivances.

3. If by reason of the elevation or the strength of its position a place cannot be bombarded, I can demolish every fortress if its foundations have not been set on stone.

4. I can also make a kind of cannon which is light and easy of transport, with which to hurl small stones like hail, and of which the smoke causes great terror to the enemy, so that they suffer heavy loss and confusion.

5. I can noiselessly construct to any prescribed point subterranean passages either straight or winding, passing if necessary underneath trenches or a river.

6. I can make armored wagons carrying artillery, which shall break through the most serried ranks of the enemy, and so open a safe passage for his infantry.

7. If occasion should arise, I can construct cannon and mortars and light ordnance in shape both ornamental and useful and different from those in common use.

8. When it is impossible to use cannon I can supply in their stead catapults, mangonels, trabocchi, and other instruments of admirable efficiency not in general use—In short, as the occasion requires I can supply infinite means of attack and defense.

9. And if the fight should take place upon the sea I can construct many engines most suitable either for attack or defense and ships which can resist the fire of the heaviest cannon, and powders or weapons.

10. In time of peace, I believe that I can give you as complete satisfaction as anyone else in the construction of buildings both public and private, and in conducting water from one place to another.

I can further execute sculpture in marble, bronze, or clay, also in painting I can do as much as anyone else, whoever he may be.

Moreover, I would undertake the commission of the bronze horse, which shall endue with immortal glory and eternal honor the auspicious memory of your father and of the illustrious house of Sforza.

And if any of the aforesaid things should seem to anyone impossible or impracticable, I offer myself as ready to make trial of them in your park or in whatever place shall please your Excellency, to whom I commend myself with all possible humility.

—Leonardo Da Vinci

APPENDIX C

■■■

Glossary

Aerial Screw
Helix-shaped flying device designed by Leonardo da Vinci that follows the idea of screwing into the air.

Armored Car
Tank-style design of Leonardo that merges the concepts of chariot and war tortoise.

Block
Graphical element of the NXT-G programming language that encapsulates functionality such as motor control, sensor access, and other configurable items.

Bluetooth
Industrial specification for wireless personal area networks, providing a way to connect and exchange information between different kinds of devices. Used by the NXT to communicate remotely with other Bluetooth-enabled devices, in particular computers and other NXT robots.

Catapult
Leonardo's design for an onager-style catapult that uses a double leaf spring to store kinetic energy.

Clos Luce
Also called *Cloux*, the manor house near the French king's residence where Leonardo spent his final years from 1517 to 1519.

Codex
Assemblies of loose sheets of Leonardo's manuscripts compiled by different collectors over the centuries, following various collection criteria.

Custom Block
User-defined subprograms in the NXT-G programming language, consisting of sequences of blocks connected by beams and data wires.

Educational Base Set
Version of the LEGO MINDSTORMS NXT kit intended for schools and universities. Contains only 431 parts and lacks the programming software, but contains a rechargeable battery pack.

Firmware

Software that is embedded into hardware. The NXT has its own firmware that can be thought of as its operating system. Released on an open source license in December 2006.

Flying Machine

Ornithopter-style flying device designed by Leonardo that mimics a bird's method of flying.

Francois I

King of France. Lived 1494–1547. Patron of arts and of Leonardo in Leonardo's later years.

Gran Cavallo

Giant bronze statue of a horse planned by Leonardo to be erected in Milan. Never completed in his lifetime because the material was used for guns instead. In 1999, a facsimile in reduced size (3 meters high instead of the originally intended 8) was created in Milan.

Input Port

Port at the NXT Brick where an input device such as a sensor can be wired in. The Brick offers four input ports.

LEGO MINDSTORMS NXT Software

Official programming environment for the NXT, provided by LEGO.

leJOS NXJ

Open source Java-based operating system and programming platform for the LEGO MINDSTORMS NXT.

Lorenzo de Medici

Ruler of the Florentine Republic. Lived 1449–1492. Considered one of the most remarkable public figures of his time. Nicknamed "Il Magnifico." Patron of Leonardo and of the arts in general.

Ludovico Sforza

Duke of Milan. Lived 1452–1508. Nicknamed "Il Moro" due to his dark complexion. Leonardo's employer during Leonardo's first sojourn in Milan (1482–1499).

MINDSTORMS Community Partner Program (MCP)

Program initiated by LEGO made up of around 20 people charged with helping establish and deepen the connection between the NXT community and the LEGO Group. Successor to the MDP.

MINDSTORMS Developer Program (MDP)

Program initiated by LEGO made up of 100 people all over the world who tested beta versions of LEGO MINDSTORMS NXT kits and helped guide the product development process for the NXT. December 2005 to August 2006.

NXC (Not eXactly C)

C-style language that can be used to program the NXT Brick. Programs written in NXC are compiled to run on the original LEGO NXT firmware. Developed and maintained by John Hansen.

NXT Brick

Programmable controller of the NXT, its central component. Also known as *The Intelligent Brick.*

NXT File System

Persistent logical file system, also named Table of Contents (TOC), that is stored in the flash memory of the NXT. Used to save artifacts such as programs and data files.

NXT-G

Programming language that comes with the LEGO MINDSTORMS NXT Software. Provides a graphical syntax.

Output Port

Port on the NXT Brick where an output device such as a motor can be wired in. The Brick offers three output ports.

pbLua

Text-based programming language for the LEGO MINDSTORMS NXT. Based on Lua, a lightweight programming language created by a team from the Pontifical Catholic University of Rio de Janeiro, Brazil. Developed and maintained by Ralph Hempel.

Renaissance

French term meaning *rebirth* and denoting an era roughly between 1500 and 1700 when the focus of the occident's highbrows shifted from metaphysical considerations to matters that from today's view may be denoted as physical: interest in the human being itself, the scientific (rather than the philosophical) heritage of the antique, the reasons for the different phenomena mankind encounters in nature, and the attempt to make use of mechanical inventions for everyday life challenges.

Retail Version

Standard version of the LEGO MINDSTORMS NXT kit, containing 577 parts.

Revolving Bridge

Mechanical bridge designed by Leonardo that could swing around on its pylons.

Robo Center

Part of the LEGO NXT MINDSTORMS Software that is not directly connected to programming but serves as a bridge to the NXT community. Provides not only onscreen building instructions for four advanced robots, but also a portal to the LEGO.com MINDSTORMS community NXT web site that hosts challenges and NXT-G related material such as sample programs, sound files, and additional building instructions.

RobotC

Programming environment based on the popular functional programming language C. Developed by the Carnegie Mellon University Robotics Academy.

Servo

Motor whose internal position and state can be controlled from an external unit. The NXT motors are servos.

Sound Sensor

Type of NXT sensor that measures the intensity of ambient sound.

Touch Sensor

Type of NXT sensor that responds to pressing and releasing. Intended to be used for short-distance detection by physical contact.

Try Me

Built-in program in the NXT that provides a graphical menu on its display to perform several administration tasks.

Ultrasonic Sensor

Type of NXT sensor that measures the reflection of high-frequency sonar signals it emits itself. Intended to be used for contact-free, long-range detection.

■■■

Bibliography

Books

Bagnall, Brian. *Maximum LEGO NXT: Building Robots with Java Brains*. Winnipeg, MB, Canada: Variant Press, 2007.

Contributors to NXT STEP Blog. *The LEGO MINDSTORMS NXT Idea Book: Design, Invent, and Build*. San Francisco, CA: No Starch Press, 2007.

Ferrari, Mario; Ferrari, Guilio; and Astolfo, David. *Building Robots with LEGO MINDSTORMS NXT*. Rockland, MA: Syngress Publishing, 2007.

Gasperi, Michael; Hurbain, Isabelle; and Hurbain, Philippe. *Extreme NXT: Extending the LEGO MINDSTORMS NXT to the Next Level*. Berkeley, CA: Apress, 2007.

Hansen, John C. *LEGO MINDSTORMS NXT Power Programming: Robotics in C*. Winnipeg, MB, Canada: Variant Press, 2007.

Kelly, Jim. *LEGO MINDSTORMS NXT: The Mayan Adventure*. Berkeley, CA: Apress, 2006.

Kelly, Jim. *LEGO MINDSTORMS NXT-G Programming Guide*. Berkeley, CA: Apress, 2007.

Laurenza, Domenico; Tadei, Mario; and Zanon, Edoardo. *Leonardo's Machines: Da Vinci's Inventions Revealed*. Newton Abbot, Devon, UK: David & Charles Publishers, 2006.

Web Sites

Apress Source Code/Download page, http://www.apress.com

Author's web site, http://mynxt.matthiaspaulscholz.eu

The Drawings of Leonardo da Vinci, http://www.drawingsofleonardo.org

LEGO Education, http://www.legoeducation.com

LEGO.com MINDSTORMS NXT, http://mindstorms.lego.com

LEGO.com MINDSTORMS NXTLOG, http://mindstorms.lego.com/nxtlog

leJOS NXJ home page, http://lejos.sourceforge.net

Leonardo3, http://www.leonardo3.net

Leonardo da Vinci: The Codex Leicester, http://www.odranoel.de

Leonardo da Vinci: War Machines, http://digilander.iol.it/debibliotheca/Arte/Leonardowar_file/page_01.htm

LUGNET Robotics NXT news group, http://news.lugnet.com/robotics/nxt

The Models in Clos Luce, http://www.castles-france.net/vinci-clos-luce/amboise.htm

The Notebooks of Leonardo da Vinci, http://www.sacred-texts.com/aor/dv/index.htm

NXC home page, http://bricxcc.sourceforge.net/nxc

The NXT STEP, http://thenxtstep.blogspot.com

NXT Tutorial, http://www.ortop.org/NXT_Tutorial

nxtasy.org, http://nxtasy.org

pbLua home page, http://www.hempeldesigngroup.com/lego/pbLua

Philo's NXT web site, http://philohome.com/nxt.htm

RobotC home page, http://www.robotc.net

Steve Hassenplug's NXT web site, http://www.teamhassenplug.org/NXT

Universal Leonardo, http://www.universalleonardo.org

Wikipedia, http://en.wikipedia.org/wiki/Leonardo_da_Vinci

Index

Find it faster at http://superindex.apress.com

You Need the Companion eBook

Your purchase of this book entitles you to buy the companion PDF-version eBook for only $10. Take the weightless companion with you anywhere.

We believe this Apress title will prove so indispensable that you'll want to carry it with you everywhere, which is why we are offering the companion eBook (in PDF format) for $10 to customers who purchase this book now. Convenient and fully searchable, the PDF version of any content-rich, page-heavy Apress book makes a valuable addition to your programming library. You can easily find and copy code — or perform examples by quickly toggling between instructions and the application. Even simultaneously tackling a donut, diet soda, and complex code becomes simplified with hands-free eBooks!

Once you purchase your book, getting the $10 companion eBook is simple:

❶ Visit **www.apress.com/promo/tendollars/**.

❷ Complete a basic registration form to receive a randomly generated question about this title.

❸ Answer the question correctly in 60 seconds, and you will receive a promotional code to redeem for the $10.00 eBook.

THE EXPERT'S VOICE™

2855 TELEGRAPH AVENUE | SUITE 600 | BERKELEY, CA 94705

Offer valid through 12/25/07.